I

About the Editors

Christine Heward is a senior lecturer at the Institute of Education, University of Warwick. Sheila Bunwaree is lecturer in the Faculty of Social Studies and Humanities, University of Mauritius.

Gender, Education and Development: Beyond Access to Empowerment

edited by

CHRISTINE HEWARD AND
SHEILA BUNWAREE

Zed Books Ltd
LONDON & NEW YORK

Gender, Education and Development: beyond access to empowerment was first
published in 1999 by Zed Books Ltd, 7 Cynthia Street, London N1
9JF, UK and Room 400, 175 Fifth Avenue, New York, NY 10010, USA.

Distributed in the USA exclusively by St. Martin's Press Inc., 175 Fifth
Avenue, New York, NY 10010, USA

Cover by Andrew Corbett
Set in Monotype Garamond by Ewan Smith
Printed and bound in the United Kingdom by Redwood Books,
Trowbridge, Wilts.

A catalogue record for this book is available from the British Library

Library of Congress Cataloging-in-Publication Data

Gender, education, and development : beyond access to
empowerment / edited by Christine Heward and Sheila Bunwaree.
        p.   cm.
    Includes bibliographical references and index.
    ISBN 1-85649-631-7 (hardcover). — ISBN 1-85649-632-5 (pbk.)
    1. Education—Developing countries. 2. Women—
Education—Developing countries. 3. Women in development—
Developing countries. 4. Education equalization—Developing
countries. 5. Education and state—Developing countries.
I. Heward, Christine. II. Bunwaree, Sheila S.
    LC2607–G46   1998
    371.822–dc21
                                            98–47783
                                              CIP

ISBN 1 85649 631 7 cased
ISBN 1 85649 632 5 limp

Contents

Tables and Figures

Tables

Figures

Abbreviations

ADB	Asian Development Bank
ASEAN	Association of South East Asian Nations
CEDAW	Convention on the Elimination of All Forms of Discrimination Against Women (UN)
CENWOR	Centre for Women's Research (Sri Lanka)
DfID	Department for International Development (UK)
EPRDF	Ethiopian People's Revolutionary Democratic Front
EPZ	export-processing zone
ERP	economic recovery programme
FAO	Food and Agriculture Organization (UN)
FAWE	Forum for African Women Educationalists
GAD	gender and development
GATT	General Agreement on Tariffs and Trade
GCU	gender coordinating unit
GEM	Gender Empowerment Measure
GER	gross enrolment ratio
GETT	Gender Equity Task Team (South Africa)
ICPD	International Conference on Population and Development
IDS	Institute of Development Studies (UK)
ILO	International Labour Organization (UN)
IMF	International Monetary Fund
LDC	less developed country
MFLS-2	Second Malaysia Family Life Survey
MMM	Mouvement Militant Mauricien
NCW	National Council of Women (PNG)
NESP	national economic recovery programme
NGO	non-governmental organization
NIC	newly industrializing country
NRSP	National Rural Support Programme (Pakistan)
OECD	Organization for Economic Cooperation and Development
PN	Projeto Nordeste (Brazil)
PNG	Papua New Guinea
PQLI	physical quality of life indicator
PRA	Participatory Rural Appraisal

SAARC	South Asian Association for Regional Cooperation
SAP	structural adjustment programme
SDP	sector development plan
SEP	Secondary Education Project
SIDA	Swedish Development Authority
TAMWA	Tanzania Media Women's Association
TGE	Transitional Government of Ethiopia
TGNP	Tanzania Gender Networking Programme
TRHG	Teenage Reproductive Health Group (Tanzania)
UDSM	University of Dar es Salaam
UNFPA	United Nations Fund for Population Activities
UNICEF	United Nations Children's Fund
UPE	universal primary education
WB	World Bank
WED	Women Education Development (Tanzania)
WID	women in development

CHAPTER I

Introduction: The New Discourses of Gender, Education and Development

Christine Heward

Gender, education and development discourses are of recent origin. A popular discourse was first established in 1995 by the highly influential World Bank statement of priorities in educational policy in which basic education, especially that of girls, became the first priority. Firmly within the framework of classical liberal economics, the Bank's statement argued that investing in the education of girls would yield externalities in reduced fertility rates and improved child health. For the first time the education of girls was at the top of the agenda for donor agencies, governments and non-governmental organizations (NGOs).

From women in development to gender and development

The roots of this new discourse lie in debates about women in development (WID) in the early 1970s. In the immediate post-war understandings of development, women were invisible. As wives and mothers they were the passive recipients of welfare policies. Notions of WID challenged this view by constructing an alternative discourse. It drew on Ester Boserup's (1970) analysis of the way in which the introduction of new technologies and cash cropping in African farming caused a gender segmentation of agricultural practice because the new methods were associated with men while 'traditional' subsistence farming became feminized and devalued. Attempting to counter this, WID emphasized women's active productive contribution to development. It used arguments of their economic efficiency to divert scarce resources to women. In doing so it focused on what women did for development, rather than what it did for them. WID is associated with development projects aimed at women only, especially income-generation projects. Such projects have been criticized for playing down the importance of welfare and ignoring the complexities of gendered distributions of resources within households.

These critiques were the starting points for discourses characterized as 'gender and development' (GAD), which have gained momentum since the 1980s. 'Gender analysis' is a widely used GAD framework and identifies differences between men and women in productive work and access to resources. This analysis is then used to plan projects that improve productivity. Gender analysis sees men and women as separate categories involved in discrete relations. However, such a view may not do justice to the complexity of gender relations within households as a fluid mix of trade-offs. Budgetary responsibilities at a particular time may depend on negotiations about perceived current surpluses. If women are seen to have more surplus cash they may be expected to take over certain responsibilities so that men can spend their money on personal consumption or group investments, such as a larger fishing boat. Women may not be passive victims in such arrangements, within the complex web of conflict and cooperation that is domestic power relations. Such critiques point to the difficulties posed by conceptualizing women as a homogeneous group with identical interests. One of the most important objectives of this collection is to stress the heterogeneity of women and their interests. Too many groups have remained invisible, lacking voices, so that their interests and needs have been ignored. For too long indigenous women have been invisible, their voices silenced. Giving voice reveals the problematic and multi-layered nature of women's experience in all its ambiguities. We can then begin to conceptualize women's individual subjectivities and relate them to the dilemmas and contradictions of power relations of households, communities and states.

During the 1980s the dominant issue for development theorists was the effects of structural adjustment programmes (SAPs) imposed by the International Monetary Fund (IMF) to stabilize debt-ridden economies. The literature on SAPs has outgrown all others in the development field. Stromquist demonstrates that, while their assumptions are gender-blind, SAPs have greatly increased the burdens on women, with severe consequences for children's welfare. The response of policy-makers to such critiques was to introduce safety nets to mitigate the effects of SAPs on the most vulnerable groups, but the effect on girls' school enrolment has been significant (Rose 1995). Stromquist (Chapter 2) and Jayaweera (Chapter 11) argue that safety nets are 'add-ons' with marginal effects.

Mainstreaming gender

Efficiency arguments are hugely popular with policy-makers as they enable them to demonstrate the pay-off from their preferred policies in simple terms of dollars expected to be produced or saved. Feminist economists have continued to analyse their conceptual frameworks and have shown that SAPs have accentuated the rigidities of gendered economic relations within households, reducing the effectiveness of the programmes. A number of analysts have argued the necessity for basing SAPs only on properly gendered models of economic development. Dasgupta's model of economic development places women at the centre, managing, saving and planning domestic economies and their households' futures (Dasgupta 1993). The application of a gendered model of economic development to the development process underlies Moser's conceptualization of gender planning (Moser 1989). One of the most important purposes of these analyses has been to ensure that gender is central to macro-economic planning rather than marginalized in low-budget, women-only projects. Influencing policy-makers towards mainstreaming gender at all levels of development planning is a crucial thrust in the emerging gender, education and development literature.

Social relations analysis

Evaluations of development projects in which making resources directly available to women was ineffective in improving their economic situation have been the starting point for more sensitive analyses of the complexities of gender relations. Social relations analysis therefore seeks to understand the social processes that sustain the unequal distribution of resources so that power can be redistributed by addressing these issues directly. Making power relations the focus of analysis highlights the differences among women and draws attention to factors other than gender through which groups have access to resources such as communities. This perspective sees the gender division of labour in terms of complex and fluid co-operation in which women and men negotiate over dilemmas and choices, perceived differently by women in different positions and stages of the life-cycle. Social relations analysis concentrates on the precise terms under which women and men cooperate and on the specific institutions, such as marriages and markets, that structure that cooperation. Such an analysis takes women's perceptions of the intricate power relations of their situations seriously as the basis for project planning. Women's empowerment thus becomes the central concern of projects that are planned from the 'bottom up', with women themselves participating directly in planning projects to improve their lives in place of the 'top-down' approach where projects emanate from professional developers (Razavi and Miller 1995).

Participatory development

In the late 1990s discourses of gender, education and development are shifting and being redefined by a wide range of interest groups. Empowerment is an increasingly important objective for projects in which women are involved. Participation is a crucial criterion for donors, and more aid from falling budgets is being channelled through NGOs as the most effective conduit to the poorest and most marginalized groups. At the multilateral level there are clear differences in policy assumptions. The World Bank remains committed to a classical liberal economic framework: 'Education is an investment which lifts individuals out of poverty by increasing their returns in the labour market' (Woodward 1997). WB lends money to governments for such schemes as government schools for girls. In contrast, UNICEF is committed to education as a human right hitherto denied to many girls and women. Its statement on these issues, 'Educating Girls and Women: a Moral Imperative', was published in 1992.

The most recent statement of the United Nations Development Programme's commitment is to address the growing inequalities between the world's poorest and the richest nations through pro-poor policies. Human poverty is distinguished from income poverty as a short life, illiteracy and lack of access to public and private resources. Education is an integral part of a platform of policies to empower women and men in the poorest communities and societies. 'Everywhere the starting point is to empower women and men and to ensure their participation in decisions that affect their lives and enable them to build their strengths and assets' (UNDP 1997: 6).

The notion of a continuum of assumptions underlying their gender education and development discourses, from the liberal economic of the WB to human rights at UNICEF, is too simplistic in the web of inter-relations of discourses, agencies and practices among multilateral, bilateral and non-governmental organizations through which aid projects are actually being delivered in the 1990s. In 1993 more than half of WB funding to Africa was channelled through NGOs, and the Bank is popularizing the model of the informal schools organized by the Bangladesh Rural Advancement Committee. Critics of NGOs point to the limitations of their short-term project mentality and their anti-state bias. While gender, education and development practices on the ground are increasingly complex, the assumptions and concerns of the dominant discourse remain those of education as a return on investment.

Closing the gender gap

Despite the efforts of the UNDP and UNICEF to broaden the context of debates about gender, education and development in the international donor community, international gatherings in the 1990s have been pre-occupied with the single narrowly conceived issue of closing so-called gender gaps in school enrolments in regions where birth rates are high, particularly Sub-Saharan Africa and South Asia. The decade opened with the meeting on 'Education for All' in Jomtien in 1990. There progress towards universal primary education (UPE) was reviewed and a new target date of UPE by 2010 was set. The fact that two-thirds of children not in school were girls was noted, and the importance of increasing access for girls strongly supported. The gender, education and development discourse was thus prominently established. In 1994 the UN conference on population was held in Cairo. This was a very difficult meeting, with strained relations caused by the issue of birth control. Opponents included the Vatican and certain Islamic states, and the USA was under contradictory pressures from anti-abortionists and those fearing a Malthusian apocalypse. Girls' education was a policy that all could support as a means of reducing population. The gender, education and development discourse was increasingly dominated by this policy as a medium-term economic investment to reduce fertility rates. In March 1995 the UN Conference on Poverty convened in Copenhagen and Hillary Clinton made a widely publicized speech in support of the USA's investment of $100 million over ten years in girls' education as a means of reducing poverty by lowering fertility, improving child health and raising women's incomes from the labour market. This was a popular summary of the World Bank policy paper *Enhancing Women's Participation in Economic Development*, published in July 1994. The most forceful statement of this position was made by the Bank's chief economist, Lawrence Summers, in 1993:

> An educated mother faces higher opportunity cost of time spent caring for the children. She has greater value outside the house and thus has an entirely different set of choices than she would have without education. She is married at a later age and is better able to influence family decisions. She has fewer, healthier children and can insist on the development of all of them, ensuring that her daughters are given a fair chance. And the education of her daughters makes it much more likely that the next generation of girls, as well as boys, will be educated and healthy as well. The vicious cycle is thus transformed into a virtuous circle (quoted in Jeffery and Basu 1996: 17).

At the UN Women's Conference in Beijing in September 1995 the rights perspective was strongly reasserted. The continuing disadvantages in women's access to health and education services was at the top of the agenda. Nevertheless, the mid-decade review of 'Schooling for All' in Amman in May 1996 noted the continuing large disparities in girls' access to schooling, despite the steady rise in primary school enrolments worlde-Yide since Jomtien.

Girls' education as contraception?

Three recent comprehensive reviews of the research show that the relationship of fertility to girls' education is complex, mediated by the social, cultural and political context of girls' and women's lives within patriarchal gender relations (Jejeebhoy 1995; Jeffery and Basu 1996; Ainsworth et al.

1996). These surveys are most valuable: Jejeebhoy reviews a wide-ranging sample, while the other two publications concentrate respectively on South Asia and Sub-Saharan Africa, where fertility is high and literacy levels among women low. Jejeebhoy provides a clear summary of the findings of studies of fertility and education from 38 different countries derived from the World Fertility Survey and the Demographic and Health Survey for the United Nations Population Fund and the International Union for the Study of Population. The studies show, *inter alia*, that there are thresholds of development, below which education has little effect on fertility. Education appears to reduce fertility in countries with higher levels of development and egalitarian gender regimes. The nature of the relationship changes over time and is stronger in more developed and urban settings. Autonomy is crucial to women's control over their fertility. The relation between education and autonomy is mediated by the cultural relations of patriarchy. Highly educated women have more autonomy than uneducated women, but in many highly patriarchal settings women's autonomy increases only when they have secondary and/or higher education. The significance of education has been investigated for five different elements of autonomy: knowledge of the outside world, decision-making in the family, mobility, emotional autonomy away from kin towards the nuclear family, and self-reliance socially and economically. In the all-important matter of age of marriage and choice of partner, cultural setting mediates the relationship of education and fertility. In patriarchal settings the relationships are weakened and it takes several years of schooling to postpone the age of marriage. While girls' schooling is associated with lower fertility, studies also demonstrate that it reduces the period of breast-feeding and abstinence from sexual relations, both of which reduce natural fertility.

Perhaps the most interesting findings are those about the relationship of schooling to desired family size. While women's education has a moderate and consistent inverse effect on desired family size, a brief period of primary schooling does not appear to change desired family size, attendance at junior middle or secondary school being necessary to do so. Cultural contexts are crucial here. In gender-stratified settings, where women's lives are characterized by seclusion and dependency, considerable education is required before women abandon their reliance on children, especially sons, for social status and security in old age. Two very important outcomes that are consistent for even a brief schooling are the practice of contraception and infant health and survival (Subbaro and Raney 1993).

Jeffery and Basu begin their editorial deconstruction of these relationships from the proposition that: 'The causal link between female schooling and fertility change has had a high profile in policy-making but a weak theoretical and empirical basis' (1996: 13). They designate the WB view as 'education as contraception', arguing that policy-makers see the causal sequence simplistically as the increased opportunity costs of educated women's children because of their higher earning power or their increased status in domestic decision-making. They cast doubt on such straightforward causal linkages in the South Asian context, where the schooling of girls is more often about inculcating piety and deference than learning how to 'insist'. Autonomy may imply 'loose morals' and there are some very puzzling inconsistencies in the relationships between girls' schooling, autonomy and fertility rates. The lives of girls and women in different parts of South Asia belie the simple logic of the World Bank experts. Educated women in South Asia may experience contradictory pressures from the families into which they marry. In rural areas, particularly, they may be expected to demonstrate their superior respectability to their uneducated neighbours by punctilious observance of the restrictions of seclusion, while at the same time advancing the education of their sons by helping with schoolwork and negotiating with schools and teachers. Jeffery and Basu suggest that at the basis of the WB argument is a patronizing assumption that the rural, illiterate poor are deluded by the belief that they need large families. Perhaps the greatest challenge to Summers' simplistic virtuous circle is the evidence from Kerala. This tiny state has attracted huge attention from development experts, academics and policy-makers alike, because of the way it has attained high literacy and low fertility, while mean income per head has remained low. Nevertheless, Visaria's measures of autonomy suggest that women in Gujarat have higher levels of autonomy than those in Kerala (Visaria 1996). Another perplexing setting for the advocates of schooling as contraception is Bangladesh, where fertility rates are falling despite the continuing marked gender gap in literacy and school attendance. There better access to credit and a vigorous birth-control policy have empowered women and increased their autonomy, enabling them to control their fertility (Schuler, Hashemi and Riley 1997). Jeffery and Basu conclude that girls' schooling will not 'resolve a wide range of social problems in South Asia: determined social reform will be required as well'.

The survey by Ainsworth et al. (1996) of the relationships among fertility, girls' schooling and contraceptive use in 14 countries in Sub-Saharan Africa comes to similar conclusions. They see the relationship of girls' education and fertility operating through four possible mechanisms:

- Wage effects: the opportunity cost of bringing up schoolchildren is greater. Educated women can also earn more in the labour market.
- Higher demand for child schooling: women who have some schooling have higher aspirations for their children – the much-debated quality/quantity trade-off (Lloyd and Blanc 1996).
- Lower child mortality: educated women are able to bring up healthier children.
- More effective use of contraception (Ainsworth et al. 1996: 86–7).

A multivariate analysis was carried out, controlling for age, area of residence, wealth, ethnicity and religion, on data drawn from the Demographic and Health Surveys in Tanzania 1991–92, Uganda 1988–90, Burundi 1987, Mali 1987, Niger 1992, Nigeria 1990, Kenya 1993, Ghana 1993, Togo 1988, Zambia 1992, Zimbabwe 1988, Senegal 1992–93, Cameroon 1991 and Botswana 1988. In general in these countries fertility rates are high, from 7.4 in Niger to 5 in Botswana, and levels of girls' schooling low, from 17 per cent in Mali to 16 per cent in Zimbabwe. A brief period of schooling did not affect fertility – completion of primary education appeared to be the threshold for the effect of school attendance on fertility. School attendance was positively related to contraceptive use. In most rural areas, however, contraceptives are not available. Countries with fertility rates greater than 7 include Niger and Mali, which are among the poorest in the world, with sparse rural populations and very few girls receiving any schooling. Zimbabwe, Botswana and Kenya, on the other hand, have made very marked progress in school attendance among girls. Widespread family planning services have also been introduced, and women have wider labour market opportunities than those in the poorest rural countries.

This recent evidence from Sub-Saharan Africa and South Asia, the regions where gender gaps in schooling are large and fertility rates high, suggests that an expansion of girls' schooling alone in the poorest countries with the most marked gender gaps and highest fertility rates is unlikely to succeed in reducing fertility there. 'Schooling as contraception' is a facile notion. However, other policies can succeed, as the falling birth rate in Bangladesh clearly shows. The country remains very poor and literacy levels are increasing only slowly, especially among women. More research is needed on the changes in Bangladesh and how Kerala and Sri Lanka have succeeded in attaining high literacy rates and low fertility without the rapid economic growth associated with newly industrializing countries (NICs). The social context within which fertility decisions are made remains all-important. Fertility rates have fallen in countries where an investment has been made in the quality of life of women and children. How far changing masculinities have contributed to these changes is another issue requiring urgent investigation. The WB has ignored these wider contexts, advocating a single narrow policy that takes no account of the realities of women's lives.

Integrated anti-poverty programmes

The 1997 *Human Development Report* (*HDR*) makes a distinction between economic and human poverty. Human poverty is defined as a short life, illiteracy and lack of access to services such as clean water and primary healthcare. The 1997 *HDR* focuses on the worsening gaps between the rich and the poor within and among countries: 'The share of the poorest

20% of the world's people in global income now stands at a miserable 1.1% down from 1.4% in 1991 and 2.3% in 1960. It continues to shrink. And the ratio of the income of the top 20% to that of the poorest 20% rose from 30 to 1 in 1960 to 61 to 1 in 1991 and a startling new high of 78 to 1 in 1994' (UNDP 1997: 9). It argues for much stronger pro-poor polices, in which debt reduction is the first priority at the macro level and an integrated platform of policies is introduced at community levels to empower women and men and reduce poverty. Knodel and Jones (1996) have argued that the continuing social class inequalities of poverty and wealth imply that the priority given to girls' education is misplaced and should now go to reducing social class inequalities in access to schooling. *HDR 1997* places women and their education at the centre of pro-poor policies. Educating girls and women is not an alternative to poverty reduction, it is crucial to achieving it.

Moving beyond the gender gap

The surveys by Kelly and Elliott (1982), King and Hill (1993) and Brock and Cammish (1997) of girls' and women's education in the developing world concentrate on access, gender gaps and fertility issues. The foundation of a critical theoretical perspective has been laid in Nelly Stromquist's progress in understanding the complexity of gender power relations at the household, community and state levels. In 1995, looking forward to the UN women's conference in Beijing, Stromquist presented a feminist critique, 'Romancing the State: Gender and Power in Education' as the presidential address to the Comparative and International Education Society. She argued that women have less power and fewer civil rights than men, and that transformative policies by states are needed to create more equitable gender orders. Despite critical feminist perspectives on the patriarchal state, the women's movement has expended considerable effort promoting legislation, which has then been poorly implemented. Urged on by the rhetoric of successive UN women's conferences, echoed by the aid agencies, many countries have put in place legislative frameworks on gender equity, which have a minimal effect on the ground. In education the focus is on access, and content is ignored. States espouse the rhetoric of gender equality, implemented in weak access policies, and this perpetuates gender ideologies and power relations. They eschew radical policies addressing content, which might transform gender orders and empower girls and women. Stromquist concludes: 'Women have obtained more symbolic than real victories from the state and have constantly underestimated the ability of education in the reproduction of conventional gender identities' (1995: 454).

In Chapter 2 Stromquist develops this analysis, linking individual, community and institutional levels in an attempt to understand the complexities in changing relations of gender, education and development. The case studies in this volume all go beyond access issues to analyse the ideological and material structural relations shaping the educational realities in girls' and women's lives. Many of the subjects for whom voice is a crucial methodological issue have been marginalized, silenced and ignored. A wide range of methodologies, often in combination, have been used, and the subjects' own words are given prominence in these accounts. Some are methodologically unique and innovatory, and all bring new evidence to bear on understandings of gender, education and development. Many shed light on the lives of girls and women from the poorest and most invisible localities in the developing world. Their objectives are:

1. To give a voice to girls and women from the developing world in an attempt to understand and interpret their roles as active agents rather than passive consumers of education and development.
2. To initiate a debate that goes beyond issues of access, enrolments and levels of attainment to an analysis of the micro-processes of schooling, curricular content, meanings, and the way in which girls and women construct their understandings of education.
3. To provide a critique of the World Bank's reductionist perspective on girls' education.
4. To make linkages among gender, education and development within diverse social, political and cultural contexts, bearing in mind such issues as race, class, religion and ethnicity.

The four chapters in Part One use a fascinating range of methodologies to document the realities of education in girls' and women's lives, which are placed within changing political contexts. In Chapter 2 Nelly Stromquist draws on evidence from a number of countries in Africa and Latin America to show how decisions about girls' education at the household level are made within the macro-economic context of SAPs, which have greatly increased the burdens on girls and women in providing for their families. Projeto Nordeste (PN) in Brazil, the biggest WB-supported project in the world, illustrates the critique of WB rhetoric. PN is designed to reduce educational inequalities in the poorest provinces of Brazil, one of the most unequal countries in the world. It focuses on rural urban inequalities, ignoring gender and ethnicity. It is judged 'highly successful' as a 'participatory' project, yet women are excluded from its committees.

In Chapter 3 Christine Fox argues that in all aspects of life girls and women in Papua New Guinea are 'othered' and subordinated to produce one of the lowest educational participation and literacy rates among women and girls in the world. In Chapter 4 Elaine Unterhalter drives the analysis of the significance of the content of education for women's consciousness into new realms, by using autobiographical evidence to compare the educational experience of two generations of high-profile women under apartheid in South Africa. She finds that for the younger generation empowerment came not from schooling, but from 'survival in traumatic times'. In Chapter 5 Sheila Aikman provides an important and powerful analysis of the experience of formal Eurocentric education among a previously invisible indigenous group, the Arakmbut, charting the erosion of their knowledge of local biodiversity.

Part Two develops our understandings of the dynamics of family and household contexts with analyses of three very different societies in Sub-Saharan Africa. In Chapter 6 Pauline Rose and Mercy Tembon use evidence from interviews with girls themselves, their parents and teachers in Ethiopia to show that despite government policies economic inequalities and the continuing cultural importance of early marriage remain the most import-ant issues in girls' educational participation. Shona Wynd in Chapter 7 considers the relation between the extremely low educational participation rates and high fertility rates of girls and women in Niger, who are among the poorest in the world. Literacy and education are valued solely as a means to a government post and a secure high income. Interviews with rural parents illustrate their belief that their daughters will not succeed, largely because educated elites corruptly ensure the success of their own children. Wynd concludes that WB policies on girls' education that take no account of local cultural understandings are likely to fail. In Chapter 8 Stella Bendera examines the experience of girls and women of education in Tanzania, where, amid the depressing effects of SAPs, girls' and women's education is the subject of continuing systematic review and research by the government, NGOs and academics.

Part Three takes the analysis of gender, education and development into issues of the relationship between gendered education and segmented labour markets in two very different middle-income countries: Malaysia and Mauritius. Sheila Bunwaree argues in Chapter 9 that the government in Mauritius protected the education of girls by refusing to implement the introduction of user fees as part of its SAP. She uses evidence from interviews with girls and their parents to illustrate the subtle processes marginalizing and devaluing girls' and women's educational experience. Mauritius had a suitably educated female labour force to staff the textile factories of the Export Production Zone. However, in the post-GATT era, other countries with lower labour costs are likely to dominate textile markets. Secondary and tertiary education in science and technology are poorly developed in Mauritius, especially among girls. Suet-ling Pong's sophisticated analysis in Chapter 10 uses quantitative and qualitative evidence from Malaysia to examine Knodel and Jones's argument that the continuing focus on gender inequalities in education is 'wide of the mark' since social class inequalities are a greater and more persistent issue. She points out that: 'Ethnic politics dominated Malaysia's post-independence education politics.' Malay women, formerly the most disadvantaged group, benefited most from these policies. The gender gap in education and in incomes has closed among the Malays but not among the Chinese communities in Malaysia, showing that gender inequalities are embedded in their larger political, economic and cultural contexts and histories.

Part Four illuminates some of the varying relations among gender, education and development in South Asia. Sri Lanka has long been a 'light in a naughty world', one of the most important examples of a country with high scores on all measures of gender equality and empowerment despite low per capita income. In Chapter 11 Swarna Jayaweera indicates the long historical development by which Sri Lanka has attained universal literacy and low birth rates among women without the rapid economic development associated with such a transition in other countries. She provides a strong critique of SAPs, demonstrating that even after the recent attempts to add a 'human face' it is the poorest and most vulnerable who pay the price of adjustment packages. Gender inequalities in access to education have been eliminated, but many girls face dilemmas and contradictions between their understandings of femininity and their educational aspirations. As do Mauritius and Malaysia, Sri Lanka provides further evidence that equal educational attainment does not translate into equal rewards in the labour market for girls and women. Jayaweera concludes with the issue of education and empowerment, arguing that education alone does not necessarily empower girls and women. While literacy levels are high, most women in Sri Lanka are subordinated in the domestic division of labour and a significant number experience domestic violence.

Mo Sibbons's chapter on Nepal is an analysis of a particular development project attempting to move from WID to GAD. Nepal is also one of the poorest countries in the world: land-locked, with poor agricultural conditions and rapid population growth. The Secondary Education Project is receiving major support from donors and aims to improve access and quality in secondary education, especially that of girls. Sibbons argues that, rather than poverty, it is the cultural beliefs about early marriage and femininity that are responsible for the low participation of girls in secondary education.

In Chapter 13 Christine Heward excoriates successive governments of Pakistan that have neglected human development for half a century since independence to spend the major part of the national budget on defence against India. Most women, especially those in the countryside, are illiterate, spending their lives bearing and rearing children and shouldering the endless domestic burdens of fetching fuel, water and fodder for their animals. The dismal government support for girls' education was excused by the belief that parents did not want it. NGO-supported projects with informal schools modelled on those of the Bangladesh Rural Advancement Committee have shown that parents do want to educate their daughters. To be supported girls' schools must be free and of good quality, be near their homes and have teachers whom the community trust, preferably women. Informal schools supported by NGOs are unlikely to be sustainable, especially in the most disadvantaged communities. Defence has been reasserted as the priority for government spending in Pakistan. Rapid urbanization may provide the possibility of a better life for girls and women in Pakistan, leaving many of those in the rural areas poor and illiterate.

A number of important conclusions may be drawn from these case studies:

- They highlight the contradictions between IMF and WB policies. Girls' education is established as a high priority in the international donor community. How far their policies will mitigate the effects of SAPs on poor households, where girls' education may be a low priority, remains to be seen.
- They illustrate the gap between the rhetoric of donors and education officials about gender equality and the reality of many women's lives, dominated by poverty and domestic responsibilities.
- They draw attention to the importance of local cultures, first of all for girls' and women's access to education but most importantly for the meaning of educational experience in their lives.
- They support the need for analyses of the content of education and the way education is experienced by girls and women, tracing the life-courses of women and making inter-generational comparisons. Such studies must take account of changing economic, political and cultural contexts, especially gender-segmented labour markets.
- They raise the issue of the extent to which the gap between the educational experience of poor and rich women within and between countries is widening. How far women in rural areas in the poorest countries will become increasingly invisible and isolated from the globalized economy and knowledge society in the twenty-first century is an all-important question for future research and policy-making.
- They make the empowerment of women and their autonomy central issues in understandings of gender, education and development.
- They demonstrate the complexity of relations among gender, education and development, exposing the simplistic view of girls' education as contraception. Gender relations in education are embedded in their changing political, economic and cultural contexts. Sensitive analyses using qualitative and quantitative evidence are needed to explicate their complexities and nuances.

Bibliography

Ainsworth, M., K. Beegle and K. Nyamete (1996) 'The impact of women's schooling on fertility and contraceptive use: a study of 14 Sub-Saharan African countries', *World Bank Economic Review* 10 (1): 84–122.

Boserup, E. (1970) *Women's Role in Economic Development*, Allen & Unwin, London.

Brock, C. and N. Cammish (1997) *Factors Affecting Female Participation in Education in Seven Developing Countries*, Department for International Development, London.

Dasgupta, P. (1993) *An Enquiry into Well-Being and Destitution*, Clarendon, Oxford.

Jeffery, R. and A. Basu (1996) *Girls' Schooling, Women's Autonomy and Fertility Change in South Asia*, Sage, New Delhi.

Jejeebhoy, S. (1995) *Women's Education, Autonomy and Reproductive Behaviour: Experience from Developing Countries*, Oxford University Press, Oxford.

Kelly, G. and C. Elliott (1982) *Women's Education in the Third World: Comparative Perspectives*, State University of New York, New York.

King, E. and M. Hill (1993) *Women's Education in Developing Countries*, World Bank, Washington, DC.

Knodel, J. and G. Jones (1996) 'Post-Cairo population policy: does promoting girls' schooling miss the mark?', *Population and Development Review* 22 (4): 683–702.

Lloyd, C. and A. Blanc (1996) 'Children's schooling in Africa: the role of fathers, mothers and others', *Population and Development Review* 22 (2): 265–98.

Moser, C. (1989) 'Gender planning in the Third World: meeting practical and strategic gender needs', *World Development* 17 (11): 1799–825.

Please, S. (1996) 'Structural adjustment and poverty – blunting the criticisms', *Development Policy Review* 14: 185–202.

Razavi, S. and C. Miller (1995) 'From WID to GAD: conceptual shifts in the women and development discourse', UN Research Institute for Social Development, Geneva.

Rose, P. (1995) 'Female education and adjustment programs: a cross-country statistical analysis', *World Development Review* 23 (11): 1931–49.

Schuler, S., S. Hashemi and A. Riley (1997) 'The influence of women's changing roles and status in Bangladesh's fertility transition: evidence from a study of credit programs and contraceptive use', *World Development* 25 (4): 563–75.

Stromquist, N. (1995) 'Romancing the state: gender and power in education', *Comparative Education Review* 39 (4): 423–54.

— (1997) 'Gender sensitive educational strategies and their implementation', *International Journal of Educational Development* 17 (2): 205–14.

Subbaro, K. and L. Raney (1993) *Social Gains from Female Education: A Cross National Study*, World Bank Discussion Paper 194, World Bank, Washington, DC.

UNDP (various years) *Human Development Report* (especially 1997), Oxford University Press, Oxford.

Visaria, L. (1996) 'Regional variations in regional autonomy and fertility and contraception in India', in R. Jeffery and A. Basu, *Girls' Schooling*.

Woodward, D. (1997) 'Economic dimensions of education and the role of the World Bank', paper presented to NGO Education Forum, London 1997.

PART ONE

Changing Political
Contexts

CHAPTER 2

The Impact of Structural Adjustment Programmes in Africa and Latin America

Nelly P. Stromquist

Analysing women's conditions and gender relations

Scholarly work on gender and the political pressure generated by the women's movement have produced a greater awareness of the need to assess both macro- and micro-institutions through a gender-sensitive lens. Deeper examination of the dynamics in place in such settings as the labour market, schools and families reveals forces that maintain patriarchal relations and identifies spaces that can be used to subvert them. While the subordination of women is expressed and resolved differently across societies and social classes, important commonalities exist. The lower the family's income, the greater the economic contribution made by the unpaid work of its unemployed members to the satisfaction of basic needs.

To understand women's situation in society, it is crucial to examine the relationship between reproduction and production – or the double role that women perform as mothers and workers. For this understanding, the household is a vital site, as 'women's consciousness is structured partly by the socialization process which enculturates the gender ideals of the dominant ideology, and partly by women's pragmatic negotiation of gender roles' (Obbo 1990: 222). In societies where few are wealthy and low-technology domestic production the norm, most women operate in unpaid family labour in the familial mode of production. In the African context, women and girls spend many more hours than men and boys in domestic work.

Poverty is an essential factor in the subordination of women because of its association with limited domestic infrastructure. In Sub-Saharan Africa, safe drinking water is accessible on average to 57 per cent of the urban population but to only 29 per cent of the rural population. Women bring home 93 per cent of the water and 95 per cent of the firewood (Spring 1987). Since roads are limited, the tasks of water and firewood procurement are both difficult and time-consuming.

Africa has a predominantly rural population and agriculture plays a

fundamental role in people's work and subsistence. For women participating in the labour market, wages are typically 60 to 70 per cent of those
paid to men. A study of 15 Latin American and Caribbean countries
found that about 40 per cent of the gender wage gap is explained by
differences in educational levels, labour market experience and the low-
paying fields in which women work, with 60 per cent attributable to gender
discrimination (Psacharopoulos and Tzannatos 1992). Education is not
sufficient to reduce salary differentials when sexual stereotypes permeate
a culture.

In rural Sub-Saharan Africa the number of women-headed households
has increased because of the concentration of wage jobs in cities, emigra-
tion to sell one's labour abroad, and the widespread phenomenon of
informal and unstable marital unions. For example, women head one-
third of households in Malawi, more than 50 per cent in communal areas
of Zimbabwe, and 40 per cent of Kenyan small farms (Gordon 1996).
These women are especially vulnerable, particularly if their skills are not
upgraded with economic and technological changes.

The role and impact of structural adjustment
programmes

Since the late 1970s economic and social policies, generally known as
structural adjustment programmes (SAPs), have been implemented in
several developing countries with the purpose of improving their overall
conditions. These policies have been drafted from a gender-blind perspective and they have had serious consequences for women. In fact, it
has been women who have articulated the most serious criticisms of the
social costs of structural adjustment, presenting evidence of the increasing
poverty and inequality among women that SAPs have generated (Jaquette
1997).

While the focus of this analysis is on the impact of structural adjustment upon education, it places education in the context of a wider socio-
economic framework. SAPs are not the only source of gender inequality
in Africa today. For example, in Africa a woman does not usually own
land but rather obtains usufructuary rights to land from her husband's
lineage group (Palmer 1991). Lack of access to land generates a number
of constraints in access to other productive resources: credit, extension
services, training, technical assistance, and membership of farmers' organizations.

The purpose of SAPs is to steer economies towards better economic
and social performance. Their basic aims are as follows:

- opening the national economy to imports;
- reducing the size and role of government;

- eliminating subsidies to agriculture;
- encouraging privatization of many economic and social sectors; and
- devaluing the local currency.

Reviews of the impact of SAPs in the many countries where they have been enacted report negative consequences (Cornia et al. 1992; Samoff 1994; Reimers and Tiburcio 1993), but there are a few dissenting views (Okyere 1990; Bourguinon and Morrisson 1992). Since 1987 the IMF has received $4 billion more than it has provided in new finance (Development and Cooperation 1997). Countries in Sub-Saharan Africa have entered a period of steady deterioration, reflected in mounting external debt and a continuous financial bleeding to meet debt service payments.

Various researchers have criticized macro-level development policies that are insensitive to any consideration of women's economic contribution and their need for incentives at the micro level. In their view, this gender-blindness has contributed to the recent food crisis in Africa (Mackintosh 1989; Gladwin 1991a and 1991b; Gordon 1996) and to the increased domestic and subsistence burdens of women (Nyoni 1991; Sen 1996). SAPs 'assume that all actors or units are equal before the market, and that gender differentiation is the result of the free choice of alternatives based on comparative advantage' (Geisler 1993: 1973). SAP policies have expanded the extraction and production of natural resources to be traded on the international market; this has favoured large over small producers, and men over women. In principle, the incentives under SAPs should shift women in agricultural labour away from food production. But since women are assigned (arbitrarily, to be sure) a social responsibility for sustaining the family, they continue to engage in food production. Even if women wanted to move into cash-crop production, family responsibilities make them less mobile than men. Men control and benefit most from cash crops, and generally have more control over use of land. As Gordon observes (1996), when food crops become major sources of cash income, men are able to redefine these food crops into cash crops and take them over for their own benefit – something that women cannot do. In other words, patriarchy, not the market, enables crucial production choices.

SAPs make assumptions about the prevalence of a formal labour market, where wages will go up on the heels of increased competition in the marketplace. But in Africa, most producers are outside the formal economy. Even in urban areas, 50 per cent of the workers are in the informal sector, and the majority are women (Gordon 1996). Wage employment represents less than 15 per cent of the total labour force in 11 of 13 African countries for which data are available (Bennell 1994, cited in Pritchett 1996).

SAPs affect women negatively through the impact of changes in income and prices, in levels and composition of public expenditures and in working conditions (Young 1993). According to IMF data (cited in Cornia et al. 1992), there was a reduction of approximately 30 per cent in the terms of trade between 1982 and 1990. Governmental cutting of services often shifts costs and work to the unpaid economy (that which concentrates on the production of non-tradable goods) (Gordon 1996). Such cuts have been said to constitute, *de facto*, a reproductive tax on women (Geisler 1993). As home managers, women have been adversely affected by the reduction or abolition of subsidies for food and other basic goods. Their role as mothers has been made more difficult by reduced social services. As workers, increasing numbers of women have had to engage in income-generating activities, especially in the informal sector, to stem the fall in household income.

Since 1988, structural adjustment lending by the World Bank to many countries has included safety-nets for the poor, including women. The World Bank 1989 *World Progress Report* noted that two of the eight fiscal structural adjustment operations in 1988 and three of the twelve fiscal operations in 1989 included action to 'help women contribute to macro-economic adjustment or to improve their future productivity' (cited in Jahan 1995). These measures have included providing nutrition programmes for pregnant and nursing mothers and healthcare for women and children, improving educational opportunities for girls in rural areas, training women in construction, and targeting credit to women (Jahan 1995). The amount of funds available through these 'safety-nets' is minuscule *vis-à-vis* the size of the groups in need of assistance. Jahan remarks quite rightly that these programmes have been 'largely palliative measures intended to soften the adverse impact, and did not challenge the basic directions of SAPs' (1995: 71).

The impact of SAPs on education

There is intense debate among scholars about the effects of structural adjustment programmes on education, because of the difficulty of distinguishing the consequences of SAPs from those of domestic civil strife and drought. There is a clear pattern of negative shifts in the distribution of national budgets during the period when SAP reforms were introduced. Moreover, comparison of educational conditions in Africa with other regions, such as Latin America, that have experienced less dramatic domestic problems shows a consistent pattern of negative impacts of SAPs upon education.

African countries that underwent such adjustments during the 1980s had a smaller growth in GNP than countries without the adjustment. Indeed, 68 per cent of the countries with SAPs experienced a *decrease* in their GNP, while only half of those without adjustment programmes did

(Reimers and Tiburcio 1993). This decrease in GNP reflected the decrease of 25 per cent in average salaries in the non-agricultural sector between 1980 and 1985 in two-thirds of African countries.

A strong association has been found between SAP measures and reductions in national educational budgets. A review of 21 African countries that adopted SAPs and ten that did not revealed that 62 per cent of those countries with SAPs decreased their educational expenditures as a proportion of the GNP; in contrast, only 20 per cent of the countries without SAPs did (Reimers and Tiburcio 1993). Case studies of Brazil, Costa Rica, Senegal, Tanzania and Hungary indicate that spending in primary and secondary education decreased as a result of SAP measures (Samoff 1994). A study of 16 low-income countries with structural adjustment programmes in 1981–85 found that primary school enrolment declined by between 3.2 and 39 per cent (Commonwealth Secretariat 1989: 82).

Reductions in educational budgets have had strong impacts on student access to primary schooling. As a region, Sub-Saharan Africa has the largest proportion of children not attending primary school, increasing from 43 per cent of the total number of children aged 6–11 years in 1980 to 50 per cent in 1990 (UNESCO 1995). Growth in enrolment slipped from 10 per cent in the late 1970s to 1.6 per cent in the 1980s, at a time when the population was growing at 3.2 per cent per year (Cornia et al. 1992). Gross primary enrolment rates in African countries without SAPs increased by 5.5 per cent in contrast to 0.41 per cent in countries with SAPs during the 1980–88 period. Access to secondary schooling has also suffered, and the rate of growth in African countries with SAPs was 3.3 compared to 9.4 per cent in countries without SAPs. Thus the decreased growth rate in primary school enrolment resulted in decreased secondary school enrolment, which fell from 14 to 4 per cent of the pertinent school-age population during that period (Cornia et al. 1992).

SAPs were instituted to improve economies that were already troubled. It is possible, therefore, that school enrolments would have decreased without SAPs. The point to be argued, however, is not merely the decrease in enrolment but the fact that SAPs were not able to create conditions that resulted in improved access to schooling. Primary enrolment rates declined, depriving some children of access to the most basic level of schooling. African countries with SAPs had a 30 per cent decrease in access to first grade compared with countries without SAPs. Decreases in educational achievement as reflected in higher repetition rates have been observed in many countries. For the children who did attend primary school, their likelihood of attending secondary school also decreased. The rate of transition from primary to secondary schooling in 1988 registered a drop from 46 per cent in countries without SAPs to 38 per cent in countries with SAPs (Reimers and Tiburcio 1993: 44).

As enrolment decreases the gender gap has widened in primary grades,

Table 2.1 Annual growth rate in percentage of girls and boys completing primary schooling in Latin America according to length of SAP implementation, 1980–88

No. of years with SAP	Girls	Boys	No. of countries
None	2.42	1.34	7
1–2	-1.90	-0.81	5
3–4	-0.77	-1.53	12
5 or more	-0.31	0.29	5

Source: Reimers and Tiburcio 1993: 53.

with 13 percentage points to the detriment of girls (Cornia et al. 1992). Comparisons between girls and boys indicate that girls have also fared worse than boys in terms of primary school completion, and that the negative impact on girls' enrolment is long-lasting. Table 2.1 presents compelling evidence about the gender-differentiated impact of SAPs on basic education, effects that manifest themselves directly through reduced expenditures in education and through household responses. While the average enrolment of girls in countries without SAPS has registered an increase over that of boys, in countries with SAPS girls' enrolment falls precipitously, especially immediately after the implementation of these policies.

Comparisons of SAP impacts on education in Latin America are particularly illuminating. Latin America did not face major natural catastrophes or political upheavals during the 1980s, thus adding some precision to the identification of impacts attributable solely to SAPs. A number of Latin American scholars, particularly Reimers (1991) and Reimers and Tiburcio (1993), have shown in categorical terms the negative association between SAPs and educational expenditure. As in the case of Africa, Latin American countries with SAPs experienced reductions in educational budgets and consequently in gross enrolment rates in primary and secondary schooling. The data for the level of educational expenditure as a proportion of total government expenditure in Latin America, which cover a period of about 16 years, reveal a negative annual growth in 14 out of 19 countries (Reimers 1991). These longitudinal data for Latin America (see Table 2.1) weaken the hope that significant educational improvements may occur after the economies undergoing SAPs pass the initial shock. It must be noted, however, that longer longitudinal data for Latin American countries would be useful, for a key question is whether governments recover their ability to invest in education as the national economies become accustomed to the new economic equilibrium brought by restructuring.

Facing pressure to reduce budget deficits, many governments look first to education for ways of diminishing expenditures. That education is easy to attack is facilitated by the fact that mainly poor families attend public schools today: their voices are weaker than those of families whose children attend private schools. Education has suffered in particular because of three factors:

1. Overall cuts in public expenditures often result in disproportionate cuts in education compared to other public sectors. This is especially so because the short-term focus of adjustment measures has not allowed for any special treatment of the education sector.
2. As the standard of living of large segments of the population falls, the household income available for investment in school (e.g. tuition, uniforms, textbooks) decreases.
3. As the need for economic survival increases among poor households, reliance on child labour – and thus their removal from school – increases (Commonwealth Secretariat 1989; Riemers and Tiburcio 1993).

A significant portion of the decrease in student enrolment can be attributed to the growing parental burden of primary education and the increasing opportunity costs of sending children to school. Changes in a number of economic and social conditions (for example, a fall in the minimum wage, an increase in unemployment, the loss of health coverage, reduction of public expenditures for child welfare) have a stronger effect on poorer families because they generally have larger than average numbers of children. Poor families are also most affected because any increase in the cost of services represents a higher proportion of their income than for other social classes. It has been estimated for Latin America that, in the absence of special policies to correct these biases against the poorest families, a reduction of 5 to 10 per cent in government expenditures as a proportion of the GDP may result in a net drop in family resources three to four times larger (Albanez et al. 1989, cited in Reimers and Tiburcio 1993). When parents are barely able to send their children to school and cannot afford additional expenses, such as textbooks (which often remain unpurchased), quality deteriorates.

To reduce the negative effects of SAPs on education, the World Bank increased the amount of lending to this sector, encouraged finance-driven education reforms, and increased its emphasis on efficiency over equity issues. Greater state support has been given to primary education. At the same time, increasing segments of secondary and higher education have been privatized and fees encouraged (Jones 1997), thus making it more difficult for lower-income groups to attain competitive levels of schooling.

An example of World Bank work: Project Northeast, Brazil Facing a pressing situation in the national economy, borrowing countries and lending institutions develop an instrumental view of education. They see access almost as the exclusive objective and fail to recognize how the effects of SAPs go against the goals of school permanence and performance. They define efficiency as the ability of school systems to prevent students from repeating school years. Equity – both gender and ethnic – assumes low priority and often becomes invisible. These dynamics are exemplified in Project Northeast (Projeto Nordeste, PN) in Brazil, recipient of one of the largest World Bank loans in the world.

PN serves nine states that are greatly disadvantaged compared to the rest of Brazil. Official sources indicate that 1.7 million children aged 7–14 do not attend school in the region. PN is a five-year project begun in 1993 and scheduled to be completed in 1998. It has a total budget of $736 million, of which $18 million come from the World Bank loan. Its coverage is enormous, as it seeks to reach 176,625 teachers, 22,386 school principals, and 6.5 million children in grades one to four.

According to loan documents, PN's main objectives are to improve the quality and equity of primary schools in the country. To this end, it proposes a set of interventions that have included creating new educational facilities and improving existing ones, providing educational materials and textbooks to schools, training teachers in basic content, providing school administrators with management skills, and promoting educational innovations. After some problems in the initial years, PN is now considered by World Bank authorities an 'exemplary model' in terms of execution (Renato 1997).

While equity concerns were clearly identified as project objectives, very little of what has taken place so far reflects a consideration of gender issues. It should be noted that in Brazil, women attain as many years of education as men: 4.9 vs. 5.1 for men, according to the Ministry of Education and Sport (Ministerio da Educacao e do Desporto 1996: 9) and the levels of enrolment at all levels of schooling are about the same for both sexes (Rosemberg 1992). In society, however, women occupy a position inferior to that of men in professional roles, political representation and access to income and property.

PN has been participatory in design, having had several committees, including a consultative group, a technical team, a research team and a coordination team, comprising in total 45 persons from research institutions, universities and government bodies. However, academic gender specialists and women from the local women's movements have not been involved. The main research products linked to PN resulted in 13 studies, published in a book focusing on educational failure (PN/BM/UNICEF 1997). The studies address important issues such as school governance, teachers' salaries, classroom practices, student performance and dropping out, politics of education, and school conditions.

Gender is discussed in two studies. The study on school drop-outs states that 'gender is not an important category among the reasons leading low-income students to abandon school', but it also observes that mothers 'wish that their daughters be, first of all, mothers' (PN 1997: 2–3). The study on the impact of the social environment on student performance finds that the mother's schooling has a greater impact on student educational performance than does the father's schooling (PN/BM/UNICEF 1997: 35). Although primary schoolteachers are almost exclusively women, gender aspects of their identity as professionals and their salaries are not discussed.

In 1997 the Brazilian government produced, with project funds, a set of ten booklets, which it called 'national curricular parameters'. These booklets cover seven core subjects and three cross-cutting issues that seek to permeate the core subjects. Gender issues and sex education are considered within the multicultural cross-cutting issues. They receive a coverage of three pages. No evidence could be found that the workshops for teachers and administrators are considering gender issues. A key instrument to facilitate educational actions is the school census, described by ministry authorities as representing 'a significant step forward in gaining access to up-to-date and consistent data to plan and formulate effective policies' (Ministerio da Educacao e do Desporto 1997: 1). The questionnaire on which the census is based (administered in 1996 and repeated in 1997) gathers data on the physical condition of the school, the enrolment of students in primary, secondary and technical schooling, and teacher numbers and their levels of education. The questionnaire includes no breakdown by sex for either students or teachers.

The work of PN will, to a great extent, continue through a ten-year loan also from the World Bank. This new phase, now expanded to cover the west-centre region, will be called the Fund for Educational Strengthening (Fundo de Fortalecimento Escolar – Fundescola). The cost of the new project will amount to $1.3 billion, of which $1.1 billion will come from the World Bank.

This example from Brazil shows how a project whose implementation has been judged excellent nevertheless deviates from original objectives, as quality issues dominate and equity is redefined to refer only to rural/ urban disparities but not to either race or gender issues. It also shows how gender equity is perceived as access to education, so that criteria of gender equity are fulfilled by parity in enrolment. The goal is 'modernization'. Without funds to explore the creation of an alternative social order, concerns for social justice are minimized.

Household dynamics impacting on decision-making

Poor families are the hardest hit by government cuts in education budgets. In the few cases where measures have been taken to promote access to schooling, definitions of quality have pre-empted considerations of equity. In rural areas, especially in Africa, it is girls within these families who have suffered the most. In more urbanized regions, such as those in Latin America, it appears that boys have suffered considerably as they have been forced to enter the informal sector of the economy at early ages, a phenomenon that appears in the lower enrolment of boys compared to girls in secondary schools in several Latin American countries during the 1980s and 1990s. To understand the gender impact it is necessary to consider the internal dynamics of households. Decisions about sex relations, domestic work and outside work are far from being unanimous, but are the product of negotiation among household key members. It is crucial to pay attention to how resources are allocated within households and communities because allocations at this level may have lasting repercussions (Massiah 1990; Kusterer 1990).

Unlike schools, which are easily observable, households are private settings to which researchers have access only rarely. It is difficult to document with precision the various negotiations and resulting decisions between husband and wife, adults and children in the households. These decisions can be reconstructed from certain indicators disaggregated by sex, such as literacy, years of schooling, health, nutrition and poverty. Because social statistics do not always distinguish between men and women and often fail to differentiate between socio-economic levels, we know relatively little about gender differences within the household. Time allocation studies in the former Ivory Coast support the findings of those in other African countries. They indicate that women do 66 per cent of the total agricultural work and that children, especially girls, and the elderly account for another 20 per cent (FAO 1983, cited in Spring 1987).

Income is also unevenly distributed within households. Men support their families while reserving substantial amounts of their resources for their own use. Given the tendency of husbands to provide a fixed housekeeping allowance to wives, it is possible that women have faced an even sharper drop in real transfers from their husbands to meet basic household needs than indicated by the declines in real wages (Commonwealth Secretariat 1989).

There is ample consensus in the literature that women tend to spend more of their income on the family than do men. In the African context, household incomes are not pooled or separated (Geisler 1993). Women control their own resources but give husbands money for house-building, festivals, children's education, and household expenditures (Afonja 1990). The reduction in consumption caused by falling incomes forces the women to produce more goods at home with reduced resources (Feijoo and Jelin 1987). Women then tend to purchase foods that are less processed; they also spend more time trying to find cheap foods and gathering fuelwood and water. Since a considerable proportion of the fuel and water procurement is done by daughters, this division of labour affects girls' participation in schooling.

Economic crises cause a disproportionate increase in the work of women and children, who are asked to participate more in household survival. This reduces the contribution of parents to the education of their children or to the improvement of their local school (Reimers and Tiburcio 1993). Both factors result in increased pressures to withdraw children, girls first, from school. In Zambia in 1985, despite 'free' primary education, parental expenditure on basic items necessary for one child to attend school was more than one-fifth of the average per capita income (Commonwealth Secretariat 1989).

Data about household decisions from one African and two Latin American countries provide insights into the dynamics affecting the participation of children in school. A study of rural areas in Mexico showed that the decrease in the purchasing power of wages has obliged women to send their children to work in agriculture. In a survey in a region of sugar-cane plantations 48 per cent of the women stated categorically that their children should not study: the households of these wives had taken older female children out of school to look after younger children while the mother was at work (Commonwealth Secretariat 1989). Studies of low-income women in Ecuador have produced parallel findings: 30 per cent of the women were able to cope with their changed economic circumstances, but 55 per cent were 'just hanging on, using future resources in order to survive today', sending their sons out to work or keeping their daughters at home to take over domestic responsibilities; the other 15 per cent of the women were no longer coping and had their young children roaming the streets (Commonwealth Secretariat 1989). Similar negative impacts were found in Nigeria through a qualitative study of 40 women in ten villages. The study sought to assess the impact of SAPs during the 1985–89 period, and found that some households had reduced meals from three to two per day, but 85 per cent of the households had only one meal per day. One-quarter of the households were found to send children out to work for income (Elabor-Idemudia 1991).

An unintended consequence of the SAPs for women is that many poor urban women have mobilized themselves in defence of their family interests. In Latin America the unemployment and inflation caused by the economic crisis had led to the creation of mothers' clubs and communal kitchens with the explicit goals of lowering the cost of feeding their families. This has been accomplished through sharing food-buying and cooking. These activities have demonstrated women's abilities to organize and manage relatively complex activities (including large-scale production of food and distribution). In turn, this has encouraged the establishment of local women-led NGOs aimed at micro-enterprise development, skills training, and savings/credit programmes. These initiatives, however, are few and have occurred mostly in urban areas. The economic crisis in Latin America has made it necessary to strengthen ties within informal mutual support networks in the neighbourhood and the wider family. According to some observers, these 'social capital' horizontal networks are based on equality, collaboration and norms such as trust and account- ability. These settings are therefore considered to have a potential for transforming women's position by making public their domestic problems and their solutions.

Consequences for women's advancement

There is a wide consensus in both Latin America and Africa that SAPs have given insufficient attention to the social costs of adjustment. There is also a belief that macro-economic analysis is biased against women because of its inability to identify distortions in resource allocations.

In the African context, it is clear that the agrarian aspects are essential. Here, three basic observations can be made. First, there is a crucial need for women to have formal access to land. Development of the food sector would require reallocation of land and capital (Royal Tropical Institute 1995), and this would entail women's right to own land by holding direct title to it. Second, land titles operate as the entry point to most other agricultural resources: credit, access to technology, technical assist- ance. Third, it is imperative to make peasant agriculture more productive rather than to eliminate it (Gordon 1996). Making peasant agriculture more productive implies the provision of technical assistance, fertilizers and time-saving tools to women farmers. Women's role in agriculture should be strengthened and not limited to production of food for family consumption – otherwise, we will be merely reinforcing women's repro- ductive roles. Both measures – land ownership and increased productivity – should result in greater wealth at the household level in rural settings.

The challenges ahead suggest that the state should play a strong role in the provision of redistributive policies as well as in the coordination of measures to improve and disseminate knowledge and technologies. This creates a major conundrum, because while the state is needed, it has historically been reluctant to act on behalf of the transformation of gender roles. Some state-based actions are necessary:

1. Strategies to improve girls' education in Africa need to work on the provision of basic fuel and water infrastructures for the household. 'No single act so reduces household labor time as the bringing of water and fuel to the household' (Kusterer 1990: 254). It will be difficult to move out of the patriarchal economy and its concomitant conditions unless investment in physical and human infrastructure increases the productivity of domestic work (Kusterer 1990).
2. There is a need to redefine the educational requirements of women and girls. Educational programmes aimed at adult women should go

beyond literacy programmes to include knowledge of soil fertility, water use, animal husbandry, forest products use, food storage, nutrition, health and marketing (Gladwin 1991a). Recent studies on the effects of education on national productivity (measured as growth of GDP per worker) show that these effects are very weak for Sub-Saharan Africa and South Asia, highlighting the need to modify the technological environment before education can be effective (Pritchett 1996).

3. To accomplish gender objectives the collection and use of social statistics will have to be improved. This requires not just accurate, regular and prompt gender-disaggregated data, but a better conceptual basis to data so that they properly reflect women's full contribution to the economy and the household (Commonwealth Secretariat 1989). The domestic and unpaid work women perform must be documented. Along with improved statistics, there should be more qualitative studies focusing on household behaviours and dynamics. The household is a site of important decisions and allocations that affect educational access, attainment and performance. Statistics must also present data about the various socio-economic classes and main ethnic groups. Without such data the extent of maldistribution of state services is unknown.

4. Financial assistance should be targeted to low-income women and should be available for low-level economic activities, including micro-credit capacity. Countries should be given incentives to invest in women and failure to address them should result in substantial sanctions. The issue of intervention in sovereign countries can be counter-argued by the assertion that international assistance should serve the entire country and that investments in areas such as the military, roads, dams, etc. do not serve women.

5. In the African context, it can be asserted that the economic crisis and the World Bank's current solution, SAPs, have brought many of women's economic and political gains to a standstill. As women have performed as the shock-absorbers of socio-economic crisis (Meena 1991), many issues regarding legal and political rights have been cast aside in the search for immediate survival.

While most governments and donor agencies have made progress in recognizing the significant contribution of women to societies and the need to end discriminatory practices against them, crucial macro-economic measures remain untouched by gendered policy analysis, and women's core agenda – such as poverty reduction and equality in human development, decision-making and entitlement – are not acknowledged in important policy dialogues (Jahan 1995). In fact, the groups more likely to represent women's interests – the women's NGOs – are usually absent from important government discussions. A recent publication (World Bank 1995) calls upon governments to work 'in collaboration' with other players from the development community and civil society. This document identifies a large set of institutions without specifically acknowledging the role of women's NGOs and feminists.

Women have shown that they are not merely victims, that they can mobilize themselves to defend their interests and those of their families. Yet it is clear that despite women's resourcefulness, the state's failure to consider the impacts of macro-structural policies on women is a major impediment to changing gender relations.

Bibliography

Afonja, S. (1990) 'Changing patterns of gender stratification in West Africa', in I. Tinker (ed.), *Persistent Inequalities*.

Blossfeld, H.-P. (1995) *The New Role of Women: Family Formations in Modern Societies*, Westview Press, Boulder, CO.

Bourguinon, F. and C. Morrisson (1992) *Adjustment and Equity in Developing Countries: A New Approach*, OECD, Paris.

Commonwealth Secretariat (1989) *Engendering Adjustment for the 1990s*, Commonwealth Secretariat, London.

Cornia, G., R. van der Hoeven and T. Mkandawire (eds) (1992) *Africa's Recovery in the 1990s: From Stagnation to Adjustment to Human Development*, St. Martin's Press, New York.

Development and Cooperation (1997) 'Borrowed burden', *Development and Co-operation 2*.

Elabor-Idemudia, P. (1991) 'The impact of structural adjustment programs on women and their households in Bendel and Ogun states, Nigeria', in C. Gladwin (ed.), *Structural Adjustment and African Farmers*.

Feijoo, M. del Carmen, and E. Jelin (1987) 'Women from low income sectors: economic recession and democratization of politics in Argentina', in UNICEF (ed.), *The Invisible Adjustment: Poor Women and the Economic Crisis*, UNICEF Regional Office for the Americas and the Caribbean, Santiago.

Geisler, G. (1993) 'Silences speak louder than claims: gender, household, and agricultural development in Southern Africa', *World Development* 21 (21).

Gladwin, C. (1991) *Structural Adjustment and African Farmers*, University Press of Florida, Gainsville.

— (1991a) 'Introduction', in C. Gladwin (ed.), *Structural Adjustment and African Farmers*.

— (1991b) 'Fertilizer subsidy removal programs and their potential impacts on women farmers in Malawi and Cameroon', in C. Gladwin (ed.), *Structural Adjustment and African Farmers*.

Gordon, A. (1996) *Transforming Capitalism and Patriarchy: Gender and Development in Africa*, Lynne Rienner, Boulder, CO.

Jahan, R. (1995) *The Elusive Agenda: Mainstreaming Women in Development*, Zed Books, London.

Jaquette, J. (1997) 'International security: the role of women's political participation', paper presented at Seminar Series on International Relations, University of Southern California, Los Angeles.

Jones, P. (1997) 'On World Bank education financing', *Comparative Education* 33 (1).

Kusterer, K. (1990) 'The imminent demise of patriarchy', in I. Tinker (ed.), *Persistent Inequalities*.

Mackintosh, M. (1989) *Gender, Class and Rural Transition: Agribusiness and the Food Crisis in Senegal*, Zed Books, London.

Massiah, J. (1990) 'Defining women's work in the Commonwealth Caribbean', in I. Tinker (ed.), *Persistent Inequalities*.

Meena, R. (1991) 'The impact of structural adjustment programs on rural women in Tanzania', in C. Gladwin (ed.), *Structural Adjustment and African Farmers*.

Ministerio da Educacao e do Desporto (1996) *Development and Education in Brasil*, Ministerio da Educacao e do Desporto, Brasilia.

— (1997) *Censo Escolar 1997*, Ministerio da Educacao e do Desporto, Brasilia, 18 February.

Nyoni, S. (1991) *Women and Energy: Lessons from the Zimbabwe Experience*, Zimbabwe Environmental Research Organization, Harare.

Obbo, C. (1990) 'East African women, work, and the articulation of dominance', in I. Tinker (ed.), *Persistent Inequalities*.

Okyere, W. A. (1990) 'The response of farmers to Ghana's adjustment policies', in World Bank (ed.), *The Long-Term Perspective Study of Sub-Saharan Africa*, World Bank, Washington, DC.

Onimode, B. (1988) *A Political Economy of the African Crisis*, Zed Books and Institute for African Alternatives, London.

Organization of African Unity (1981) *Lagos Plan of Action for Economic Development in Africa, 1980–2000*, ILO, Geneva.

Palmer, I. (1991) *Gender and Population in the Adjustment of African Economies: Planning for Change*, ILO, Geneva.

Pritchett, L. (1996) *Where Has All the Education Gone?* Policy Research Working Paper No. 1581, World Bank, Washington, DC.

Projeto Nordeste (1997) *Licoes e Praticas 7. A Evasao do Ponto de Vista de Pais e Alunos*, Ministerio da Educacao e do Desporto/Banco Mundial, Brasilia.

Projeto Nordeste/Banco Mundial/UNICEF (1997) *Chamada a Acao. Combatendo o Fracasso Escolar no Nordeste*, Projeto Nordeste/Banco Mundial/UNICEF, Brasilia.

Psacharopoulos, G. and Z. Tzannatos (1992) *Women's Employment and Pay in Latin America: Overview and Methodology*, World Bank, Washington, DC.

Reimers, F. (1991) 'The role of organization and politics in government financing of education: the effects of "structural adjustment" in Latin America', *Comparative Education* 27 (1).

Reimers, F. and L. Tiburcio (1993) *Education, Ajustement et Reconstruction: Options pour un Changement*, UNESCO, Paris.

Renato, P. (1997) 'Demos um grande salto', *Boletim Tecnico* 2 (16): 3–4, Ministerio de Educacao e do Desporto/Banco Mundial, Brasilia.

Rosemberg, F. (1992) 'Education, democratization, and inequality in Brazil', in N. Stromquist (ed.), *Women and Education in Latin America: Knowledge, Power, and Change*, Lynne Rienner, Boulder, CO, pp. 33–46.

Royal Tropical Institute (1995) *Advancing Women's Status: Gender, Society, and Development*, Royal Tropical Institute, Amsterdam.

Samoff, J. (ed) (1994) *Coping with Crisis: Austerity, Adjustment and Human Resources*, Cassell and UNESCO, London.

Sen, G. (1996) 'Gender, markets and state: a selective review and research agenda', *World Development* 24 (5): 821–9.

Spring, A. (1987) *Women Farmers and Food Issues in Africa: Some Considerations and Suggested Solutions*, Working Paper No. 139, Office of Women in International Development, Michigan State University, East Lansing.

Tinker, I. (1990) *Persistent Inequalities: Women and World Development*, Oxford University Press, New York.

UNESCO (1995) *1995 Trends and Projections of Enrollment by Level of Education, by Age and by Sex, 1960–2025*, UNESCO, Paris.

World Bank (1995) *Toward Gender Equality. The Role of Public Policy*, World Bank, Washington, DC.

Wright, E. (1985) *Classes*, Verso, London.

Young, K. (1993) *Planning Development with Women: Making a World of Difference*, Macmillan, London.

CHAPTER 3

Girls and Women in Education and Training in Papua New Guinea

Christine Fox

Introduction: gendered images

This chapter discusses the education and training of women and girls in Papua New Guinea, where female participation rates in all levels of education are among the lowest in the world. Papua New Guinea is vast and the contexts of women's lives complex and diverse. Nevertheless the most important single influence on girls' and women's access to and participation in formal education is an overwhelming image of women as subordinate, dominated by men in society. Systematic subordination of women in households and communities continues as the reality for women. Government rhetoric encouraging a gender analysis of development as part of the global movement among donors and government officials is far removed from women's lives and has made little difference to them.

Some of the information about education and development in Papua New Guinea presented in this chapter is based on recent reviews of the education system by international education consultants, including an extensive joint review completed in 1995 by Australian and Asian Development Bank teams (PNG/AusAID/ADB 1995). Much of the information, however, was gathered by this writer interviewing a number of women and men, singly and in groups, formally and informally, in various parts of the country during 1995, recording their perceptions from their personal accounts, and comparing their views with what has been documented about women and development in many countries. The evidence presented illustrated a sense of Otherness about women, a sense that there was some logic about their lack of voice. As Edwaid Said has noted, people become locked into particular stereotypical positions of subordination (Said 1978, 1983). The idea of Otherness is a logic of binary oppositions, and constitutes a dangerous twist to the way people see themselves, 'a logic of subordination and domination' (Benhabib 1992: 15). Such a danger seems present in many aspects of Papua New Guinea's education system. Girls face several disadvantages, which together serve to compound the difficulties of becoming educated in a system still faced with problems of development.

Many men interviewed by the writer during her research in Papua New Guina claimed that women are subordinate because it is a time-honoured cultural reality of Papua New Guinea society. This claim is disputed by most of that small minority of women who now have an authoritative voice in the urban or rural sectors, and by many of the men who support equity. However, the perpetuation, or reification, of the image of a gendered other tend to project the unequal state of affairs to the public 'as if it were permanent, natural and outside of time' (Thompson 1990: 65). The illusion is reinforced by images of women depicted by the local media, in the community, in schools and other educational institutions and in workplaces.

Nowhere is the 'Othering' of the female gender group and the gap between government rhetoric and the reality of women's lives clearer than in the local media. The daily and weekly newspapers published in the capital city, Port Moresby, nearly always show females in the background, or carrying out tasks that relate to serving roles. Often they are not in the picture at all, or else news of women is found on a separate 'women's page'. This lack of a sense of active participation is contrary to the intent of the Papua New Guinea Constitution, which calls for equal participation by women citizens in all political, economic, social and religious activities (Avalos 1993: 275). Indeed, Avalos points out that the ideological principles of the constitution show a strong commitment to equality and the right of every individual, male or female, to participate. Culturally, women play a complementary role to men in the sphere of work and family in both rural and urban daily life, and in the overall economic and social development of Papua New Guinea. But rarely is this complementarity recognized. The question is whether anyone is listening to the voices of women, or whether they are silenced by their gendered Otherness (Stromquist 1990, 1996).

Social and cultural factors

During the 1990s, development in Papua New Guinea has had a positive impact in some sectors of the economy, and for some people this has allowed more people, including some women, to enter the education system. However, the picture for the majority has not improved, and one of the greatest sources of inequality is an increasing differentiation of power and wealth between men and women (Johnson 1993: 183). By international standards, including less developed countries (LDC), UNDP data show that participation rates for women in Papua New Guinea are among the worst in the world.

Papua New Guinea's rate of female illiteracy is one of the highest in the world, at between 68 and 80 per cent. Life expectancy was only 40.5 years in 1970 and rose to 49.6 in 1980 and to 55 in 1994, according to UNDP estimates (Andrew 1994: 6). The same source estimated that neighbouring Solomon Islands women had a life expectancy of 70 years. The maternal mortality rate in Papua New Guinea is far higher than that of most countries, and is currently estimated at between 7 and 18 per 1,000 live births. UNICEF estimates that one in every 22 rural mothers dies during pregnancy or childbirth. Infant mortality rates are still the highest in the Pacific. In 1980, approximately 114 of every 1,000 children born alive died before they reached the age of 5 years. By 1990 the figure had only decreased to 75 of every 1,000 children. The statistics for access to safe water supply are also among the worst in the world, with only 22 per cent of the population having a safe water supply. Only five countries in the world have lesser access to safe water (UNICEF/PNG 1993). The UNDP's comparative social and economic indicators of human development rank Papua New Guinea as 129th out of 173 countries with its low life expectancy, low GNP per capita, low education enrolment ratio and high infant and maternal mortality rates (Andrew 1994).

Studies of women's social situation indicate that there is a greater investment in the health of boys compared with that of girls – for example, more boys than girls are immunized in infancy (AIDAB 1993). Moreover, the physical well-being of girls and women is seriously threatened by increases in domestic violence, in child abuse, and in the fear and experience of sexual assault and violence in schools, further education, workplaces and public places. Each of these factors tends to militate against the equal participation of women in education and employment.

Generalizations about differences between 'traditional' and 'urban' women in Papua New Guinea are of limited value. Vast differences are found in a country with an estimated 4.1 million people, about 48 per cent of whom are women. Over 85 per cent of the population lives in rural communities, at great distances from each other. Some 800 language groups have been identified, and the country contains examples of many different cultural traditions and social expectations for women. Even so, the activities expected of rural women in the family and in her community tend to be similar, including home-making, childbearing, gardening, livestock rearing, producing food and handicrafts and operating small businesses. Most of all, the identity 'woman' is about being a 'wife' and 'mother'.

The institution of marriage has a tremendous impact on the welfare of women and the status of men. Data from the 1990 census indicate that about 20 per cent of women are already married by the time they reach 15 years of age, and over 80 per cent are married by about 25 years of age, compared with about 50 per cent of males by 25 years of age. Maria Kopkop's analysis of the status of women (1992) describes marriage in kinship-based societies as a contractual arrangement between two clans that establishes networks of reciprocal rights and duties. The practice of presenting brideprice to the girl's family is believed to give the husband and his clan rights over the women's reproductive capacity and labour. This includes the right to punish the woman physically by beating her, according to customary law. A few Papua New Guinea communities allow polygamy, a system that tends to deprive the wives of power or status. Some abuse of this customary practice has been reported when wives are maltreated, indicating an increase in domestic violence. In the 1990s the media have been reporting an increase in the numbers of women who have retaliated against the abuse of their human rights. There are reports of women being imprisoned for attacking or killing their husband or another wife.

Cultural production or gendered subordination?

The effects on women's lives of 'traditional' cultural expectations relative to contact with other values are debatable. One commentator argues that the relative status of rural women within the family is declining, leading to loss of self-esteem and deteriorating mental health among some rural women (M. Andrew, pers. comm., June 1995). One reason for the decline of traditional status is reflected in changing lifestyles with the influx of imported values, goods and images. For example, more families are able to bring home processed foods from stores, and homes are being exposed to commercial messages from the mass media.

As these symbols of change filter into communities, there are some indications that the so-called customary rights of men over women are being used as a camouflage for male aggression and social irresponsibility. In the public and private employment sectors, male dominance is used to restrict promotion and training opportunities for women, and to discriminate against women in other ways. Time and again it was suggested by the interviewees that any moves to increase female participation in education and employment must involve a change in male attitudes and behaviour towards women.

Yeoman reported in 1985 that many parents believed it was more important for boys than for girls to gain an education in the formal sector, and that if money was short, sons would be educated before daughters (APEID 1987). Parents also feared for the safety of their daughters in school, or believed that family labour requirements, marriage, and pre-marriage arrangements were more important. Some families, particularly where the parents had not had more than a year or two of schooling, tended to show a general lack of interest in formal education. A girl's participation often depended on whether her father supported the idea and was prepared to pay school fees or other costs.

The fear of their husbands, or future husbands, that many women expressed is borne out by the very high levels of domestic violence reported in a large-scale investigation published in 1992 (PNG Law Reform Commission 1992). The Law Reform Commission's special committee of enquiry noted that 'everything depends on whether males will allow females to do anything; for example, teachers don't take up promotion partly through fear of being beaten more by their husbands' (1992: 24). It reported that of rural wives surveyed during the 1980s, at least 67 per cent in Highland regions had experienced domestic violence (estimates were of 100 per cent in one community). In urban areas, 56 per cent of women from low-income families and 62 per cent of women from elite families reported that they had been hit by husbands. The Women and Law Committee, based at the Law Reform Commission, has carried out a well organized campaign against domestic violence for several years. It is difficult to establish how successful this campaign has been, but, importantly, it has raised women's level of awareness of the issues (Cox 1996). With more education, women may be better equipped to protect themselves against violence or at least have greater access to legal representation. For the majority of women, such a solution is too simplistic. For example, women teachers, and female students, may find it more difficult to stay on in school if they try to challenge the system, and many feel isolated as well as physically threatened. As the evaluator of the anti-violence campaign, Elizabeth Cox, has said, the opportunity to participate in society, in particular through education, is nevertheless an essential part of the struggle to do something positive to counteract increased subordination through violence (pers. comm., June 1995).

The gap between government rhetoric and women's realities

At the local level, there is no system in place to ensure women's representation so that they could have some influence over the enforcement of laws against violence and other crimes. In 1978 there were only seven women in the local government councils compared with 4,313 men, and there is no indication that the situation has improved in the 1990s. In the National Parliament in 1995 there were no female MPs to promote the cause of women. In Papua New Guinea women are primarily valuable economic 'commodities'. A report of a UNDP/ILO Mission on Human Resource Development pointed out that women should be seen as economic contributors, not as social welfare problems (ARTEP 1993). Rapid economic change has led to even further marginalization of women on the one hand and an increase in women's workloads on the other (ARTEP 1993: 241). Women do not lack ingenuity in finding new ways to create income or increase supplies. There is considerable evidence around the world to show that community participation in non-formal education and training has meant significant improvements to the quality of life in many rural communities, by providing women with new skills and new ways of saving labour and time (Gannicott and Avalos 1994). The main constraints on greater participation are lack of initial working capital, lack of technical and marketing knowledge, and a continued lack of basic training and education for the majority of women.

In the urban sector, a minority of women (approximately 10 per cent of female urban dwellers) are wage-earners. Much depends on the balance of power between males and females in both private and public spheres. Where women have supportive husbands, decision-making can be shared, and the status of women improves to the mutual social and economic benefit of family and community (pers. comm., discussion workshop of women public servants, Milne Bay 1995). On the other hand, women are often excluded from decision-making and, in many cases, they are excluded from control over their earnings or from the right to use their earnings for the benefit of their children. The 1980 census data indicated that only 1.5 per cent of all women employees occupied executive or managerial positions. By 1995, the percentage had increased to 2.8, or no better than one in 35 of the top four grades of the public service (PNG Department of Personnel Management 1995). The UNDP/ILO Mission report of 1993 (ARTEP 1993) recommended that the promotion of women to senior positions would lead to an overall improvement in the situation of women, but such a change involves recruitment, training, promotion strategies and, most importantly, the creation of a work environment more conducive to and supportive of women.

Women interviewed by the writer indicated that harassment in the workplace is a major problem and contributes to a reluctance to pursue the issue of promotion, or even training for promotion. In 1995, the Department of Personnel Management provided data showing that 88 per cent of all the overseas training opportunities in the national public service in 1994 and 1995 were given to men, a further illustration of the gulf between government rhetoric and the realities of women's lives. While some of this discrepancy can be attributed to a lack of available positions, much of the problem relates to discrimination against women in the workforce, the result of deeply embedded socio-cultural factors, and the positioning of men as powerful, leaving an image of women as subordinate to men.

Gannicott and Avalos maintain that there is little to be gained at the government level by demonstrating the extent of discrimination. At the government and international donor levels the argument that education and training of women 'makes hard-headed economic sense' is more persuasive (Gannicott and Avalos 1994: 3). Be that as it may, the views of women who formed the Steering Committee to prepare the National Plan of Action, presented at the Beijing International Women's Conference of September 1995, clearly also saw the advantages of female participation in education as a means not just to better economic outcomes, but also to better health outcomes for all Papua New Guineans.

It appears that only a fine line divides traditional cultural attitudes and more recent attitudes of male aggression and arrogance. Moreover, there is a growing social belief that if jobs are scarce, it would not be appropriate for women to compete with men for such jobs, in the same way that if money were scarce, it would not be appropriate for a daughter to 'take' a son's place at school. An ADB Report (Schoeffel-Melissea 1987) on women and development in Papua New Guinea noted that: 'Girls are socialized to accept their secondary status and few perceive the existence of greater opportunities and wider choices in life than those assigned to them by tradition' (Schoeffel-Melissea 1987: 20).

Changing the attitudes and behaviour of boys and men is one of the keys to increasing the participation of girls and women in society at large and education in particular. Whether the argument of 'good economic sense' will be sufficient to change these gendered cultural images is conjecture at this stage. The writer recently witnessed a 'critical incident' in the ethnography of gender relations in education in Papua New Guinea. A student in an urban high school told her that the water had been cut off, and there was no access to safe water for miles around. Students were told to bring their own containers of water when they came to school. Some boys grabbed the containers that girls had brought with them. Other boys actually went without water and risked becoming sick rather than carry their own to school – 'that is a girl's job,' they said.

Education and development

In 1993 the government of Papua New Guinea initiated two major reforms of its education system designed to reduce drop-out rates, increase access and facilitate greater equity. Pre-schools taught in local languages are being introduced. Many communities have volunteer pre-schools at the moment, and there are signs that communities are not happy with the anticipated changes because the centres are no longer seen as belonging to a voluntary service provided by the local community. There are conflicting reports about the implementation of the reform. Apparently some of the new government-funded Tok Ples Skuls (Talk Place Schools, or pre-schools) are already closing because government funds are not always forthcoming. There are also more optimistic reports that Community Teachers' Colleges are enthusiastically training early childhood teachers.

The second reform is the removal of Grades 7 and 8 from secondary schools to local primary schools, postponing the costly need for children to board away from home at distant high schools, a frequent reason for

Table 3.1 Projected enrolments for primary and secondary schools, Papua New Guinea, 1994–2004

Year	Elementary (Prep–E2)	Primary (G1–G8)	Junior (G7–G10)	Senior (G11–G12)	Total secondary	Total enrolments
1994	660	495,918	65,038	3,370	68,408	564,986
1995	3,762	516,017	68,157	4,286	72,443	592,222
2000	213,625	489,810	66,348	8,364	74,712	778,147
2004	429,226	519,304	60,775	13,275	74,050	1,022,580

Source: PNG/AusAID/ADB 1995 Draft Report.

dropping out of education. A summary of projected student enrolments consequent on the reform plans for Grades 7 and 8 moving over to the primary school is shown in Table 3.1. At present there is a large drop-out rate between Grades 1 and 6, with many students leaving before they have completed even one year of school. Of the students who enrol (about 80 per cent of the school-age population in total, but fewer females than males, even fewer in rural areas), about 40 per cent of students who complete Grade 6 go on to Grade 7. The rate is lower for females (about 30 per cent). After Grade 8, another 20 per cent drop out. By the end of Grade 10, another 90 per cent (of those who have completed those two years) leave school. Fewer than 1 per cent of those who start in Grade 1 manage to continue through to Grade 12. For girls the figure is closer to 0.3 per cent. In 1988, a total of 818 students were enrolled in Grade 12, the final year of high school, in the whole country. In 1994, 1,094 were enrolled. The target progression rate means that over 5,000 students will be studying in Grade 12 by 2004.

The debate on school reform and female participation must consider the context of the 'late development effect' discussed by Sheldon Weeks in his review of the last 20 years of education in Papua New Guinea (Weeks 1993). The context of schooling is all-important, and change must be seen in relation to Papua New Guinea's history and connections with British, German and Australian education systems, both public and church-based (and see Crossley 1992; Bray 1993; Johnson 1993; Preston 1993). In this sense, the neglect of any emphasis on universal primary education before the 1960s may account for some of the problems the education system faces today. The lead-up to independence in 1975 involved the development of national goals and eight directive principles for government, which assumed large-scale plans for educational development. Yet, as Weeks notes, by 1982 there was a feeling of frustration with the pace of change, and a sense that there was a significant gap between the rhetoric and the reality (Weeks 1993: 262). This frustration re-emerged and led to the reforms of 1993.

While female participation rates at all levels of education are markedly lower generally, what these national statistics do not indicate is the enormous disparities by region, and by distance from an urban centre. For example, the enrolment of all school-age children for at least one year of schooling is about 99 per cent in Manus, compared with only about 54 per cent in the Southern Highlands.

In community schools that serve several villages, some children have to board during the week. This reduces the participation rate of girls further, and in such schools there are fewer girls than in urban areas or in single village schools. In Papua New Guinea, as in other countries, sexual harassment, sexual liaison and rape are reported as major difficulties for some of the children and teachers. A study undertaken in the East Sepik area by Tom Seta (1993) shows that a major problem for the girls was their being away from home. They felt threatened by male teachers' sexual harassment, and harassment by *rascals* (roaming unemployed males).

The apparent lack of incentive to learn on the part of some girls, and their difficulties in competing or setting high goals for themselves, could be accounted for by the problems they face in many schools. It was reported, for instance, that in the co-educational schools nearly all leadership positions and responsibilities are given to boys, so that girls rarely have an opportunity to develop confidence and self-esteem. In one province it was reported that in some schools teachers have been known to have sexual liaisons with girls in Grade 4 of primary school (10–11 years of age), and have paid the parents not to report the 'incidents'. Stories were related of girls becoming pregnant at the age of 12, some of whom die in childbirth if they do not have access to appropriate medical help.

The evidence available suggests six important reasons for low female participation in addition to the economic and social factors commonly cited in the development literature. Further research is necessary to confirm these findings:

1. the high cost of schooling;
2. lack of education for parents for improving skills and sharing work in family life: time-saving, health-improving, capacity-building skills that are the prerequisites to easing the burden of girls' work at home so that they can go to school;
3. lack of recognition of the rights of all humans not to be sexually abused, beaten or discriminated against – a basic right and the prerequisite for feeling safe to attend school, university or a place of employment outside the home;
4. discriminatory practices of selection and promotion;
5. insufficient understanding by trainers, planners, administrators, teachers and non-formal education facilitators of gender issues in curriculum and instruction; and

6. lack of information, role models or opportunity to have raised expectations as to how females can contribute to society, family and community.

The overriding issue identified and named here as the first key point is cost. If parents have to pay fees, and money is short, then the boys in the family take precedence over the girls. All the key informants for the present study mentioned the economic cost as being the major factor preventing girls from enrolling and continuing at school. If a family had a high enough income, girls tended to be allowed to go to school. Moreover, if the family lived close to an urban area, where some of the schools provide places for day-students, the costs were less than for boarding. The cost for a girl to go to high school for a year in Milne Bay, for example, is now about 400 kina, which is over half the average family income in Papua New Guinea.

The high quality of Papua New Guinean schooling in urban areas

In many respects, the quality of schooling in Papua New Guinea for those who can afford to attend the better-resourced urban schools is high by national and international standards. The responsibility for the school curriculum rests with the Department of Education. Interviews with female staff in the Curriculum Development Division and in the Inspections and Guidance Division revealed a high level of gender awareness. For example, at the Editorial Office of the Department of Education's publishing unit, a recently produced Grade 11 and 12 language book was sent back for re-writing and re-illustrating because all the examples given about sport were male. The Examinations Unit also works to ensure that there is gender inclusiveness. In Schools Broadcasting, it was reported that two subject areas, Community Life and Expressive Arts for primary schools, had plenty of female role models portrayed. In the English syllabus, children's readers are now tackling gender issues, including domestic violence and health. In higher grades, there is greater use of overseas texts, but where the curriculum features Pacific novelists, female writers are often selected. A 1990 video on Techniques in Counselling, which was addressed particularly to the problems of girls, was produced by the Guidance Branch of the Inspections and Guidance Division.

While quality of teaching and resources are unevenly distributed, standards of classroom teaching are protected by the relatively high level of qualifications of teachers in PNG. Unlike many smaller nations in the Pacific, most of Papua New Guinea's teachers are qualified and have a personal education of Grade 10 or above. In PNG poor housing, high absenteeism and high turnover are the main factors affecting the quality of education (Andrew 1994 and pers. comm. 1995). Some schools also have discipline problems among the teachers themselves.

In PNG there is a long tradition of input from international advisers in curriculum planning and teacher education. Bilateral projects with Australia are currently concentrating on further upgrading of teacher education. The curriculum is based largely on foreign ideologies. In the view of a leading educationalist in the Pacific, this has been a vehicle for subordinating rather than strengthening and transforming local indigenous cultural values (Konai Helu Thaman 1993 and pers. comm.). The informed and gender-aware work of the Curriculum Development Unit has tried to redress the balance in Papua New Guinea.

Vocational education

In many countries the structure of the vocational school curriculum reinforces the division of labour between women and men, and contributes to the 'subordination of local cultures to that of capital' (Preston 1993: 111). In Papua New Guinea, vocational schools are still dominated by male students. In 1994 the proportion was about three to one for boys. The current government reform aims to have equal male–female participation in the next eight years. Vocational centres suffer from serious resource deficiencies. For example, in one centre examined by Marjorie Andrew in 1995, a teacher reported that she had been allocated only 160 kina (approximately £75 sterling) for one term to teach 50 girls in home economics, often with no teaching aids or ingredients to use. The course was strongly biased towards home improvement rather than promoting self-employment or employment in the waged sector. Girls have few chances of self-improvement through vocational training, which is accorded low status in the community. In PNG, as elsewhere, study at a post-Grade 10 institution is of much higher status. There are two universities and about fifty smaller institutions in PNG. In 1995, about 3,500 school leavers were enrolled in some form of higher education. The overall enrolment was around 8,500, of whom about 35 per cent were female. For the universities, the proportion was around 25 per cent, although at the University of Technology the proportion was only 19 per cent female students in 1995 (PNG Commission for Higher Education 1995).

The development of women's organizational structures in PNG[1]

For decades the global movement of 'women in development' has attempted to assist women to improve their position, and to resist subordination. In the 1990s the movement towards 'gender and development' is an attempt to create a positive climate that includes both men and women in collaborative development initiatives. In Papua New Guinea, as in other countries in the Pacific, a strong core of women have been campaigning for change for decades. In 1975, the United Nations International Women's Year, Papua New Guinea held its first National Women's Convention, to which delegates from each province were sent. A National Council of Women (NCW) was formed officially in 1978 and incorporated by an Act of Parliament the following year. A Women's Services Division of the government was created to:

1. provide a policy framework for the national government and provincial governments to set up appropriate programmes for women;
2. establish and maintain a management system capable of implementing these programmes at national and provincial levels; and
3. provide avenues, structures and the processes for women in government, non-governmental and community sectors to work together for achievements of the objectives in the policy framework.

The NCW was involved at every stage of the policy and programming work of the Division, but had no policy function in either its Act or Constitution and was not representative of all provinces or churches. An integrated National Women's Development Programme was launched as a major initiative to be funded for four years under the overall responsibility of the Women's Division. Training was one of the key components of the programme. Its implementation was thwarted time and time again.

National Policy for Women In 1990 a National Policy for Women was launched with four guiding principles:

1. equality and participation;
2. dignity and respect for women;
3. Melanesian values; and
4. productive action.

The Constitution specifically calls for 'everyone to be involved in our endeavours to achieve integral human development of the whole person for every person and to seek fulfilment through his or her contribution to the common good'. It further calls for 'equal participation by women citizens in all political, economic, social and religious activities'.

The reality does not meet the rhetoric (Avalos 1993). The globalization of gender awareness has meant that virtually all of the international funding agencies have adopted mandates for the integration of women. While some of these agencies claim that the only reasons for lack of participation can be lack of access or lack of motivation, the reality appears to be a systematic blocking of female endeavours, by dint of the organizational structures and funding processes. The trend in Papua New Guinea among female change agents is not to move away from a focus on women, but to focus as well on gender sensitization, and on gender and development, as noted in Chapter 1 of this book.

Dialoguing interculturally

How effective has the globalization of gender issues in the international donor community been in the specific context of PNG? The women involved in the preparation for and the debriefing from the Beijing Conference, and women working with international gender-focused projects, unequivocally agreed that support internationally was particularly useful when working in the non-formal sector. The benefits of this interaction on gender-based issues in formal education and training are not so clear. Planning and development in formal education appear to be male territory in which 'partnerships ... are held together and sustained by mutual interests' (Baba 1989: 43). The review of resourcing of education undertaken by a joint Australian, Asian Development Bank and Papua New Guinea team in 1995 scarcely mentioned the issue of gender differentiation, other than in vocational education (PNG/AusAID/ADB 1995).

The women face a dilemma in identifying their needs as those of women from a less developed country. There are many dangers in being determined by cultural or gendered relativity. Gayatri Spivak, a vocal advocate of establishing more genuine ways to dialogue interculturally, has frequently objected to being positioned as 'a Third World' person, or 'a woman', or a 'post-colonial': 'we who are from the other side of the globe very much fight against the labelling of all of us under that one rubric [Third World], which follows from the logic of neo-colonialism' (Spivak 1990: 114).

Labelling and fixing the Other is a form of colonial discourse that perpetuates unequal relationships of power, and it is perhaps nowhere more overt than in Papua New Guinea, with the male fixed as powerful and the female as Other.

> An important feature of colonial discourse is its dependence on the concept of 'fixity' in the ideological construction of otherness. Fixity, as the sign of cultural/historical/racial difference in the discourse of colonialism, is a paradoxical mode of representation: it connotes rigidity and an unchanging order as well as disorder, degeneracy and daemonic repetition ... The stereotype ... is its major discursive strategy (Bhabha 1994: 66).

With the high level of activity and energy from women in all parts of the country, the notion that female participation is not culturally appropriate becomes questionable, to say the least. The positioning of women as subordinate is deeply imbedded in the social practices of men, but does this mean that women's subordination is culturally acceptable? Increasingly, both men and women in Papua New Guinea are attempting to tear away the mask that hides the troubling experiences of women and that creates the semblance of cultural acceptance. Those who struggle against the image of the subordinated woman are creating new metaphors to depict the meaning of unity. What these metaphors indicate is a view of the world as a web – interconnected planning, networks, awareness, community – a web of communication, a web of combined strength.

At the government level the cultural dialogue about gendered Otherness has been subverted by those in the donor community who fear upsetting cultural sensibilities. The distortions of power (see Fox 1997) have thus lingered and even been strengthened by the tendency of representatives of international agencies to deal mainly with men in their deliberations about economic development. Most of the funding for development is channelled through male-dominated organizations following decisions based on male perceptions of what is needed. In PNG it makes 'good economic sense' and 'good human rights sense' to encourage girls and women to participate in education, employment, development and social transformation.

Note

1. This section was written in collaboration with Ruby Zarriga, head of the Gender and Development Unit in the Department of Finance and Planning, PNG.

Bibliography

AIDAB (1993) 'Women in development in Papua New Guinea Sector Program development', briefing for PNG Sector Working Groups, AIDAB, Canberra.

Andrew, M. (1994) Draft paper presented to PNG government on demographic data (unpublished).

APEID (1987) *Universal Primary Education for Girls: Papua New Guinea*, Asian Program of Educational Innovation for Development (APEID), UNESCO, Principal Regional Office for Asia and the Pacific, Bangkok.

ARTEP (1993) *Papua New Guinea: Challenge for Employment and Human Resource Development*, Report of the UNDP/ILO Employment Strategy and HRD Mission to PNG, ILO Asian Regional Team for Employment Promotion (ARTEP), New Delhi.

Avalos, B. (1993) 'Ideology, policy and educational change in Papua New Guinea', *Comparative Education* 29 (3): 275–92.

Baba, T. (1989) 'Australia's involvement in education in the Pacific: partnership or patronage?', *Directions* 11 (2): 43–53.

Benhabib, S. (1992) *Situating the Self*, Polity Press, Cambridge.

Bhabha, H. (1994) *The Location of Culture*, Routledge, London.

Bray, M. (1993) 'Education and the vestiges of colonialism: self-determination, neocolonialism and dependency in the South Pacific', *Comparative Education* 29 (3): 333–46.

Cox, E. (1996) 'Campaigning against domestic violence: an evaluation of the PNG Women and Law Committee's Campaign Against Domestic Violence', draft report from 1992, to be published with the support of UNICEF, Port Moresby.

Crossley, M. (1992) 'Teacher education in Papua New Guinea: a comment on comparative and international observations', *Journal of Education for Teaching* 18 (1): 23–8.

Flaherty, T. (1993) 'Educational opportunities for high school girls in Milne Bay and East Sepik provinces', in C. Thirlwall and B. Avalos, *Participation and Educational Change*, pp. 237–48.

Fox, C. (1997) 'The authenticity of intercultural communication', *International Journal of Intercultural Relations* 21 (1): 85–104.

Gannicott, K. and B. Avalos (1994) *Pacific 2010: Women's Education and Economic Development in Melanesia*, Pacific Policy Paper No. 12, National Centre for Development Studies, ANU, Canberra.

Johnson, P. L. (1993) 'Education and the "new" inequality in Papua New Guinea', *Anthropology and Education Quarterly* 24 (3): 183–204.

Kopkop, M. (1992) *Status of Women 1992: Country Report Papua New Guinea*, report presented to the Seminar on Improving the Status of Women, Tokyo, Japan, September/October.

Nakikus, M., M. Andrew, A. Mandie-Filer and B. Brown (1991) *Papua New Guinea: Women in Development Sector Review*, UNDP, New York.

Phillip, A. (1993) 'Trying to cope: the struggle of women in Port Moresby to continue their education by distance', in C. Thirlwall and B. Avalos, *Participation and Educational Change*, pp. 237–48.

PNG/AusAID/ADB (1995) *Education Sector Resources Study*, Final Report, April (draft).

PNG Commission for Higher Education (1995) unpublished data from the Selection Branch, Boroko, May.

PNG Department of Personnel Management (1995) *Human Resource Development: a Discussion Paper*, Government Printing Office, Boroko.

PNG Law Reform Commission (1992) *Final Report on Domestic Violence*, Report No. 14, PNG LRC, Government Offices, Boroko.

Preston, R. (1993) 'Gender and relevance: decentralised vocational education in Papua New Guinea', *Oxford Review of Education* 19 (1): 101–15.

Said, E. (1978) *Orientalism: Western Conceptions of the Orient*, Penguin, Harmondsworth.

— (1983) *The World, the Text and the Critic*, Harvard University Press, Cambridge, MA.

Schoeffel-Melissea, P. (1987) *Women in Development: Papua New Guinea*, Country Briefing Paper, December, ADB Programs Department (East), Manila, the Philippines.

Seta, T. (1993) 'Why low female retention in secondary schools? An East Sepik experience', in C. Thirlwall and B. Avalos, *Participation and Educational Change*, pp. 249–62.

Spivak, G. (1990) *The Post-colonial critic: Interviews, Strategies, Dialogues* (ed. S. Harasym), Routledge, New York.

Stromquist, N. (1990) 'Gender inequality in education: accounting for women's subordination', *British Journal of Sociology of Education* 11 (2): 137–54.

— (1996) 'Mapping gendered spaces in Third World educational interventions', in R. Paulston (ed.), *Social Cartography*, Garland, New York.

Thaman, K. Helu (1993) 'Culture and the curriculum in the South Pacific', *Comparative Education* 29 (3): 249–60.

Thirlwall, C. and B. Avalos (eds) (1993) *Participation and Educational Change: Implications for Educational Reform in Papua New Guinea*, UPNG Press, Port Moresby.

Thompson, J. B. (1990) *Ideology and Modern Culture*, Polity Press, Cambridge.

UNICEF/PNG Department of Health (1993) *Profile of Children in Papua New Guinea*, PNG Department of Health for UNICEF, Waigani, PNG.

UNDP (1994) *Papers and Proceedings of a National Employment Summit*, UNDP, Waigani, PNG.

Weeks, S. (1993) 'Education in Papua New Guinea 1973–1993: the late development effect?', *Comparative Education* 29 (3): 261–74.

World Bank (1995) *Priorities and Strategies for Education,* World Bank, Washington, DC

CHAPTER 4

The Schooling of South African Girls[1]

Elaine Unterhalter

The racism of the South African education system was an important and well-documented feature of the apartheid era. One of the key objectives of the first democratically elected government of South Africa has been the development of policies to overcome the inequities of the racially segregated schooling system of the past. The gender inequities of the schooling system have been less well delineated and less promptly tackled by government, partly because they are more diffuse.

Unlike in a number of countries in Southern and Central Africa, girls are not excluded from school or higher education in South Africa. Superficially girls and women may appear to be privileged over boys and men in certain features of the education system. Table 4.1 demonstrates the differential retention in favour of girls for a cohort of pupils who began schooling in 1976. Table 4.2 looks at a cohort that began schooling in 1983 and completed Standard 10 (the end of secondary school) in 1995. While these calculations are based on incomplete data,[2] they indicate that there has been a considerable expansion in the enrolment of girls in school, particularly among those racialized as African under apartheid, for whom education was not compulsory until 1995 (Unterhalter 1991). Although fewer girls may be enrolled they are more likely than boys to complete primary schooling and to remain in school until the end of the secondary phase.

Table 4.1 Percentage of girls and boys completing schooling in South Africa, by phase completed: 1976 cohort[3]

Phase completed	Girls	Boys
Primary	56.8	46.9
Junior secondary	43.4	34.8
Senior secondary	31.9	25.9

Source: Compiled from Central Statistical Services 1997: Table 5.12.[4]

Table 4.2 Percentage of girls and boys completing schooling in South Africa, by phase completed: 1983 cohort

Phase completed	Girls	Boys
Primary	61.1	51.8
Junior secondary	58.7	45.5
Senior secondary	53.5	38.1

Source: Compiled from Central Statistical Services 1997: Table 5.12.[4]

The trend identified in Tables 4.1 and 4.2 for the population as a whole is replicated for the population classified as African under apartheid, who, under the apartheid regime, were denied access to compulsory education and provided with school facilities that were inadequate for their needs and considerably inferior to those of the population classified as white.

Table 4.3 Percentage of girls and boys classified African completing schooling in South Africa, by phase completed: 1976 cohort

Phase completed	Girls	Boys
Primary	51.2	40.6
Junior secondary	35.8	29.0
Senior secondary	21.9	16.8

Source: Compiled from Central Statistical Services 1997: Table 5.34.[4]

Table 4.4 Percentage of girls and boys classified African completing schooling in South Africa, by phase completed: 1983 cohort

Phase completed	Girls	Boys
Primary	59.1	48.5
Junior secondary	50.1	37.0
Senior secondary	50.6	35.3

Source: Compiled from Central Statistical Services 1997: Table 5.34.[4]

Tables 4.3 and 4.4 show that even though survival in the school system was so much harder for Africans, the national trend for greater retention of girls in school was replicated despite the hardship and discrimination experienced by this group. Budlender's work indicates that women comprised 44 per cent of all university students in 1988, but that African women comprised 49 per cent. (Budlender 1994: 130–1). Women were heavily concentrated in courses dealing with education and healthcare. In 1993 women accounted for 49 per cent of all students enrolled in universities, with 63 per cent concentrated in social science, education, business and healthcare (Budlender 1997: 10).

Successful survival in schooling and progress to higher education for South African girls has not translated into labour market advantage or higher earnings. While it is undoubtedly true that regardless of racial classification women with more education fare better than those with less, it also clear that women and men with equivalent levels of education do not earn similar amounts or work in jobs of similar status (Budlender 1997; Erwee 1994). Labour market segmentation, discriminatory practices at work and lack of social welfare, particularly childcare and health service provision, may explain this pattern. Gender discrimination crosses class boundaries and affects women regardless of the length of their education. Women continue to experience discrimination in personal, private and public spheres, as well as high levels of violence and low levels of self-confidence (Lessing 1994).

The extent and nature of gender discrimination has been highlighted in South Africa by an articulate women's movement and a number of women's campaigns. Gender discrimination, including that by customary law, was outlawed by the Constitution of 1997. Work by feminist lawyers has been important in expanding the concept of human rights, protected by the Bill of Rights, to include social and economic rights and so make visible the areas where many women faced the worst abuse of their rights. The White Paper on Education of 1995 committed the government to investigating developing gender equity strategies in education. In 1996 a Gender Equity Task Team (GETT) was appointed; it reported in 1997 on the need to establish 'gender desks' at strategic points in the national Ministry of Education, and for increased gender sensitivity in drafting education policy documents (Motala 1997). In late 1997 some provincial departments of education, for example Gauteng, were beginning to formulate gender policy documents through limited exercises in participatory planning procedures.

All these initiatives rest on the assumption that access to education is the key to the social and economic well-being of girls and women. Being present in a classroom is somehow transformative. Factors such as content and pedagogy, and issues about how education changes subjectivities, are ignored. Many of these initiatives on gender equity in education rest on scant local knowledge. Policy-makers have frequently imported outside experts and sometimes sought to incorporate unamended policy proposals from Australia or the United Kingdom. While GETT has criticized these initiatives at conferences, it has been slow in putting forward counter-proposals and mobilization of women in the education sector on issues of gender discrimination is rare.

This chapter is about subjectivities and education. It examines the development of identities and schooling among two generations of women in South Africa. It explores the extent to which the disjuncture between girls' success in school and lack of success in the labour market can be attributed not only to structural features but also to constructed features of identity formed in schools. It draws on work from the developed world that points to the ambiguous experience of school for girls and boys (see for example Kenway and Willis 1993; Mac an Ghaill 1994; Gordon 1996; Holland, Blair and Sheldon 1995; Giroux 1992). It explores this complexity, raising questions about the silences in the literature on gender, pedagogy and processes of identity formation in schools. Finally it assesses the extent to which access to schooling leads to empowerment.

Exploring these issues demands access to the changing subjectivities of girls and women during their experience of education. One of the consequences of apartheid has been the denial of a voice to the majority of women and girls. In such circumstances, the analysis of autobiography for social enquiry has been used to powerful effect by Steedman (1986) and Stanley (1992). To illuminate the changing constructions of gendered identities within education, the autobiographies of six South African women (four African and two white) who went to school in two different periods have been selected. The first group of older women – Ellen Kuzwayo, Phyllis Ntantala and Phyllis Lewsen – had their schooling in the 1920s and 1930s (Kuzwayo 1985; Ntantala 1992; Lewsen 1996). The second group – Mamphela Ramphele, Sindiwe Magona and Gillian Slovo[5] – had their schooling in the 1950s and 1960s (Ramphele 1995; Magona 1991; Slovo 1997). All are or have been influential in discussions of education policy, either because they are key players (one is a member of parliament and one the vice-chancellor of a university), or because they are close to powerful networks of political decision-making either in the African National Congress (ANC), or in particular institutions (universities or the media). They are not representative, and reflect the voices of a tiny fraction of the population. These are all women who have succeeded not only politically or professionally, but also in terms of being able to write their version of their lives and have it published. How do they see both their success and their schooling?

Autobiographies of schooling

The six autobiographies represent experiences of women strongly marked by the brutality and violence of racialization in apartheid South Africa. All the texts are deeply engaged with the way 'race', often much more than gender, shaped the possibilities in a life. But below the diversity articulated by differentially racialized voices lie another set of comparisons among th texts. There are notable similarities between the autobiographies of the black and white women of the older generation, and difference with the autobiographies of the younger generation. The older women remember their schooling in both co-educational and single-sex schools as a mixture of pleasure and pain. The younger women remember school only as pain. This colours their accounts whether they depict single-sex or co-educational schools. What are the specific elements of school they remember? Why are the differences so striking? How do these published memories articulate with current strategies in policy-making?

The older generation of women (Phyllis Ntantala, Ellen Kuzwayo and Phyllis Lewsen) all come from families that had considerable material wealth, linked to farming, compared to the majority of the population. However, in childhood and youth the benefits these women could derive from this wealth were circumscribed by gendered family politics. Moreover, despite their relative wealth, all the women of the older generation suffered discrimination and prejudice – on the grounds of race for the two African women, and on the grounds of Jewish ethnicity for the white woman. The burden of that suffering was most acute for Ellen Kuzwayo, who was detained in prison for over a year without trial and then prevented through banning orders from participating in any social activities outside her home.

The younger generation of women (Mamphela Ramphele, Sindiwe Magona and Gillian Slovo) do not come from so uniform a background. Two (Slovo and Ramphele) are the daughters of professionals, although a vast gulf separates Slovo's parents' urban world of lawyers and journalists from Ramphele's parents' rural world of teaching and preaching. Of the six Magona is the only one from an impoverished family: she grew up in the townships of the Cape Flats. Her father was a labourer, and her mother worked in the informal sector, sewing and hawking. While her parents strongly believed in schooling as the tool by which their daughter's 'lot was to be improved' (Magona 1991: 48), their understanding of the length of that schooling was considerably shorter than the parents of all the other writers.

The apartheid era was exceptionally brutal for all this group of women. Mamphela Ramphele's friends and lover were imprisoned, tortured and murdered in police detention; she too was imprisoned, humiliated by police and then banished to a remote rural area, where she lived for seven years under police scrutiny and intimidation. Gillian Slovo's mother was murdered by an apartheid security service assassination team. As a young girl she experienced first the imprisonment of her parents and grandparents for long periods, followed by the exile of her family from South Africa to London. These losses and separations marked her whole perspective on adult life. Sindiwe Magona's pain was not so dramatic, but was nevertheless a wound constantly reopened by the humiliations and proscriptions of racism and by the distress of friendships corrupted and disrupted. She had to take difficult decisions as a lone parent, and struggle constantly to find some voice.

Similarities and differences across generations

The autobiographies of Phyllis Ntantala, Ellen Kuzwayo and Phyllis Lewsen have many points in common. They all evoke an idyllic rural childhood, where the natural landscape is a source of aesthetic pleasure, and of learning about birds, plants and history that is of enormous significance to each, writing some 50 years later in urban settings. In all three accounts the countryside is a place where they are free from constraints of femininity, where they can cross boundaries and play as boys. Phyllis Ntantala is encouraged by her father to be the son her parents never had, to help her father around his farm (Ntantala 1992: 41–2). Ellen Kuzwayo revels at certain moments in abandoning the constraints of her separate Christianized and schooled identity when joining the work-parties of tenant farmers or observing the circumcision rites of her neighbours (Kuzwayo 1985: 68–9; 70–2). Phyllis Lewsen is allowed by her parents to roam about the countryside with her brother, exploring and playing imaginative games. She alone, however, recalls incidents where she was sexed and named as inferior by her father:

> One treat that Harry was allowed, but I was forbidden, was riding a horse. My father ... was very proud of Harry's pluck and daring. To encourage these traits, he bought Harry a lively black pony for his sixth birthday ... I begged to be allowed to go riding as well. For once my father gave into me. He hoisted me onto the back of Harry's pony – and I promptly and ignominiously fell off ... My father angrily declared that I was behaving 'just like a girl!' and could not be allowed to ride again (Lewsen 1996: 12).

This is in striking contrast to Ntantala, who comments on her father's stress to all his daughters 'not to take second place to anybody, because we were as good as the best, including men' (Ntantala 1992: 14).

For the older generation of writers there is thus a sense of landscape as a natural setting, where the bonds of the femininity imposed by 'society' are loosed and the markers of 'race' are not noted.

But the landscape is not felt or portrayed elegiacally by the younger generation. The brutalities of the apartheid regime are not a disruption of a largely idyllic childhood, but are present in the very fabric of that childhood, marked on the roads through the veld, built into the children's perception of the land. Their homes provide no protective boundaries. Before she is five, Sindiwe Magona is aware of the racism of the white tourists travelling in fast cars through the Transkei, stopping to buy goods from her and her friends standing at the roadside, choking with dust as they go by (Magona 1991: 10–12). One of her first experiences on moving to Cape Town at five was of a police liquor-raid on her parents' home and the fear in her father's eyes (ibid.: 19–20). Home was not a place of safety, nor the veld a place of simple beauty.

Similarly Mamphela Ramphele evokes both the warmth of an extended family – its exchanges of food, childcare, poetry and ideas – and the oppression of a village where men were absent as migrant workers and where the cruelty of the Dutch Reformed Church minister, who could turn half the village off their land for disobeying his orders, was relentless (Ramphele 1995: 24, 31). Gillian Slovo also mixes the vitality of her parents' exciting and interesting lives with the consequences of police raids on her home, her parents' detention without trial and the disappearance of friends and family into exile. This home that is not home is partly made so because as a child she sees the casual cruelty experienced by black dustbin-workers running after the lorry with their heavy loads every day. For her the landscape is a place of danger out of which two black women stumble bleeding. They had been robbed and attacked in the veld, but the police did not believe they were important enough to take statements from them (Slovo 1997: 44). For all three the landscape confers 'race'; it does not obliterate it. But the power of learning 'race' seems to overarch and diminish an awareness of gender.

Relations with mothers

All three writers of the older generation set the beauty and tranquillity of the rural landscape against their evocations of their immediate families as places of stress and distress. They lost their mothers when they were children. Phyllis Ntantala's mother died when she was four and her father remarried a woman who neglected her. Ellen Kuzwayo's mother, somewhat stigmatized as the divorced daughter in the home of her parents, died when her daughter was 16. Her stepmother later turned Ellen out of her family home. Phyllis Lewsen's mother sent her away when she was four to stay in a small town with her grandmother and aunts so that she could go to school. While some of her relatives were warm and welcomed her, her grandmother was particularly cold and forbidding, punishing and insulting her (Lewsen 1996: 31). Although her mother was not dead, she was lost to the young child by distance and the pressures of caring for younger siblings.

The significance of these absent mothers is important in each text of this generation in two ways. First, in each it means that a beloved male relative is identified as the source of inspiration for the world of culture and learning. Phyllis Ntantala learned lessons in Xhosa history from her father that are crucial to her self-identity and to the narrative line of the story she tells (Ntantala 1992: 42–5). Ellen Kuzwayo remarks that, as a young girl, she was encouraged to read and understand newspaper articles by her stepfather (Kuzwayo 1985: 67). Phyllis Lewsen identifies her uncle, with his knowledge of European art, music and opera, and his large record collection as her source for widening horizons (Lewsen 1996: 28–9).

As we see below, the absence of mothers means that women teachers assume great importance in each autobiography of this generation. By contrast, for the younger generation of women, mothers are a more significant presence, although all three have long periods of absence from their mothers. For each of these writers their sense of self is partly derived from their sense of their mother's identity. Sindiwe Magona spends her early years with her mother and grandmother in the Transkei, revelling in its beauties and her freedom. She joined her mother and father in Cape Town when she was five. In that new life her mother is portrayed as the efficient provider, who could make ends meet. She earns the money for schooling; she is the role model for her daughter's dogged survival after she has left school. Mamphela Ramphele describes how she loved to be close to her mother, to do the work around the house with her, helping to carry babies and small children. However, although her mother is a teacher, like her father, it is her father's library of books she remembers, and her father's practice as a teacher (Ramphele 1995: 21). Gillian Slovo's relationship with her mother and her father is the subject of much of her book. School is incidental to the drama of this relationship. Nothing that is learned at school has any of the power or significance of what she learned from her mother while she was alive and after her death. Unlike the older group of women, where mothers are not role models, because they are absent, for this group of women mothers are powerful figures as exemplars, and providers of both material and emotional well-being. But their power does not eclipse fathers, and fathers, even though often absent, are themselves not displaced in significance by other male relatives.

All three mothers of the younger generation of women worked outside the home and two worked in education, one as a teacher, the other one as a journalist. The third mother is dedicated to the cause of her daughter's education. But this positioning of their mothers with regard to education does not make schooling pleasurable for this generation. In strong contrast with the earlier generation, for whom some teachers assumed the role of mother, for this generation teachers are dubious figures with none of the compassion or intellect of their mothers.

Relationships with teachers

For each writer in the older generation there is a particular teacher, or group of teachers, who were inspiring, enabling them to excel through a mixture of learning and love. In each text these teachers are named, fully described, and linked to a sense of joy in learning. What is interesting, however, is that the greatest pleasures their former pupils remember is the learning they inculcated outside the formal curriculum. It was not so much that they were taught facts that they recall, but that they were taught ideas or attitudes which they felt deeply and which lived with them for decades. Women schoolteachers are singled out as formative. It is the affective dimensions of their pedagogy that are remembered.

Phyllis Ntantala recalls her English teacher, at Fort Hare, 'who loved literature and ... made it live' (Ntantala 1992: 71). The experience of reading Wordsworth's *On Westminster Bridge* with this teacher remained with her as a most powerful experience. Many years later, standing on that spot with her daughter, she was able to recite the poem by heart (ibid.: 72). This delineation of a highly emotional bond with English literature is particularly significant, for earlier in the text Ntantala comments critically on how much of the curriculum she studied stressed England and English culture, while remaining completely silent, or in some cases wrong, about South African history, writing and culture (ibid.: 30).

Ellen Kuzwayo names three teachers at Adams College who 'made a lasting impression on me' (Kuzwayo 1985: 87). Her mother died shortly before she went to Adams College. An idealized femininity that she longed for in her dead mother came to be embodied for her in these three teachers. From the first came knowledge of sex, and a role model of married life and motherhood, from the second knowledge of charm, elegance and good taste in clothes, and from the third knowledge of domestic science (ibid.: 87–9). She also names a number of other inspiring women teachers, who she singles out particularly for their musical abilities (ibid.: 78, 93). Here, as in Ntantala's text, it is the teacher's ability to talk to feelings, aesthetics, and a sense of self that is important.

Phyllis Lewsen names two teachers as formative in her life, and both are particularly significant because of the teaching that they gave outside formal lesson time. Her English teacher was 'cultured, elderly, and alarmingly sarcastic' but gave to a chosen group of girls literary 'feasts' out of class time, introducing them to the canon of classical literature (Lewsen 1996: 55). Her history teacher's work in class was 'brilliant: filled with life, humour, tragedy and excitement – yet rational and coherent, so that history had meaning as well as enchantment' (ibid.: 56).

The powerful emotions of love and inspiration that flow from these teachers pervade much – but not all – of the evocations of schooling for this older generation of writers. This contrasts with the younger generation. For all three, schooling, like childhood, is cruel. It is never remembered as uplifting but is recalled as brutalizing, a crushing of creativity, a harsh bodily regime.

Ramphele and Magona describe the lack of food at their boarding schools, the discomfort of their dormitories, the controls on their movement beyond the school's perimeter (Ramphele 1995: 36, 40, 42; Magona 1991: 79, 74). They both remark on the racism of their generally white teachers, who would not allow them to write the truth, and who impressed on them that they were lowlier (Ramphele 1995: 37, 38, 47; Magona 1991: 77, 85). Like Magona, Ramphele records the girls in her class having to do domestic work for the white teachers (Magona 1991: 83). Ramphele notes the teachers' assurance to them: 'You are born to work for us' (Ramphele 1995: 38).

Slovo's school was marked not by physical discomfort, but by emotional dislocation. It had no connection with the world of everyday racism or of resistance against that racism and the repression of that resistance. This was the world she lived in because of her parents' activism, but her school and teachers denied its reality. Behind the teachers' apparent sympathy for their young pupils, whose parents had been imprisoned, raged a vitriolic hatred of their ideas. After one of her books was published in South Africa, Gillian Slovo received a hate letter from one of these women teachers (Slovo 1997: 61).

Ramphele, Magona and Slovo all name significant teachers. For Ramphele these are two male English teachers and a science teacher who were kind and helped her with her work (Ramphele 1995: 37, 46). For Magona it is the teacher who reads out to the whole school that she had passed and gives her a feeling of achievement and pleasure in school (Magona 1991: 48–9). For Slovo it is a teacher she envies for her certainty in the power of god (Slovo 1997: 61). But, in contrast to the earlier group of writers, where significant teachers were portrayed with great affection as key figures in the process of identity formation, here their importance is noted but mixed with doubt and self-mockery.

All the autobiographies provide evidence of the ambiguities entailed in the construction of femininity through schooling. For the three older women school is a place where female docility is learned as much as creativity and critique. Women teachers are as significant for these lessons in obedience as for their lessons in the powers of emotion and the breadth of knowledge. Ellen Kuzwayo describes graphically how the hem of her dress, considered too short, was cut with a blade in front of her whole class by a vengeful teacher (Kuzwayo 1985: 82). Female teachers rigidly policed their pupils at Heladtown, in Ntantala's account, stigmatizing and ridiculing any contact with male pupils (Ntantala 1992: 67). Some of the white teachers arouse bitter antagonisms because of their racism, not so much to their black pupils, but to the cook and gardener (Ntantala 1992: 71). In Lewsen's autobiography, it is not so much the teachers as fellow students who are singled out for delivering painful lessons in appropriate femininity. This quality entailed sportiness (which she was able to attain) and not too much cleverness (which she was not). Lewsen also points out how, although she excelled in sport, as was considered appropriate, some of her experiences of school life were marred by anti-Semitism, articulated both by pupils and by some staff (Lewsen 1996: 40, 54–5).

The pivotal women teachers are not able to command authority in the narrative in their own right. Each is situated in relation to a wider notion of the good, and this realm of the good is strongly sculpted around dominant male figures. For both Lewsen and Ntantala this good is equated with the canon of English literature, largely male-authored. In remembering important teachers, notions of male superiority, and of 'efficient' femininity subordinated to that, are significant components of perceptions of 'the good' for both Lewsen and Kuzwayo. An implication of this is that female teachers cannot be remembered, even by their most academically or professionally successful female students, outside a gendered framework of male dominance. While to differing degrees the subsequent texts of all three autobiographies are about struggling with the inequities of patriarchal relations – in work, in the family and in relation to the state – it appears that those struggles take place from a standpoint where forms of male dominance are, to some extent, naturalized and equated with 'the good'.

For the younger generation of women, part of their sense of the irrelevance of school is their awareness that what is taught there has no bearing on 'life', whose real meanings reside in political struggle. Just as for the older three an awakening to knowledge – an awareness of literature, history or music – was linked to an initiation into a world shaped by men, so too for the younger women the passage into politics is depicted as emerging largely through relationships with a world shaped by important men – fathers or lovers.

Nevertheless, the process of forming racialized, ethnicized and gendered identities in school settings does not go uncontested by either generation of women. All the autobiographies of the older generation highlight strategies of resistance employed by the girls to imposed identifications. Ellen Kuzwayo, after her humiliation when her skirt was cut, was welcomed with sympathy by her classmates; Ntantala and her friends organized a strike against the racist teacher, refusing her offers of mouthwatering cakes and pleasant Sunday afternoon teas; Lewsen describes herself clearly calculating how to overcome the handicaps she was aware she suffered as a clever Jewish girl entering high school. But while they could marshal good defences against oppressive regimes of racism, they appear much less supported, either by teachers or fellow pupils, with regard to sexism. Indeed, none of the writers comments on the extent of male power in the schools they attended, although it is evident from their accounts that male teachers command all the senior positions.

But all three younger writers transmute these strategies of resistance to injustice. Resistance strategies for them turn from the triumphs of collaborative action portrayed in the first set of books to wry ironic vignettes of attempts at survival. Ramphele describes the bonding of home-girls, sharing their food parcels as a way of surviving the near starvation of boarding school, but tells how she decided to separate herself from her home-girl group, because the rituals of sharing meant she did not get enough food (Ramphele 1995: 40). Magona remembers how at high school she joined the IDC (I don't care) group, as a rebellion against the lack of friends and the boredom of lessons, but that her only benefit from membership was to fail at the end of the year (Magona 1991: 76–7). Gillian Slovo knows of her mother's imprisonment for a noble cause and yet cannot understand it, given the incomprehension and pretence of all around. Her response is to act out a defiant conformity, a desperate pretence to herself that denied what she so admired in her mother and thus suggested that she was really like the other girls in her class (Slovo 1997: 76).

Does schooling entail empowerment for these women?

The question is not easy to answer, but I think part of the answer lies in unravelling in the two groups of texts the narrative function of the section on schooling. For all three women of the older generation schooling is crucial in positioning them for marriage. For Ntantala and Lewsen marriage, while not without difficulties, brings access to emotional happiness and secure incomes from which their intellectual and political interests can develop.

At the end of her book, after the death of her husband Phyllis Ntantala remarks that people can now see her as a person in her own right and not as 'the appendage of a great man' (Ntantala 1992: 230). On one level Phyllis Lewsen ends her book on a much more impersonal note. She remarks on 'the miracle' of the South African elections and the inauguration of Nelson Mandela as president. The text ends almost abruptly. Beneath it is a picture of her holding her grandson on her knee (Lewsen 1996: 220). Both texts thus appear as affirmations of independent identity, despite the acknowledged racist and largely unacknowledged sexist conditions of their times.

Ellen Kuzwayo's marriage did not bring happiness and after some years she was able to leave a relationship that was brutal and debilitating. Bringing up her children alone, struggling to make a living and to achieve support for the social work she was doing, imprisoned without trial in the late 1970s, she is much more aware than the two other writers of the extent of discrimination against and hostility to women in South Africa. Yet interestingly, where both the others affirm their independence, she commits herself to service to the community (Kuzwayo 1985: 221–2) and identifies with a history of resistance by generations of South African women (ibid.: 258–63).

For all three writers, despite their learning, their scholarship and their activism the note they end on is one of motherhood. Ntantala celebrates the support of her children in helping her to survive (Ntantala 1992: 236),

Lewsen cradles her grandson, and Kuzwayo commits herself to stand with her community – 'our menfolk and our children' – in the struggle against apartheid. She quotes a Setswana proverb: 'The child's mother grabs the sharp end of the knife' (Kuzwayo 1985: 263). There are very different emphases in these portrayals of motherhood, but in these narratives the journeys that began with schooling have returned each woman to the space their own mothers made empty. The work of their substitute-mother teachers is both incorporated and forgotten. Well-being carries a sense of independence, but simultaneously affirms an apparently non-controversial meaning of femininity.

For the younger generation of writers schooling is emphatically not empowering. Schooling, in all three texts, is not a realm separated from the racism of society. But, interestingly, the gendered dimensions of that racism are barely remarked on. The harshness of male teachers is not differentiated from that of female teachers. Fellow schoolgirls inflict the cruelties of initiation ceremonies and rebuff friendship (Ramphele 1995: 39; Slovo 1997: 76), and while there are occasional references to friends who have to leave school because of pregnancy, the world of male students appears very far away. All three feel the shadow of male relatives, whose power is often set against their powerlessness. Sindiwe Magona's older brother has the freedom of the street and the admiration of his peer group, in ways his sister never does (Magona 1991: 47, 74). Mamphela Ramphele and Gillian Slovo are both aware of their fathers as political strategists (on different terrains) who do not or cannot put the needs of their children above the needs of their constituencies. But these perceptions about gendered power in the family are not utilized in relation to school.

In these texts the narrative purpose of the section on schooling is different from that in the autobiographies of the older generation of women. For Ramphele, Magona and Slovo there is virtually no link between formal schooling and their acquisition of insight into their society or themselves. Schooling for all three is a rather unpleasant disjunctive interlude. It leads nowhere. There is of course some connection, predicated on exam results, between Ramphele's schooling, her entry into medical school and the development of her political consciousness through her work with her fellow students there. But the link is tenuous. Similarly the education Magona receives is from the harsh realities of work as a domestic servant, the difficulties of keeping a teaching job, the burden of bringing up children, for the most part on her own (see also Magona 1992). These are her, in her words, 'finishing school'. Slovo learns the significant lessons about her parents and their history by painful research, when her father is dying and her mother dead. Her schooling was irrelevant to this search. All three writers of this generation pay considerable attention to the sexism of South African society in subsequent chapters of their books. The sexism is delineated both in their families and in the repression of the state. They uncover this sexism through living it. This narrative structure means that as their schooling played no role in alerting them to sexism, it is not subjected to the same critique they level at other institutions.

In contrast to the older women's texts, in which schooling is seen to be catalytic to empowerment, the younger generation of women portray it as irrelevant. Empowerment for all three flows from survival in traumatic times. They rely on their courage, their wits, the support of friends and family, and dogged persistence. To some extent these may have been qualities cultivated through the harshness of their schools, but they are portrayed as qualities dredged from deep recesses of endurance in adult life.

The autobiographies of the younger women end on notes very different from those of the older women. Not one evokes motherhood. All three portray a sense of themselves in a larger world, a world of the struggle against apartheid for Ramphele; of people guarding secrets and signalling meanings for Slovo; a world of the spirits and all humanity for Magona. It is a world they are confident in, even though they have been battered by it. They do not see themselves completing circles.

Whatever the sexism of South African schooling, neither set of auto-biographies delineates it closely. They are silent on this for different reasons. For the older women, I believe, this is partly because of the powerful positive memories they have of schooling, linked to an age somehow *before apartheid*. For the younger women their silence might be linked with their powerful negative memories of the very recent past, a deep trauma entailing gendered identities with which it is not easy to come to terms.

Stories, statistics and strategies

The autobiographies show the ambiguities, dilemmas and contradictions entailed in schooling for a group of women whom, according to the statistical data, we should count as successful and empowered. The narratives the women construct undermine the simplistic certainties of the numbers. These figures, like the women's feelings, are each only part of the picture. But the significance of these stories and the process of telling life stories has, to date, been given less weight than the statistics in formulating strategies for gender equity in schooling and carrying out research for policy. The views of imported experts on gender policy, working within supposedly neutral general frameworks, are often valued more than local storytellers. Neither group has an exclusive or authentic voice to contribute. What emerges so clearly from these autobiographies is how complex the process of remembering schooling is, and how nuanced the ways in which it shapes a voice. In this complexity, I believe, lie some of the clues to the ways in which patriarchal relations persist so viciously in South Africa, despite the many decades of schooling for girls.

Notes

1. Thanks to Debbie Budlender of CASE (Community Agency for Social Enquiry) in Cape Town for invaluable help with statistics.

2. Under apartheid there was little consistency in the collection of data on school enrolments. These data must be seen primarily as indicating trends. Second, it must not be assumed that the students enrolled in the last year of primary or secondary schooling in any year comprise a proportion of all students who enrolled in the first year of primary schooling seven years before. Before 1995 primary schooling was not compulsory, which resulted in a very skewed age balance in South African schools with all grades having a varying proportion of students who were under and over the correct age (*Edusource Data News* 1997).

3. The South African school phases referred to here entail a seven-year primary phase, a three-year junior secondary phase and a two-year senior secondary phase. Enrolment in the final year of primary school or any phase does not ensure progression to the next.

4. These tables have been compiled taking a cohort of girl and boy pupils who enrolled in 1976 (for Tables 4.1 and 4.3) and 1983 (for Tables 4.2 and 4.4) and calculating the gendered distribution of enrolments was seven years (Std. 5), ten years (Std. 8) and twelve years later (Std. 10).

5. Gillian Slovo left South Africa for exile in the UK when she was eleven and since the unbanning of the ANC in 1990 has lived in South Africa only for periods of a year or less. She is the only white woman of her generation to write an autobiography. She was active in the ANC in exile and remains close to key players in South Africa.

Bibliography

Bozzoli, B. (1991) *Women of Phokeng*, Raven, Johannesburg.

Budlender, D. (1994) 'Women in tertiary education', in M. Lessing (ed.), *South African Women Today*, pp. 129–38.

— (1996) 'South Africa: gender and education', paper prepared for the Gender Equity Task Team, National Department of Education, Pretoria.

— (1997) The Second Women's Budget, IDASA, Cape Town.

Central Statistical Services (1997) *South African Statistics 1995*, Government Printer, Pretoria.

Edusource Data News (1997), October.

Erwee, R. (1994) 'Scaling the economic ladder', in M. Lessing (ed.), *South African Women Today*, pp. 35–53.

Giroux, H. (1992) *Border Crossings: Cultural Workers and the Politics of Education*, Routledge, London.

Gordon, T. (1996) 'Citizenship, difference and marginality in schools: spatial and embodied aspects of gender construction', in P. Murphy and C. V. Gipps (eds),

Equity in the Classroom: Towards Effective Pedagogy for Girls and Boys, Faler Press and UNESCO Publishing, London, pp. 34–45.

Holland, J., M. Blair and S. Sheldon (eds) (1995) *Debates and Issues in Feminist Research and Pedagogy*, Multilingual Matters, Clevedon.Kallaway, P. (ed.) (1984) *Apartheid and Education*, Ravan, Johannesburg.

Kenway, J. and S. Willis (1993) *Telling Tales: Girls and Schools: Changing Their Ways*, Department of Education and Training, Canberra.

Kotecha, P. (1994) 'The position of women teachers', in M. Lessing (ed.), *South African Women Today*, pp. 69–97.

Kuzwayo, E. (1985) *Call me Woman*, Women's Press, London.

Leidenberg, S. (ed.) (1995) *The Constitution of South Africa from a Gender Perspective*, David Philip, Cape Town.

Lessing, M. (ed.) (1994) *South African Women Today*, Maskew Miller Longman, Cape Town.

Lewsen, P. (1996) *Reverberations*, University of Cape Town Press, Rondebosh.

Mac an Ghaill, M. (1994) *The Making of Men: Masculinities, Sexualities and Schooling*, Buckingham, Open University Press.

Magona, S. (1991) *To My Children's Children: An Autobiography*, Women's Press, London.

— (1992) *Forced to Grow*, David Philip, Cape Town.

Meintjes, S. (1995) 'Relationships in transition: the Women's National Coalition in South Africa', paper presented to conference on Gender in Empire and Commonwealth, February 1995, Institute of Commonwealth Studies, University of London.

Miller, J. (1990) *Seductions: Studies in Reading and Culture*, Virago, London.

— (1997) 'Autobiography of the subject', paper presented at the American Research Association Annual Meeting in Chicago.

Motala, S. (1997) *EPU Quarterly Review*, issue titled 'From policy to implementation: ongoing challenges and constraints', Education Policy Unit, University of the Witwatersrand, Johannesburg.

Muller, J. (1996) 'Dreams of wholeness and loss: critical sociology of education in South Africa', *British Journal of Sociology of Education* 17 (2): 177–96.

Muller, J. and N. Cloete (1993) 'Out of Eden: modernity, post apartheid and intellectuals', *Theory, Culture and Society* 10: 155–72.

Nkomo, M. (ed.) (1990) *Pedagogy of Domination*, Africa World Press, Trenton, NJ.

Ntantala, P. (1992) *A Life's Mosaic*, David Philip, Cape Town.

Ramphele, M. (1995) *A Life*, David Philip, Cape Town.

Slovo, G. (1997) *Every Secret Thing: My Family, My Country*, Little, Brown, London.

Stanley, L. (1992) *The Auto/biographical I*, Manchester University Press, Manchester.

Steedman, C. (1986) *Landscape for a Good Woman*, Virago, London.

Tom, P. (1985) *My Life Struggle*, Raven Press, Johannesburg.

Unterhalter, E. (1991) 'Can education overcome women's subordinate position in the occupation structure?', in E. Unterhalter et al. (eds.) *Education in a Future South Africa: Policy Issues for Transformation*, Heinemann, London.

Unterhalter, E. et al. (eds) *Apartheid Education and Popular Struggle*, Zed Books, London.

CHAPTER 5

Schooling and Development: Eroding Amazon Women's Knowledge and Diversity

Sheila Aikman

Indigenous women have hitherto found little space within debates about gender education and development to air their specific concerns. Similarly, discussion of education for and/or by indigenous peoples has rarely focused special attention on indigenous women. The Fourth World Conference on Women held at Beijing in September 1995 provided a platform for indigenous women's organizations from around the world to give voice to common concerns about forces of globalization and a capitalist growth model of development, and the impact of these on the biodiversity, indigenous women's oral knowledge and informal processes of learning and teaching.

This chapter looks at the relationship between gender, education and development with particular reference to the Beijing Declaration of Indigenous Women, a document submitted to the Fourth World Conference by the Indigenous Women's Caucus. This Declaration critiques the UN Platform for Action produced at the World Conference for failing to address the wider political and international influences on women's education and development and the failure of the global economic growth model of development to meet the fundamental material and spiritual needs of the majority of peoples of the world (Indigenous Women's Caucus 1995). The Declaration also directly criticizes Western formal education for discriminating against indigenous peoples and eroding cultural diversity and indigenous peoples' own education systems.

Taking the case of Arakmbut women of the Southeastern Peruvian Amazon, the chapter examines the dynamics of gender, education and development for indigenous women. It investigates the constraints and challenges for Arakmbut women from the hegemonic economic development model and questions the role of formal education in promoting this model at the expense of indigenous Arakmbut alternatives. It provides evidence to suggest that formal education, embedded in a modernizing and developmentalist ideology, is leading to the 'growth of ignorance' (Shiva 1993b) and poverty for the Arakmbut, not only as women, but as indigenous people. In a region where boys and girls have equal access to formal education and an almost 100 per cent completion rate for primary education, the case study examines the two-pronged attack by schooling and the market economy on the Arakmbut people's own forms and processes of learning and teaching. Learning and teaching in Arakmbut society are based in culturally and historically developed gender relations, themselves embedded in particular material and spiritual relations with the physical environment. Formal education contributes to a devaluation of these relations and of the knowledge created and passed down through generations according to indigenous learning and teaching practices.

The Arakmbut in context

The Arakmbut live in five communities in a region of lowland tropical rainforest in the Department of Madre de Dios, a region of cultural, linguistic and biological diversity. Each community has legally recognized lands that are located within their wider traditional territory. The Arakmbut are one of five Harakmbut peoples who speak variants of the Harakmbut language and together number some 1,500 individuals. The Arakmbut comprise the largest Harakmbut people today, with a population of approximately 1,000. In all, there are estimated to be some 4,000 indigenous people in Madre de Dios (Moore 1985). The population of Madre de Dios has burgeoned over the last two decades as landless migrants, capitalist entrepreneurs and international companies have been lured by the rich natural resources, particularly Brazil nuts, timber, rubber, gold and oil, and by opportunities for cattle ranching and agriculture.

The Arakmbut people are by tradition hunters, fishers and mixed agriculturalists. In the last 20 years they have also begun to pan for gold and to participate to a limited extent in the regional economy. Each Arakmbut is a member of one of seven clans, and gender is a fundamental aspect of the division of labour. The women are the agriculturalists while men work gold and do some hunting. Women plant and tend swidden gardens and cook the meat or fish that the men bring from the forest and rivers (Gray 1996).

The Arakmbut world has an invisible dimension, inhabited by spirits but no less real for the Arakmbut than the visible world in which they live. Men and women develop the capacity to understand and interpret the spirit world through dreaming. Sickness is usually the result of an attack by spirits. A shaman or curer is someone who has intimate knowledge and experience of the spirits and forest and can use this knowledge to identify which spirit is causing the sickness. The spirit, which takes the form of one of the forest animals, is lured away from the sick person by chanting. The spiritual dimension to the Arakmbut universe is ever-present and underlies every aspect of their life. It emphasizes a coherence and unity of knowledge. Thus Arakmbut 'economic' activities such as agriculture or fishing are embedded in relations with the spirit world and bound up with their specific territory and identity. As with many other hunter-gatherer peoples, existence is based on principles of cooperation and coexistence both with the natural world and with other people (Teasdale and Teasdale 1994) and of caring for and nurturing their environment and the flora and fauna that provide them with their physical and spiritual needs.

Although Arakmbut women did not participate in the Beijing Conference they are part of the global indigenous movement for recognition of their rights to land, to freedom of cultural and linguistic expression and to their continued freedom to teach their children their principles of cooperation and coexistence with the natural world. The changes that have been taking place over the last 20 years in the traditional livelihoods and non-economic activities of the Arakmbut, largely as a result of outside pressures and influences, have brought them together with other indigenous peoples of the Madre de Dios to form a representative organization to lobby for their rights to land and their freedom of cultural expression. This chapter investigates the impact of the pressures and influences on Arakmbut women that have contributed to changing gender roles and undermining women's position and status in the community.[1]

The Beijing Declaration of Indigenous Women

Over a hundred indigenous women, representing many different indigenous peoples from around the world, participated in the Indigenous Caucus at the NGO forum held from 30 August to 8 September 1995 at Huairou, outside Beijing. Their experiences of discrimination and oppression as indigenous and their common participation in the indigenous movement united them. The Beijing meeting and the regional preparatory meetings provided them with a forum for examining their specific relations as colonized and racialized women with a common experience (see Myles and Tarrago 1996; Pettman 1996; Marchand 1995). Their common self-identification as indigenous is based on their spiritual relationship with their land, their non-custodial and non-materialist relationship to their land and natural resources, their different world view (for definitions of 'indigenous' see Burger 1987), and on a struggle for recognition of common demands, such as land, cultural and linguistic freedom and self-determination. The Caucus comprised representatives of indigenous organizations from Hawaii to Colombia and the Arctic (for a full list see Indigenous Women's Caucus 1995).

The Indigenous Caucus presented the Beijing Declaration of Indigenous

Women to the official conference, highlighting areas of special concern to indigenous women that they believed were not being acknowledged in the draft UN Platform for Action. The Indigenous Women's Declaration recognizes that the Platform for Action 'rightly identifies unequal access to education and health as an area of concern' (paragraph 13) but takes global inequalities as its level of analysis, stating that strategic objectives for ensuring women's equal access and full participation in decision-making are hollow and meaningless if the inequality between nations is not addressed. It decries a lack of critique of the 'New World Order', which it considers has a clear bias in favour of large industry, which has been responsible for the decimation of the traditional livelihoods and economic activities of indigenous peoples, such as hunting, food-gathering and harvesting and subsistence agriculture. It identifies institutions such as the World Bank and the International Monetary Fund as major forces for global economics and trade liberalization, which it condemns as a process of recolonization by the rich industrialized nation-states, transnational corporations and financial institutions (paragraph 6). The World Bank considers gender equality as a matter of good economics: 'Women tend to be less educated than men, to work more hours, and to be paid less, which creates inefficiencies, hampers growth and lowers the potential well-being of society' (World Bank 1995: 3). Indigenous women, however, decry 'powerful nations and interests which impose their economic development model and monocultures on us' and reject such an economic focus because 'it ignores the non-economic activities of indigenous women and does not recognise indigenous values of sharing knowledge and mutual exchange' (paragraph 7).

With regard to education, the Platform for Action makes specific reference to the need to 'develop non-discriminatory education and training' for indigenous peoples and states that governments, educational authorities and other educational and academic institutions should: 'Promote a multi-cultural approach to education that is responsive to the needs, aspirations and cultures of indigenous women ... in the languages of indigenous peoples and ... provide for the participation of indigenous women in these processes' (A/CONF.177/L.5/Add.6 85n).

Despite this, the Platform for Action, just as with the World Bank's *Towards Gender Equality* (1995), does not question the basic Western orientation of the prevailing education system or 'acknowledge the role of Western education ... in eroding the cultural diversity which exists among indigenous peoples' (paragraph 13). The Indigenous Women's Declaration demands indigenous peoples' rights to self-determination, to their territories and to their own development, education and health (paragraph 25), as well as to their intellectual and cultural heritage, and continuance as the guardians and custodians of their knowledge and biodiversity (paragraph 43).

Arakmbut education – in touch with the land and its spirituality

For the Arakmbut 'education' is experienced as two distinct practices: the learning and teaching that take place as part of daily life and engender a sense of indigenous identity based in the intellectual and cultural heritage of the people, and the formal schooling children receive at the hands of lay-missionary teachers. The two practices are not accorded equal status in wider society. Formal education is embedded in an economic maximizing development ideology and denies the legitimacy of indigenous knowledge and values, while the very development it promotes undermines the biodiversity and indigenous ways of life (see Aikman forthcoming). It ignores women's subsistence livelihoods and their position as teachers and guardians of Arakmbut knowledge and spirituality. At Beijing, the indigenous women called for the right to continue to educate their children according to their own indigenous practices and for an end to ethnocidal Western (formal) education, which respects neither indigenous women nor men. For Arakmbut women neither of these rights is recognized.

Around the world today there are examples of indigenous-controlled intercultural bilingual education, representing a creative, challenging alternative to formal schooling, which excludes and denies indigenous peoples (e.g. Lipka and Stairs 1994). The strong indigenous political movement of the Peruvian Amazon combined with state neglect and missionary domination of schooling have produced a fertile context for experimental intercultural programmes (see Aikman 1994). The Amazon-wide Association for the Development of the Peruvian Amazon – AIDESEP – has been very active in developing and establishing an intercultural bilingual teacher-training programme for indigenous teacher trainees nominated by their representative ethnic organizations (see Trapnell 1990, 1991; ETSA 1996; Tuesta Cerron 1997). To date, however, the Arakmbut have not participated in this programme.

Schooling for the Arakmbut is controlled and run by lay-missionaries working for the Dominican Educational Network (RESSOP). Each community has a primary school, which is an edifice to the Spanish language and the national 'Westernized' culture, yet strikingly devoid of books and any other equipment with which to impart the national curriculum with its entirely literate focus and completely urban bias.

In stark contrast to this primary schooling, the Arakmbut's people's own education system is interactive, oral and relevant to the lives of the students. The learning and teaching are practical and task-oriented and the 'curriculum' is organized according to age, clan and gender. This Arakmbut way of life and sense of identity as Arakmbut is transmitted over generations through their 'informal' learning and teaching practices and processes. Using and caring for their territory as its custodians for future generations is a vital part of the learning process. A girl will learn from her mother how to grow barbasco, a root used for fishing, but she will also know that the barbasco plant comes from the forest and will learn how to treat it and the relations with the spirits that this implies.

For the Arakmbut learning is lifelong, acquired through practical experience, listening to the elders and understanding the significance and meaning of the myths, and communicating with the spirit world through dreams. It is punctuated by different stages at which new knowledge and new experiences become available. In the past boys underwent one ceremony to mark their passage from childhood to youth and another to mark that from youth to adulthood, which defined their ability to learn about the forest animals and spirits. A girl's passage from childhood to womanhood is indicated by her first menstruation and her maturity by the birth of her first child. These events indicate her entry into new phases of learning, responsibility and the ability to earn recognition of it.

Learning for Arakmbut children is based in values of trust and respect for the teacher and the obedience and patience of the learner. Teachers are parents, siblings, peers and elders. Learners and teachers interact in a familiar social context where the interaction leads towards an anticipated mutually satisfactory outcome (for more details and discussion see Aikman 1994). Lave argues that knowledge-in-practice, that is knowledge constituted in the course of participating in communal activities, is the locus of the most powerful knowledgeability of the peoples in the lived-in world (1988: 14). As McCarty et al. note of indigenous Navajo learning: 'knowledge is built through the recursive expansion of children's prior understanding, in meaningful dialogue and socially significant interaction. Learners in this process play a determinant role; they are active seekers and users of knowledge' (1991: 51–2). In Arakmbut society the participatory nature of learning and teaching as well as the clearly divided stages of knowledge and skill acquisition ensure that a child or young person is not expected to perform a task of which she has no prior experience and with which she cannot cope, either physically or in relation to the invisible world.

Arakmbut women – guardians and custodians of knowledge and biodiversity

Shiva (1993a) states that diversity is the principle of women's work and knowledge, but that this diversity is not only overlooked but under threat from the forces of development. This section will look at the nature of the learning and knowledge that Arakmbut women accumulate throughout their lives according to the principles of an Arakmbut education.

Learning is structured according to age and gender in Arakmbut society and at different periods in a woman's life she has access to new learning. A woman's activities are centred around the house, and especially the kitchen, her several gardens and the nearby forest. Women work together in small clan or affine groups, with their gardens clustered together, and make trips into the forest for different barks, dyes and seeds they might need for making bags and utensils, and in appropriate seasons visit fishing sites and beaches for tortoise eggs, bamboo grubs or peach palm fruits. Many of their diverse activities take place in the course of one day, en route to their gardens. This 'multi-tasking' characteristic of women's work belies sharp divisions between household tasks and productive tasks. A fishing trip may also be a feast of fish cooked on the beach in which the men participate; it is a meaningful context for expanding women's learning and encouraging children's learning, it is a 'social occasion' when issues of importance may be discussed and it may be an opportunity for a consultation with elder women over a pregnancy or a child's illness.

As a girl grows to womanhood, she will know and use a wide range of edible fruits and grubs from the forest, and plant and tend a diversity of types of crop. She will also develop an extensive knowledge and expertise in different varieties of each crop. For example, a young recently married woman in the community of San José grew seven different types of pineapple in her gardens, all which she knew by name and characteristics. Another woman, some ten years her senior, grew ten or eleven types. But together with one of the elders, she named, in all, 17 types of pineapple, which were grown in two or three gardens mixed together on soils suitable for pineapples. The elders could name and recite their characteristics – sweetness, colour, size, rate of growth. These are only a few examples of the diversity of knowledge and activities Arakmbut women displayed in my presence. They must surely be only a small fraction of their knowledge and understanding of their forest environment, its ecology and the medicinal plants and oral literature embedded in it. Women's work is undisputedly diverse, as is their understanding of the rich tropical biodiversity of a region recognized as one of the most diverse habitats of the world.

As hunters men bring in food (wild pig, tapir, monkey, birds, fish) that is vital for the growth, sustenance and health of the individual and the society, both physically and spiritually. Men hunt and develop a deep understanding of animal behaviour and forest and river ecology throughout their active hunting lives, but they cannot cook meat, which is essential to transform it from its raw state, imbued with the spirit of the dead animal, into beneficial food. It is the combined strengths of a woman and man, derived from their complementary bodies of knowledge and relationships with the physical and spiritual worlds, that ensure a healthy family (see Gray 1996).

Global economics and 'development'

The Indigenous Women's Declaration makes specific reference to re-colonizing processes of globalization and trade liberalization, highlighting the competition between transnational corporations and other agents of the rich industrialized countries for access to the last frontiers of the world's natural resources located on indigenous lands (paragraph 6). The Madre de Dios region is no exception, and there have been dramatic effects on the livelihood of the Arakmbut in general and Arakmbut women in particular.

The Arakmbut should not be seen as vainly trying to cling to a 'traditional' way of life in the face of change. On the contrary, they entered into gold-panning in the 1970s with enthusiasm, although until the mid-1980s it formed only a small part of their economic activities and was structured according to collaboration between kin and clan groups, with the products of the labour distributed evenly among everyone. Extended families erected temporary huts around a gold-bearing stream where they would live for several months at a time, much in the way they did in the past in their temporary hunting camps. In the early 1980s forest game was still abundant and men did not have to go far or spend many hours to bring in enough meat to cover the family's needs. But by the mid-1990s the situation had changed. Illegal settlements were a permanent feature on Arakmbut titled land and lawless gold-seekers threatened the Arakmbut with their lives. Hunting waned due to the scarcity of large game and fish stocks dwindled because of disturbed breeding grounds and mercury-polluted rivers. The village-wide collective fishing expeditions of the late 1970s stopped. What little money the gold-panning brings in today goes to buying rice and pasta, which has replaced meat and fish in the diet. For the first time, Arakmbut children are malnourished and gastric illness, tuberculosis and malaria regularly claim lives.

The marginalization of Arakmbut women

There have been several studies of the marginalization of women in the process of insertion into the market economy for Amazon peoples whose way of life has been a non-accumulative, egalitarian, subsistence practice (Stocks and Stocks 1984; Barclay 1985; Tizón 1985). These studies examine the loss of women's control over the production and distribution of valued resources and illustrate that where value is placed on purchased items, women's production becomes less valued or replaced (D'Emilio 1987). Changes in Arakmbut women's lives echo the findings of these studies.

In the late 1970s, when I first knew the Arakmbut, senior women in the community of San José made beer for village-wide parties. They received a lot of respect for this because a good party was contingent on the ability to make and supply all the beer. Making beer demanded having enough gardens not only to feed the family throughout the year but to provide a surplus from which to make *masato* (manioc beer). It was also contingent upon being able to call upon clanswomen and affines to help masticate the manioc to make the beer. By the mid-1980s beer for parties was bought by men with their money from their gold-working.

In gardening too, women's knowledge and skills are being marginalized. Over the last 20 years several crops, once important parts of the diet, have ceased to be grown by younger women. Workers from other regions of Peru who live in the village and work gold refuse to eat the produce of women's garden – manioc, plantains, sweet potato – and demand crops imported from the Andean region, such as carrots and onions. These have to be bought by Arakmbut with scarce money from gold-panning. However, with the drop in gold production there is no longer money to buy carrots and onions and, as the Arakmbut work less in gold, they are beginning to ask what happened to the varieties of tropical tubers, fruits and seeds they were accustomed to and liked in the past. The diversity of Arakmbut gardens has been decreasing, yet, on investigation, it is not all lost. Some crops can be recovered through the exchange of seeds between communities.

The loss of certain crops and types is not necessarily a new phenomenon. Over time the Arakmbut have used their diversity in different ways with different preferences. However, today for the first time, a few young women are turning their backs on agriculture and leaving the community to follow non-Arakmbut gold-miners to gold-camps in other parts of the region, often having been promised exciting futures. They end up taking jobs as cooks in squalid settlements.

Men have always been the main interlocutors with people from outside Arakmbut society and they have also been the overt decision-makers. But this has never implied that women have been powerless in external relations. On the contrary, Arakmbut women have always had a very important role in decision-making at the household level, where community-level decisions are first discussed and strategies formulated. The Arakmbut meet only when decisions have already been made through this informal face-to-face process. However, with increasing participation in the gold economy and the encroachment of their territory by settlers, traders, extractive companies and local government, the Arakmbut are engaging in new forms of interaction and relations with outside agents, who are predominantly male (traders, politicians, migrant labourers, NGO workers, local government officials). Formal community meetings are instigated and run according to the agenda of outsiders without the prior informal household discussions in which women participated actively. This process has been accelerated by the imposition of a leadership structure on communities by the Law of Native Communities. Positions of community president, vice-president, treasurer, etc. are often taken by young men who have had some formal education in Spanish, but they do not necessarily have authority within the community.

The interaction and complementarity between Arakmbut men and women have been undermined as men's economic activities assume more importance than women's through their participation in the market economy and their control over the product of their labour – gold. Men are travelling increasingly to trading posts and the department capital to negotiate with gold patrons or the municipal authorities. The shift of the context for decision-making from the community to the town not only excludes women from decisions about their lives and over community-wide issues but highlights the inexperience of many men in this non-Arakmbut sphere, where they are often cheated and hoodwinked. Nevertheless, we must avoid un-nuanced generalizations of women as subsistence farmers and men as participants in the capitalist economy. Occasionally women sell a sack of manioc to local gold-miners and they often take a bag of lemons or a hen to sell at the trading post in order to buy clothes for themselves and their children. Some women do accompany their men to town and take part in meetings with the authorities, although they are in the minority at present. It is also important to note that one Arakmbut community did for a period have a woman president, a role overwhelmingly assumed by men.

The growth of 'poverty'

Today most Arakmbut are experiencing an economic poverty unknown 20 years ago. This is the outcome of violations of their territorial rights, which have undermined their mixed subsistence economy. For the last 50 years Dominican missionaries in Madre de Dios have been trying to 'develop' the Arakmbut, encouraging them to take up skills of carpentry, to keep cattle, to sell wood and find ways of 'earning a living'. Over this period they have also carried out a campaign of proselytization and 'civilization' of the Arakmbut. In the eyes of the missionaries and the wider society, 20 years ago the Arakmbut were poor, poor in terms of their lack of Western-style development (Lohman 1993). The indications of this poverty were to be found in their social organization, language and material way of life, which had to be changed and 'improved'.

Today, the Arakmbut participate in the market economy and consume commodities produced for and distributed through the market, signs of 'development' but not necessarily 'improvement'. But we have to ask whether this entry into the market economy signifies development in terms of 'improvement'. As Shiva emphasizes: 'Development as a culturally biased process destroys wholesome and sustainable lifestyles and instead creates real material poverty, or misery, by denying the means of survival through the diversion of resources to resource-intensive commodity production'

(Shiva 1993c: 72–3). It is the insatiable search for raw materials on and around indigenous lands that has destroyed the diversity-based hunting and fishing activities of the Arakmbut and has forced them to rely increasingly on the gold economy. As Lohman states, the eradication of self-sufficiency, frugality and traditions of stewardship that are widespread in common property regimes in the name of eradicating poverty only creates more of the sort of 'poverty' that destroys the forests (1993: 30).

Schooling – the growth of ignorance

What are the effects of this development on indigenous education practices? For Arakmbut men and youths the effects are startling. Their relationship with the spirit world, nurtured and developed through hunting and dreaming, is being seriously undermined with the destruction of the forests and the flight of the fauna. Older men still try to find time to hunt, but with a physically demanding regime of gold-panning six days a week, and game becoming ever more scarce and distant, hunting is decreasing, and in some Arakmbut communities has almost stopped. As a result young men are not building up the diversity of knowledge and understanding about the forest ecology and animal behaviour necessary to be a good hunter but also necessary to protect the physical health and the spiritual health of the community.

For women, their economic activities continue but have decreasing status within Arakmbut society as market processes undermine their influence over decision-making. Women's economic activities continue to be unrecognized outside the society or are at best devalued as low-productivity activities because they do not contribute to commercial interests and economic returns. The dynamic relationship between men and women's productive work becomes broken and with it the integrated nature of women's productive and reproductive labour, which further undermines their position in society (Moore 1988).

The loss of learning and knowledge is one of the consequences of formal schooling. Primary school follows a national curriculum designed for, in the main, urban Mestizo children living in the coastal towns of Peru. Although girls still accompany their mothers to tend gardens and harvest forest fruits and fish, their obligation to attend school diverts them away from the diversity of participatory learning, which contributes over time towards a woman's intimate knowledge of the environment and its biodiversity. Children from the age of four to five years attend the missionary-run primary school in their communities and spend between five and eight hours each weekday in school, depending on individual teacher's regimes. Schooling therefore takes young Arakmbut away for long periods during the week from the context in which they learn about the Arakmbut way of life. Today, when families move to temporary gold or fishing camps, school-age children are left behind in the semi-deserted village and one woman will remain to cook for them. Thus they are restricted from taking part in many of the daily or seasonal activities and obliged to follow a strict school regime in a language they do not know.

Throughout the 1980s most Arakmbut children attended primary school, but both those who dropped out and those who graduated subsequently dedicated themselves to working with their parents and families. Since the 1990s the percentage of children completing primary schooling has increased, due to the missionary teachers' dedication, and by 1997 almost 100 per cent went on to attend secondary school (albeit after repeating several grades), the majority boarding with missionaries in towns several days' travel from their communities. They remain there for over eight months of each year, often with little or no contact with their families or their people (the exception being in the community of Shintuya, where a Dominican secondary school was opened in 1996). With the decrease in gold-panning and the impoverishment of the communities, both children and parents are putting their hopes in formal education to provide them with an opening into an alternative way of making a living.

Secondary schooling – hastening ethnocide

Formal education denies Arakmbut knowledge and the legitimacy of their way of life. Not only do educators teach and preach a hegemonic discourse, but the school as an institution has colonized Arakmbut space and time. Formal education takes place within the four walls of the school building, usually the only concrete building in the community. The school timetable and calendar force Arakmbut time into the rigid strictures of institutionalized learning.

Secondary schools offer differentiated curricula and the majority of Arakmbut students attend rural secondary schools, which emphasize a vocational agricultural education. A brief look at this curriculum displays not only its divergence from Arakmbut learning practices but its alienation of Arakmbut agricultural knowledge and skills through an emphasis on a technology-biased market-oriented rationale. At the mission secondary school of Shintuya, Arakmbut students who do not live in the adjacent community of Shintuya board at the mission under the jurisdiction of the priest. Each night all boarders must attend mass, which lasts between one and one and a half hours.

The students are taught in Spanish by lay-missionary teachers recruited through the Dominican network in the highlands and coastal areas of Peru. The focus of the agricultural dimension of the curriculum (it also includes maths, Spanish language, science, history and geography) is to provide young people with the skills and knowledge necessary to make them productive peasant farmers, able to generate an income on which to support a family. Practical experience is gained in the mission vegetable garden where, under plastic awnings, the priest attempts to grow tomatoes, maize and other crops not indigenous to the rainforest. In reality, the children I interviewed in Shintuya and Boca Colorado schools spend most of their time clearing high grass and undergrowth from around the mission compounds and school, an exhausting labour-intensive job that demands no skills other than the ability to wield a machete, which they have all been expert at since they were very young. For girls most of their out-of-school time is spend in domestic chores, usually in the kitchens, dormitories and sewing-room, or else cleaning or clearing weeds with the boys. The way of life of the boarding-school student is therefore one that encourages girls' domesticity and boys' unskilled labour.

In the past, the missionaries have encouraged the participation of the Arakmbut and Wachipaeri peoples living in the community of Shintuya in economic ventures, but with limited success. Through the 1980s the missionaries ran a sawmill and paid Arakmbut for hardwoods felled from their official territory. However, with no forest management strategy the territory is now depleted of hardwoods. The ailing timber business was supplemented with cattle-herding, and areas of land cleared to grow pasture, yet domesticated meat and pastoral activities never became very popular with the Arakmbut, and this has saved their territory from deforestation for cattle pasture. Both these activities and the approach to agriculture imply an exploitation of the natural resources that is alien to the Arakmbut people's sustainable use of their territory. This is a clear example of the economic efficiency and growth model of development supported by the World Bank (see p. 65) that the Indigenous Women's Declaration decries. The attraction of timber and cattle derives from the high prices they fetch on the global and national markets respectively.

The agricultural tasks that Arakmbut students were being obliged to carry out at the beginning of the 1997 academic year in both Shintuya and Boca Colorado verged on child labour. The agricultural lessons were *ad hoc* and experimental, under the guidance of teachers with little or no knowledge of the Amazon environment, whose agricultural experience – if any – was with Andean or coastal crops and animals in Andean or coastal contexts. The mission-run school and the mission station persist with a curriculum inappropriate for the delicate and fragile ecology of the rainforest, despite a wealth of expertise among the indigenous and agricultural organizations of the region.

The Arakmbut boarders find the school curriculum constricting and stultifying, and it discourages any student initiative. It ignores the knowledge they already have of their environment and forest and river ecology when they arrive at secondary school. Moreover, it lumps the students into culturally preconceived gender categories so that boys are groomed to become efficient peasant farmers and girls to be good peasant wives and mothers. The mission experience with timber and cattle is not a salutary example and does not give much basis for hope that its horticultural teachings will prove more environmentally sustainable or culturally sensitive.

The differentiation of roles into which these students are being socialized at boarding school contributes to a new sexual division of labour founded in the dismissal of prior knowledge and the growth of ignorance. The curriculum makes no reference to Arakmbut learning and teaching practices. Teachers denigrate indigenous children's knowledge and skills that do not derive from the school and mission. The collective nature of the Arakmbut way of life is not valued and the complementarity of women and men's activities and knowledge unrecognized. Thus, girls are marginalized from activities that the teachers and missionaries associate with 'men's work' and are steered away from gardening towards reproductive activities. The diversity and interrelatedness of women's productive and reproductive activities are not valued, nor is their position as guardians and custodians of the biodiversity. As Shiva notes in another context, women's work is often discounted by economists because of the limited concept of economics they apply (Shiva 1993b). In Madre de Dios, the school founds its agricultural curriculum on a patriarchal capitalist model of economics embedded in a development ideology that is not only unsustainable but totally destructive.

The Beijing Declaration of Indigenous Women and the Arakmbut

The Indigenous Women's Declaration highlights the dangers of these global economic trends. Taking the case of the Arakmbut, we have investigated infringements of indigenous rights by agents and participants in the market economy intent on maximizing production and resource extraction in the name of development. The case study has spotlighted the collusion of formal education with the forces of global economics and an unsustainable development model. This development model is leading to the decimation of Arakmbut livelihoods and economic activities. Moreover, it undermines women's social status by denying the legitimacy of their non-economic and subsistence activities.

The example of Arakmbut women and their situation today serves to highlight the contradictions between indigenous educational practices and formal 'Western' education, where the latter aims to inculcate this global message of progress and economic maximization. Such teaching not only contributes to the destruction of the Amazon environment but erodes and undermines women's position as guardians and custodians of biodiversity. The vocational school curriculum experienced by Arakmbut students in Madre de Dios promotes a poverty-stricken alternative to indigenous educational practices that are inherently meaningful and highly motivating. It also promotes a reconceptualization of gender according to Western patriarchal concepts and channels young Arakmbut women and men into new gendered relations, further devaluing Arakmbut women's knowledge and skills.

Education has been a weapon of oppression for many indigenous peoples through policies aimed at their cultural and linguistic eradication. However, in some parts of the world and in some areas of the Amazon, indigenous peoples are developing their own formal intercultural education in order to ensure that it respects their knowledge and way of life (see examples in Hornberger 1997). When it is under their control, some Amazon peoples have found that formal education can be an ally (for example, ETSA 1996) but, as was noted at a Latin American preparatory meeting for the Beijing conference, intercultural bilingual education is scarce and limited at present and even where it does exist, indigenous women have very limited access to it (ALAI 1995). The Arakmbut and their representative organizations have been investigating possibilities for developing an indigenous-controlled schooling that would contribute to the strengthening and support of their indigenous way of life and know-ledge. Arakmbut women must play a strong part in this development to ensure that it safeguards their profound wisdom and knowledge, and their dynamic and integral place in society.

Note

1. The case study is based on my first-hand experience of living and working with the Arakmbut women of the community of San José. It repres-ents my understanding of the changes I have witnessed over a 20-year period and, consequently, is the perspective of a marginal spectator yet also an active participant in their lives. It is also a picture built upon an arbitrary selection of observed behaviour (Caplan 1994). In trying to present my understanding of the Arakmbut women's situation over this period, I have necessarily had to present them in broad brushstrokes, at the expense of emphasizing the diversity among them and the individual and collective strategies and actions they have developed to help them direct their lives.

Bibliography

Aikman, S. (1994) 'Intercultural education and Harakmbut identity: a case study of the community of San José in Southeastern Peru', PhD thesis, Institute of Education, University of London.

— (1995) 'Language, literacy and bilingual education: an Amazon people's strategies for cultural maintenance', *International Journal of Educational Development* 15 (4): 411–22.

— (forthcoming) 'Alternative development and education: economic interests and cultural practices in the Amazon', in F. Leach and A. Little (eds), *Education, Culture and Economics: Dilemmas for Development*, Garland, New York.

ALAI (Agencia Latinoamericano de Información) (1995) '"Indigenous Women in America", conference of women's NGOs of Latin America and the Caribbean', I*WGIA Newsletter* 2, April/May/June: 8–11.

Barclay, F. (1985) 'Para civilizarlos mejor. Reflecciones acerca de programas de desarrollo para mujeres en sociedades Amazónicas', *Shupihui* 85 (25–6): 289–300.

Burger, J. (1987) *Report from the Frontier*, Zed Press/Cultural Survival, London.

Caplan, P. (1994) 'Engendering knowledge: the politics of ethnography', in S. Ardener (ed.), *Person and Powers of Women in Diverse Cultures*, Berg, Oxford, pp. 65–88.

D'Emilio, A. L. (1987) 'La mujer indígena: educación y participación en los procesos de cambio', *Arisana* 6/7: 5–36.

ETSA (1996) 'Brought together, informal and formal education in an indigenous programme in the Amazon', unpublished manuscript.

Gray, A. (1983) 'The Amarakaeri: an ethnographic account of the Harakmbut people from Southeastern Peru', D.Phil. thesis, University of Oxford.

— (1996) *Mythology, Spirituality and History in an Amazonian Community*, Berghahn Books, Oxford.

Hornberger, N. (ed.) (1997) *Indigenous Literacies in the Americas: Language Planning from the Bottom Up*, Mouton de Gruyter, Berlin.

Indigenous Women's Caucus (1995) 'Fourth World Conference on Women: Beijing Declaration of Indigenous Women', *Indigenous Affairs* 4, October–December: 27–32.

Lave, J. (1988) *Cognition in Practice: Mind, Mathematics and Culture in Everyday Life*, Cambridge University Press, Cambridge.

Lave, J. and E. Wenger (1991) *Situated Learning: Legitimate Peripheral Participation*, Cambridge University Press, Cambridge.

Lipka, J and A. Stairs (1994) 'Editor's introduction', special issue 'Negotiating the Culture of Schooling', *Peabody Journal of Education* 69 (2), Winter: 1–5.

Lohman, L. (1993) 'Against the myths', in M. Colchester and L. Lohman, *The Struggle for Land and the Fate of the Forest*, World Rainforest Movement/The Ecologist/ Zed Books, Penang, pp. 16–34.

McCarty, T. L., R. H. Lynch, S. Wallace and A. Benally (1991) 'Classroom inquiry and Navajo learning styles: a call for reassessment', *Anthropology and Education Quarterly* 22: 42–59.

Marchand, M. H. (1995) 'Latin American women speak on development: are we listening yet?', in M. H. Marchand and J. L. Parpart (eds), *Feminism, Postmodernism, Development,* Routledge, London, pp. 56–72.

Mies, M. (1993) 'The need for a new vision: the substistence perspective', in M. Mies and V. Shiva, *Ecofeminism*, pp. 297–324.

Mies, M. and V. Shiva (1993) *Ecofeminism*, Zed Books, London.

Moore, H. (1988) *Feminism and Anthropology*, Polity Press, Cambridge.

Moore, T. (1985) 'Movimentos populares en Madre de Dios y Regionalizaçión', in *Promoción Campesina, Regionalización y Movimentos Sociales*, Centro de Estudios Rurales Andinos 'Bartolome de la Casas' and Centro de Estudios y Promoción del Desarrollo, Lima.

Myles, H. and I. Tarrago (1996) '"Some good long talks": cross-cultural feminist practice', in S. Walters and L. Manicom (eds), *Gender in Popular Education: Methods for Empowerment,* Zed Books, London, pp. 181–201.

Pettman, J. J. (1996) *Worlding Women: a Feminist International Politics*, Routledge, London.

Shiva, V. (1993a) 'Women's indigenous knowledge and biodiversity conservation', in M. Mies and V. Shiva, *Ecofeminism*, pp. 164–73.

— (1993b) 'Decolonising the North', in M. Mies and V. Shiva, *Ecofeminism*, pp. 264–76.

— (1993c) 'The impoverishment of the environment', in M. Mies and V. Shiva, *Ecofeminism*, pp. 70–90.

Stocks, K. and A. Stocks (1984) 'Status de la mujer y cambio por aculturación: casos del Alto Amazonas', *Amazonia Peruana* 5 (10): 56–77, CAAAP, Lima.

Teasdale, R. and J. Teasdale (1994) 'Culture and schooling in Aboriginal Australia', in E. Thomas (ed.), *International Perspectives on Culture and Schooling*, Institute of Education, London, pp. 174–96.

Tizón, J. (1985) 'Subordinación de la mujer amazónica: modernización y desarrollo', in *Extracta: La Mujer y el Cambio*, CIPA Cultural Survival, Lima.

Trapnell, L. (1990) 'El programa de formación de maestros bilingües de la Amazonía Peruana', *Amazonía Reruana* 18: 103–16.

— (1991) 'Una alternative en marcha: la propuesta de formación magisterial de AIDESEP', in M. Zuñiga, I. Pozzi-Escot and L. E. López (eds), *Educación Bilingüe Intercultural: Reflexiones y Desafíos*, Fomciencias, Lima, pp. 219–39.

Tuesta Cerron, N. (1997) 'Beyond land rights: indigenous intercultural education', in S. Buchi, C. Erni, L. Jurt and C. Ruegg (eds), *Indigenous Peoples, Environment and Development*, International Work Group for Indigenous Affairs, Copenhagen, pp. 251–8.

World Bank (1995) *Towards Gender Equality: The Role of Public Policy – An Overview*, World Bank, Washington, DC.

PART TWO

Africa: Changing Family and Household Contexts

CHAPTER 6

Girls and Schooling in Ethiopia[1]

Pauline Rose and Mercy Tembon

This chapter investigates educational trends in Ethiopia, a country with one of the lowest per capita incomes in the world, where extremely few school-age children attend school. The negative consequences of the war in the 1980s are found to have a greater impact on boys' enrolment, largely through the fear of conscription and deterioration in economic conditions resulting in a narrowing of the gender gap in primary enrolment. The relatively narrow gender gap during the war period was not, however, caused by a change in perceptions of gender roles. Thus recent increases in primary enrolment, thanks to government commitment to education and the restoration of peace and stability after the war, have benefited boys much more than girls. While improvements in the political and economic environment have increased boys' educational opportunities, the complex, varied and often mutually reinforcing constraints on girls' schooling continue to restrict their chances of attending and completing school. It is proposed that more fundamental societal change, giving women and girls greater control over their own lives and resources, is necessary to overcome these constraints.

The chapter begins by providing a brief socio-economic background of Ethiopia, and an overview of historical trends in education. This is followed by an investigation of gender disparities in primary education at the national level. Explanations for observed differences in girls' and boys' enrolment are sought, using the results from intensive school-based surveys carried out in 1995. The chapter ends with a review of recent government policies and strategies to improve girls' schooling, and assesses whether these are likely to succeed in achieving gender equity in education.

Socio-economic background of Ethiopia

Ethiopia's population is the second largest in Sub-Saharan Africa, estimated at 53 million in 1994, with 45 per cent below the age of 15. The population is growing at a fast rate (approximately 3 per cent per annum), implying that there will be continued demographic pressure on school places in the foreseeable future. Over 85 per cent of the population live in rural areas and there is considerable ethno-linguistic diversity across the country, with approximately eighty ethnic groups and languages. Almost two-thirds of the population are estimated to be Orthodox Christian, and one-third Muslim.

Indicators of socio-economic development do not compare favourably with those of other developing countries. GDP per capita is estimated to be only US$100. Large parts of the country are prone to drought and soil erosion and the economy is heavily dependent on rain-fed agriculture, which employs 80 per cent of the labour force, mainly as peasant farmers. Consequently, agricultural production and national income are extremely volatile. This has resulted in erratic GDP growth rates and, although there are some reports of economic recovery in recent years, sustained improvements in the economy are not guaranteed. According to the 1996 United Nations *Human Development Report*, Ethiopia ranks among the seven lowest in the world in terms of social development, as indicated in Table 6.1.

Ethiopia is one of the most educationally disadvantaged countries in the world. The adult literacy rate is extremely low (44 per cent for males and 24 per cent for females). Furthermore, only about one-quarter of children attend school, a larger proportion of whom are boys than girls, especially in rural areas. To put Ethiopia's educational situation into context, an overview of historical trends in primary enrolment and the gender gap in the country is provided below.

Trends in enrolment and the gender gap at the national level

Educational development has been strongly linked to the political changes in the country, which can be categorized into three key periods, namely the Monarchy, Derg, and Federal Democratic Republic (FDRE). Schooling was established in 1908 during the Monarchy period. When the Derg (Provisional Military Administrative Council) came to power in 1974 it adopted a new education policy reflecting its socialist philosophy. During the first decade under the Derg, there was an expansion in enrolments at all levels. However, despite the government's stated aims of achieving social equity, a substantial gender gap in enrolments was still evident. Beginning in 1983/84, the rate of expansion slowed down as the country was hit by drought and famine and the civil war in the north of the country intensified. From 1988/89 until the fall of the government, enrolment declined sharply. In May 1991, as the political and economic situation worsened, the Ethiopian People's Revolutionary Democratic Front (EPRDF) gained control, leading to the formation of the Transitional Government of Ethiopia (TGE). In November 1991 an economic policy

Table 6.1 Ethiopia, socio-economic indicators, 1993

	GDP pc (US$)	LEB	FR	MMR	IMR	ALR (%) Male	ALR (%) Female	Access to (%) Drinking water	Access to (%) Health facilities	Access to (%) Sanitation facilities
Ethiopia	100	48	7.0	1,400	118	44	24	25	46	19
SSA	555	51	6.3	929	110	65	45	45	57	37
LDCs	210	51	5.8	1,015	70	58	36	52	50	31

Note: ALR = adult literacy rate; FR = fertility rate; IMR = infant mortality rate; LDC = less developed country; LEB = life expectancy at birth; MMR = maternal mortality rate; SSA = Sub-Saharan Africa.

Source: UNDP 1996.

Table 6.2 School and socio-economic characteristics of zones, Ethiopia

	Jimma	East Gojjam
Females as % of total primary enrolment, 1994/95	Rural 32 Urban 50	Rural 39 Urban 49
Female primary teachers, 1994/95, %	Rural 19 Urban 41	Rural 24 Urban na
Economic activity	Cash-crop (coffee and *chat*)	Cereal crops
Main ethnic group	Oromo	Amhara
Main language spoken at home	Oromigna	Amharic
Main religion	Muslim	Christian

Source: EMIS, MOE, various years.

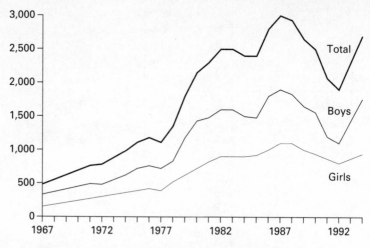

Figure 6.1 Ethiopia, primary enrolments by gender, 1967–94
Source: EMIS, MOE, various years

was produced for the transitional period, reinforcing the country's move away from socialism.

In 1992/93, the primary GER was at its lowest for ten years at 20 per cent. At that time, females comprised 41 per cent of total enrolment. It is clear from Figure 6.1 that, although boys' enrolment is greater than that of females for all years, the decline between 1987/88 and 1992/93 was greater for boys than for girls. In general, when the GER was lower the gender gap was narrower, indicating that the demand for boys' schooling was more vulnerable to the changes in the economic and political conditions than the demand for girls' schooling, which remained low throughout the period. One important explanation for this trend is that fewer boys were enrolled in school because they were conscripted into the army, or in order to avoid conscription.

Enrolment continued to fall until 1993/94, after the change in government, because of the uncertain political and economic environment. Parents, who were sometimes forced to send their children to school under the Derg, decided to exercise their 'democratic right' not to send them to school once they were given the freedom to choose, contributing to the decline in enrolment. Furthermore, some schools were looted during the early 1990s and had to be closed.

A reversal in the downward trend is apparent from 1993/94, with a steep increase in enrolment, especially for boys. Over this period, therefore, a narrowing of the gender gap is observed due to a worsening of boys' enrolment rate (rather than an improvement in that of girls). In contrast, increasing enrolments from 1993/94 have benefited boys more than girls, and the gender gap has begun to widen again. Reasons for these trends are investigated in more detail below. National averages disguise rural/ urban and regional disparities in enrolment and the gender gap. Enrolment is lower, and the gender gap wider, in rural areas compared with urban areas (where there is near equality in enrolment between the sexes).

Under current conditions of lower admission rates and higher repetition and drop-out rates for girls relative to boys, the gender gap is projected to widen further. There is, therefore, an urgent need to investigate the reasons for the inequalities in educational opportunities in Ethiopia, and to examine whether it is possible to reverse this trend.

Methodology of fieldwork

In order to understand the reasons for low enrolment and the persistence of the gender gap at the local level, surveys were carried out in two areas of the country, using both quantitative and qualitative research tools. Qualitative methods, including focus group discussions and interviews, were used to provide a more detailed understanding of the processes and issues which are the focus on in the quantitative work. The survey work was not intended to be statistically representative of the country as a whole, but was designed to gain insights into the constraints on schooling from the perspective of different members of the community (including education officials, school directors, teachers, pupils, school committees, parents and community elders).

Two areas of the country were chosen according to selected criteria, including GERs, females as a proportion of total primary enrolments, and variations in socio-economic conditions such as economic activity, ethnicity and religion. The areas chosen were Jimma Zone in the Amhara Region and East Gojjam Zone in the Oromiya Region. The school and socio-economic characteristics of the two zones are summarized in Table 6.2. In general, Jimma is more heterogeneous in terms of socio-economic characteristics compared with East Gojjam. Further details of the areas visited are provided in the following section.

In each of the two zones there were two *weredas* (districts): Maanaa and Saqqa Coqorsaa in Jimma, and Machakel and Gozammin in East Gojjam. Within each of the selected areas, both rural and urban schools were visited. More emphasis was given to rural areas, since over 85 per cent of the population reside in these areas. A total of two town schools and nine rural schools were visited. The selected schools and their catchment areas provided the basis for the fieldwork.

Attempts were made to ensure that voices of girls and women were heard. Separate discussions were held with female pupils and, in some cases, female teachers. Mothers were encouraged to attend parent meetings and, on some occasions, these meetings were held only with mothers. At the decision-making level in schools, it was apparent that women's voices were not being heard – school management committees in all schools visited were exclusively male, and all school directors were male.

Socio-economic background of areas visited

Maanaa *wereda* in Jimma is predominantly a coffee-growing area. Discussions with the local communities revealed that a significant amount of farming is devoted to cereal crops, which are produced mainly for subsistence. While it was suggested that Maanaa is probably better off relative to some of the neighbouring *weredas*, it was also noted that the owners of coffee plantations live mainly in Jimma or Maanaa town and hire labour to work on the plantations. In contrast, Saqqa Coqorsaa *wereda* in Jimma is involved primarily in subsistence cereal-crop farming. Women and girls are involved in farming and household activities, and girls also trade coffee in towns at harvest time. It is mostly men and boys who are involved in farming activities, and boys help to pick coffee at harvest time.

The main crops grown in Machakel and Gozammin *weredas* in East Gojjam are cereals. These are grown primarily for subsistence, and farmers also keep livestock. On the farm, men are involved in ploughing, while women are involved in weeding. In addition to farming activities, women are also involved in domestic business activities, such as making and selling *injera* (staple food) and local alcoholic drinks, usually to men. As a result of the war, a number of women are widows and head the household, which puts pressure on them to earn money to support the family. Girls and women do most of the work in the household, and prepare dung cakes for fuel.

Although most of the schools visited were reasonably accessible by dry-weather or all-weather road, there was not much public transport available, and what was available was too expensive for the rural population. None of the rural schools visited had electricity, and telephone connections were uncommon. The enrolment trend observed over the last five years is similar in the schools visited to the national patterns – enrolments declined until the end of the war and have subsequently begun to increase again. Furthermore, the gender gap has widened as enrolment has increased.

Results of the fieldwork

This section will focus on cultural and socio-economic constraints affecting household demand for girls' schooling, with an examination of how these are reinforced within the school environment.[2] Girls are expected to get married at an early age and work in the household, for which it is perceived that schooling provides few benefits. When household resources are limited, parents are forced to make choices about which of their children attend school. The decision is frequently made on the basis of gender.

Socio-cultural attitudes and traditions often determine the status of girls and women in society. Culturally, the place of a woman is in the home. The expectation that girls will eventually marry and become house-wives means that what they learn at home is considered by mothers to be as important as, if not more important than, what they learn at school. Therefore the norm would be for girls to stay close to their mothers as they grow up and to learn household skills and behaviours that prepare them for their future roles as wives and mothers. These socio-cultural beliefs cause parents to see the formal education of a girl as a deviation from accepted societal norms and practices. Formal education is, therefore, sometimes not perceived as appropriate for girls and is consequently not valued. Cultural attitudes are so entrenched that even young girls of school age feel that they need only to learn how to cook: 'Girls are not allowed to go to school because of tradition ... girls are born for boys and it is enough for a girl if she knows how to cook *wat* and how to keep house. Therefore no one sends girls to school.'

In both areas visited, schooling was sometimes considered to have negative consequences for girls. As one father in Jimma noted:

> There is a big problem faced by girls who go to school ... They cannot find a husband. They do not have employment opportunities. They cannot stay with their family when they get older because they will bring shame on them. The only option they have is to migrate to bigger towns and lead a miserable life. Parents are aware of such dangers. In effect, they refrain from sending their daughters to school.

In towns such girls would be employed as house-servants or would become prostitutes.

Mothers themselves are not always ignorant of the potential harm of their attitudes towards girls. One mother noted, for example, that they do not give girls the same freedom they give boys. Because of the lack of freedom and strict control of parents, girls feel dependent and lack confidence in themselves and their education. In response to this, a father in the group said that they control girls for their own good: 'If she is not controlled, she will lose her purity and even get pregnant. A boy has nothing to lose. Girls are victims and they are also scared.'

One father noted that:

> Parents, including myself, prefer to send boys to school. This is because, if a boy does not go to school he will easily develop bad characteristics and may be engaged in crime. Girls could stay at home without causing any trouble. You can always find them something to do in the house.

This view was supported by a mother, who reported that, since parents usually cannot send all their children to school, they often prefer to send boys because they are difficult to control at home, whereas girls are easy to manage. The attitudes of boys and girls and their ability to go against their parents' decisions also influences whether or not they go to school. Some parents noted that girls observe their decisions, whereas boys refuse to accept them and continue at school even if their parents disagree. Boys are in a stronger position to disobey their parents because of their financial independence.

Parents fear that their daughters will become pregnant out of wedlock. This is thought to be shameful to the family, and causes parents to be protective of their daughters. Parents generally do not allow girls who become pregnant to continue with their schooling because of the disgrace they would bring on the family. To avoid any potential family humiliation, they tend to give daughters early in marriage. In East Gojjam, girls are married as early as the age of eight. In this area, it is often considered an embarrassment if girls are not married by the age of ten. One father reported that he had withdrawn his daughter from school because he had observed that if a girl stays in school beyond the age of ten she will not find a husband. As a father, he felt it was his responsibility to be concerned about her future and was afraid that the community suspects the purity of girls who stay in school a long time. An important reason for his concern was that he wanted to be respected by the community and believed that 'schools are less likely to guarantee us respect and fame'. A reason for girls getting married at a very young age is also related to economic constraints. As one farmer noted, families with four children, for example, may arrange a marriage ceremony for all the children on the same day in order to save money, and this is particularly true for daughters. There are, however, certain choices that are made in the allocation of a family's scarce resources. For example, one community elder suggested that, if parents were wise, they would use the money spent on their daughter's wedding ceremony to cover the cost of their education at primary school instead.

Parents in East Gojjam perceived that there were fewer early marriages under the Derg because families had to obtain the approval of a committee of government officials, who would not permit early marriage. However, some parents managed to avoid this by organizing wedding ceremonies in the evening out of the sight of the officials. In recent years, parents have been able to marry their daughters when they choose, resulting in girls being withdrawn from school at an earlier age.

In Jimma, although girls are married at a slightly later age (from about the age of 13) there is a common practice of 'kidnapping' girls for marriage. Boys' parents kidnap girls from the streets or even from the school compound itself and, as a result, parents are reluctant to send their daughters to school because of fear for their safety. Girls in school noted that kidnapping is practised if a boy's family does not have enough money to spend on a wedding ceremony. They reported that, if the girl resists, she and any others who try to help her will be physically assaulted. One father admitted that fathers sometimes agree that their daughters should be kidnapped even if the girl resists. This is an important reason why girls are forced to leave school in Jimma.

Once married, it is very unusual for girls to continue with their schooling. They are considered as adults and cannot participate in school activities, which are considered childish. Furthermore, other children in school tease them. It is not so uncommon, however, for boys to continue with their schooling after marriage. Parents recognized that the problem of drop-out was accentuated when girls start school at a late age, because they reach puberty when they are still in lower grades. Parents in different groups suggested that older girls become attracted to the opposite sex and are less attentive in lessons. As one mother in Jimma commented: 'When they start to think about marriage they are easily distracted and affected by love. Thus, whenever they face an obstacle or difficulty in their education, they give in and drop out.'

In both areas visited, a high proportion of children, especially boys, in school were above the official school age. Those starting at a later age were observed to be more likely to drop out. While some boys in Jimma who dropped out during the period of instability have returned to school, few girls have returned, because they have reached puberty. Another reason why over-age enrolment was more prevalent for boys was that, in some cases, boys go to school on their own initiative when they are able to finance themselves. In addition, boys may go to mosque school when they are younger and start primary school at a later age.

The interplay between religion and culture is also important for understanding the low enrolment of girls in school. In Jimma, the influence of Islam on local culture was proposed as a reason why girls were not attending school. In East Gojjam, the cultural influence of Orthodox Christianity also appeared to influence girls' enrolment. In a discussion with community members in East Gojjam, a priest explained the lower enrolment of girls in religious terms:

> The Bible says that God created man (Adam) first. Next He created woman (Eve) from the rib of Adam. The woman is obliged to serve the man. As a result, we give due care to our male children and we wish them all the best. We send the boys to school. We want the girls to marry at an early age. Religion explains why many female children are not going to school.

In some areas, priests were involved in task-forces set up to encourage parents to send their children to school. As a *wereda* education official noted, priests themselves were not convinced of the importance of educating girls and were not, therefore, promoting their education in the sensitization campaigns.

Cultural practices leading to girls' low self-esteem have an impact on parents' perceptions of their daughters' abilities. Although many parents recognized that the poorer performance and higher repetition of girls was related to their work burden in the home, others were not convinced of this and considered it to be a natural phenomenon. For example, one father proposed that enrolment is higher for boys because they have greater aspirations, since girls are usually only interested in their work in the house and marriage. He concluded that they are therefore less interested in school and make less of an effort to join school and, as a result, parents send boys to school. This view was not supported by girls themselves, who, like boys, often expressed a desire to continue to secondary school and obtain professional employment, for example as a teacher, government official or doctor. It appears more likely that girls' role in the household and early marriage are imposed on them. For example, some girls in school expressed their desire to break free from the burden that early marriage places on them:

> While my friends are eager to marry I am eager to learn. From marriage we only get the burden of giving birth and becoming mothers at an early age. Knowledge comes from education ... Marriage at an early age is a barrier for life.

The tradition of early marriage was therefore found to be an extremely important constraint on girls' schooling. However, these cultural constraints were found to be strongly interlinked with economic factors. For children to attend school, their parents must be both willing and able to allow them to enrol. Parental inability to cope with the expenses that are incidental to schooling at the primary level was found to be a significant reason for non-attendance. Schooling at the primary level in Ethiopia is not free, even when school fees are not charged. Parents are expected to buy exercise books, pens and appropriate clothing. The total cost often adds up to a substantial proportion of family income. In the course of providing an explanation for low enrolments at the primary level, a mother in Jimma said:

> We are not cash crop-producing farmers. We mainly produce maize, teff, sorghum and enset. These products are very cheap in the market and hence we are always poor. So how can we afford these payments in school? Besides, one farmer may have many children and how can he pay for all the children?

Similar points were made by another mother in East Gojjam:

> If you want to send your children to school you need to buy clothes, textbooks, exercise books and pay school fees and other expenses ... as

you know our life is hand-to-mouth and most of the farmers have three or more children, so how can we afford these things?

Lack of money was mentioned by parents in all the areas visited, indicating that the difficulty of high direct costs of schooling is widespread among parents, especially the poor in rural areas. Furthermore, given the large number of children in most households, parents often cannot afford to send all their children to school and have to choose among them. This choice is often made on the basis of gender. According to one father:

If the parents have three or four children, they would only send one of their children to school because they cannot afford to pay school expenses for all of them ... Since we look down on girls, we prefer to send boys to school.

Related to parents' inability to pay for schooling is the opportunity for children to contribute towards the costs of their own schooling. Girls tend to be more negatively affected by parents' financial inability because, unlike boys, many of them are unable to work to earn cash that can help with the costs of their schooling. This is reflected in the experience of one mother:

When his father died, I faced a problem earning money to pay for my son's registration fee. However, he did not stop going to school. He earned money through self-employment and paid his own registration fee. His sister dropped out of school because girls cannot find such a job.

A father echoed this view:

Boys sell firewood, plant trees, keep chickens and are involved in other trading activities. Thus they buy their own books and pens to assist us by sharing the cost of their education. Girls are involved in household chores and some farm activities, so they do not help us much in sharing the cost of their education.

Consequently, more boys can enrol or continue in school because they are able to solve the problem of costs themselves.

The gender division of labour is a reflection of the overall societal expectations of gender roles. The significant contribution that girls make to the household – preparing food, cooking, fetching water, looking after siblings – is vital to production and reproduction within the household. This contribution goes unrecognized and unrewarded, resulting in their inability to attend school for financial reasons because, unlike boys, they are not economically independent and because the resources of other family members are not pooled within the household. In contrast, there are often circumstances where girls are also involved in income-generating activities (for example, coffee-trading in Jimma), but their income is usually pooled within the household, and their 'spare' time outside of trading activities is needed for work in the household. While girls are busy at home performing these household tasks, boys are free to play and study. The opportunity costs of girls' time for the household tend to be higher than that of boys' time because their household tasks are extremely important to the well-being of the entire family and must be performed on a daily basis. The opportunity costs of girls' time for the household increase as they get older. However, the opportunity costs of boys' time (which in any case are lower) are personal, and have a more limited effect on the family because they tend to have greater control over their own time and resources.

Boys and teachers in East Gojjam noted that the work performed by boys is not necessarily incompatible with their schoolwork. For example, they can study while they are working in the fields looking after cattle, whereas girls are unable to do so while performing their household chores, which do not give them a breathing space. Moreover, boys in both regions reported that they were able to study in groups, while parents would not allow their sisters to do so for fear of them forming relationships with boys. Boys in Jimma were also able to interact and study while attending the mosque in the evening, whereas girls did not have this opportunity.

The stereotypical role of men as household heads and breadwinners and women as housewives is sometimes an over-simplification of reality. A relatively large number of households are headed by females, either because of the high divorce rate in the country or because many husbands died or migrated during the war. Girls in these households are often withdrawn from school to look after the household while their mother is engaged in income-generating activities to support the family. Furthermore, boys in school in East Gojjam remarked that mothers do not usually work at home if they have a daughter as she is expected to take over the household duties while the mother goes out to work. In addition, if there are females at home, boys are not allowed to work at home. Boys in school recognize the constraint that household work places on their sisters. One boy noted:

> When at home, boys don't help in the house. They refuse. Girls cannot refuse working in the house. Girls like to work in the house. Attendance depends on how many girls there are in the house – if many, they can have time to study. If not, others depend on her.

Many children drop out during harvest time, when opportunity costs are highest. In Jimma, children and parents are more interested in earning money from coffee picking and trading, which are often considered more important than attending school – this affects both boys and girls. Thus children start school at the beginning of the year but drop out a couple of months later at harvest time. The same children may re-enrol the following year, only to drop out again.

One male teacher considered the view that parents do not send their children to school because they do not see the benefits as shallow and incorrect. Rather, he saw the problem in terms of the lack of job opportunities. This is more apparent for girls, for whom the lack of employment prospects is itself determined by cultural discrimination in the job market. Thus boys have a better possibility of obtaining employment in the formal sector, which many parents in Ethiopia consider as the most important return on their investment in education. Furthermore, since boys are more likely to get jobs, parents prefer to send them to school because they will no longer be dependent on them, unlike girls. Some parents recalled the situation under the Derg when those completing Grade 12 would be guaranteed a job and were, therefore, in a position to support their parents.

Parents in some areas are disheartened and have lost confidence in schooling. Many children in whom they have invested considerable resources to send away to secondary school in the nearest town have failed the school-leaving certificate after Grade 12. One father noted that these children are sometimes frustrated, and parents also despair. The frustration felt by some unemployed school-leavers leads them to get involved in crime. Some parents felt that education leads to alienation, and it was mentioned that education sometimes creates a rift between parents and children. Parents claim that children have forgotten how to do physical work after completing schooling, and girls in particular cannot do demanding housework and farmwork. Furthermore, educated girls cannot find husbands because they are considered too old for marriage. A father questioned why parents should destroy a girl's life by sending her to school. In many discussions, parents commented that they considered it enough to send children to school for the first two grades in order to learn the basic skills of reading and writing – there was little point to schooling beyond that. Furthermore, the lack of secondary schools in rural areas is considered a constraint on sending girls to school at all, since parents are not happy about their daughters' security if they send them away to study in town.

Cultural beliefs reinforce gender stereotypes outside and inside school. Girls are expected to behave in a culturally accepted manner, to be obedient and submissive and to perform certain tasks that society assigns to them. Socio-cultural expectations are often held by teachers (both male and female), who are themselves part of the wider society. This is reflected in the tasks that teachers expect girls and boys to undertake during school time. Both boys and girls in school revealed that, in general, girls spent more time performing non-school activities during school hours. Their tasks include cleaning the classroom and offices, cleaning the latrines (which in some cases was proposed by boys to be 'girls' work'), fetching water for the school, and undertaking tasks for teachers. Girls in one school, for example, reported that teachers sometimes order them to work in their houses, where they prepare food and make coffee.

The vast majority of teachers (both male and female) considered girls to be less intelligent than boys. This view was also expressed by members of the school management committees and by *wereda* education officials. The reasons given for this perception were that girls' performance in school was often lower than that of boys, and that they participated less in class. Although, as mentioned, there was generally a recognition of the heavier work burden on girls, teachers did not always link this with their lower performance, even if some did acknowledge that there were exceptional cases of girls who performed better than boys.

There was some awareness among female teachers of a need to review the way in which society is structured. Some female teachers were sensitive to girls' shyness and low self-esteem in class and tried to address this problem. Teachers recognized that girls' inhibitions often started in later grades. The younger ones in Grades 1–3 have no inhibitions about interacting and mixing. Beyond that, however, boys and girls do not sit at the same desks and do not feel free to talk to each other. This was observed in Grade 6 classrooms in rural areas, where there were very few pupils. The boys were huddled together in one corner of the classroom, while the girls were bunched together in another corner. In an attempt to address this, a female teacher once asked a girl in class to sit next to a boy. This did not have the desired impact, however. The girl wept for the whole day, and would not even look at the textbook of the boy sitting beside her even though she did not have her own. The teacher realized that other measures would be necessary to give girls more confidence to interact in class.

In many rural areas there are very few female teachers. The presence of female teachers might be desirable for a range of reasons, but particularly since female teachers are often the only women in positions of authority in rural areas who are able to act as role models. Their presence is likely to encourage parents to send their children to school, both because they see opportunities for their daughters outside the household, and because of the increased sense of security for girls when female teachers are present. The problem of a lack of female teachers is evident from one school in which all the teachers were male. The teachers themselves were aware of the problems girls face when they reach puberty. They noted that they were unable to provide guidance concerning menstruation directly, because girls were shy and they were afraid that girls might take it as sexual provocation. They were conscious, however, that girls stopped coming to school when they started menstruating. These teachers took the initiative to address the problem indirectly. They bought some cloth and made sanitary towels and displayed them, and they considered that this had proved successful. One of the girls in East Gojjam commented that the community in her area considered that a girl who is menstruating is not a virgin, so that a girl hides the fact that she is menstruating from her parents. This ignorance reinforces the way in which negative cultural attitudes and practices can hinder girls' personal development.

Conclusion

Substantial progress has been made in educational opportunities in Ethiopia in recent years. However, girls' enrolment has increased at a much slower pace than that of boys. Culturally determined factors (for example, the gender division of labour and early marriage) are often used as an excuse to explain the futility of educating girls. As long as women continue to be perceived (and perceive themselves) as subordinate, they will be denied the opportunity of education. Furthermore, economic constraints have less of an impact on boys than on girls, who lack the opportunity to generate their own resources. The interplay between economic inability to pay and cultural unwillingness to change are interlinked and mutually reinforcing. This is a reflection of broader societal gender power relations and has resulted in a perpetuation of the gender gap in education. It is, therefore, critical that cultural and economic constraints are addressed simultaneously to ensure that girls themselves, and the society more generally, receive the benefits of their education.

Notes

1. The work presented in this chapter is part of a research programme on Gender and Primary Schooling in Africa, directed by Christopher Colclough. The first phase of this programme has been conducted in three African countries, under the auspices of the Forum for African Women Educationalists (FAWE), with funding from the Rockefeller Foundation. Fieldwork was undertaken with a team from the Ministry of Education supported by university graduates, teacher trainers and local secondary school teachers.

2. A detailed discussion of these constraints can be found in Rose et al. 1997 and Al-Samarrai 1997.

Bibliography

Anbesu, B. and B. Junge (1988) *Problems in Primary School Participation and Performance in Bahir Dar Awraja*, Ministry of Education and UNICEF, Addis Ababa.

Asseffa, B. (1991) *Female Participation and Performance in Rural Schools in Ethiopia*, ICDR, MOE, Addis Ababa.

Ministry of Education (1995) *Education Statistics Annual Abstract, 1986 EC (1993/94)*, Education Management Information Systems, Ministry of Education, Addis Ababa.

Ministry of Education (1996) *Education Statistics Annual Abstract, 1987 EC (1994/95)*,

Education Management Information Systems, Ministry of Education, Addis Ababa.

Rose, P. and S. Al-Samarrai (1997) 'Household constraints on schooling by gender: empirical evidence from Ethiopia', IDS Working Paper No. 56, IDS, Brighton.

Rose, P., Y. Getachew, B. Asmaru and N. Tegegn (1997) 'Gender and primary schooling in Ethiopia', IDS Research Report No. 31, IDS, Brighton.

Transitional Government of Ethiopia (1994) *Education and Training Policy*, TGE, Addis Ababa.

UNDP (1996) *Human Development Report*, Oxford University Press, New York.

USAID (1994) 'The demand for primary schooling in rural Ethiopia. A research study', mimeo, USAID, Addis Ababa.

Weir, S., and J. Knight (1996) 'Household demand for schooling in rural Ethiopia', mimeo, World Bank, Addis Ababa.

Yelfign, W. et al., (1995) *Primary School Female Participation and Performance in Cheha District*, Ministry of Education, Addis Ababa.

CHAPTER 7

Education, Schooling and Fertility in Niger

Shona Wynd

Niger is one of the poorest countries in the world, and its poverty is excerbated by one of the highest fertility rates. The World Bank is leading the donor community with its sector development plan (SDP), which focuses on basic education, especially that of girls. The argument for universal basic education assumes that by increasing levels of literacy and numeracy, countries increase their own human resource capacity and accelerate development. The anticipated effect of education on health and fertility is not as clear. There is widespread confidence among donors and governments in the potential of education, particularly of girls, to affect broad social patterns, but the complexities of just how the relationship works remain poorly understood. Initiatives to increase levels of girls' education focus on increased access and a decrease in drop-out rates, ignoring quality, curriculum content and teacher training (Stromquist 1995: 4). Exploring the underpinning local social systems, which define what is valuable in an education system, is the key to these issues. Sensitive analysis of the intricacies of the relationship between fertility and education at the local level is essential to any informed debate at the global level.

Education and development in Niger

Bordered by Mali, Burkina Faso, Chad, Nigeria and Libya, Niger has the very poor education indicators that are characteristic of the Sahelian region – Niger's primary school enrolment rate for 1993–94 was 28.5 per cent. Of this low number, only 36 per cent were girls, mostly from urban areas, and in the rural areas girls often make up as little as 10 per cent of the enrolled pupils (Ministère de l'Éducation Nationale, de l'Enseignement Supérieur et de la Recherche 1993).

Nigerien girls become wives and mothers at a very young age, with 75 per cent of adolescent girls having at least one child (Kourgueni et al. 1992). Niger's vital health statistics are also among the worst in the world, with maternal mortality rates of 700 per 100,000 and, perhaps the most startling indicator, an infant and child mortality rate of 326 per 1,000 (ibid.).

This chapter examines the complexities of the relationship between education and fertility in the context of the Sahelian country of Niger as it is perceived at policy implementation and community levels.

Background of the study

The fieldwork was carried out during two visits to Niger, in 1993 and 1995. Using a combination of interviews, focus groups and Participatory Rural Appraisal (PRA) techniques, data were collected from international and national education and health organizations, ministry officials, education and health staff and local individuals.

During most of the fieldwork periods the country was politically and economically unstable, with strikes, rallies and protests creating a tense environment. Schools and health centres remained closed for the majority of my 18-week stay in 1995, although most health centres offered a minimum of emergency healthcare throughout the strikes. The strikes were a response to the government's failure to pay any salaries to civil servants for several months. Disruption continued after the elections in January 1995 with the threat of school closures, creating a potential fourth *année blanche* in six years. The strikes affected those who lived in the capital, Niamey, far more than the 85 per cent of the population living in rural areas.

Contextualizing education and schooling in Niger

There are no reliable statistical data about the number of children recruited into the first year of school in Niger. Three or four different values are given for the same indicators in official Ministry of Education documents. One senior Ministry of Education official stated that the government of Niger simply does not have accurate data for how many children there are in the country, how many go to school, or how many actually sit exams. The most recent study indicates that for the 1992–93 and 1993–94 school years, the contrast between urban and rural male–female ratios is marked (Ministère du Développement Social, de la Population et de la Femme 1994) (see Tables 7.1 and 7.2). The numbers of male and female students are more balanced in the urban areas than they are in the rural areas, possibly because of the high concentration in cities of male and female civil servants who have themselves benefited from a formal education and are more likely to insist that all of their children attend school. Moreover, the demand for household labour is lower in urban areas and urban mothers are less likely to be as dependent upon their daughters for help

Table 7.1 Number of children attending primary school in urban areas of Niger, 1992–93 and 1993–94

Department	1992–93			1993–94		
	Boys	Girls	Total	Boys	Girls	Total
Agadez	1,736	1,373	3,109	1,824	1,446	3,270
Diffa	391	330	721	530	381	911
Dosso	1,478	1,139	2,617	1,363	1,212	2,575
Maradi	2,093	1,362	3,455	2,384	1,427	3,811
Niamey	6,803	6,680	13,483	7,202	7,092	14,494
Tahoua	10,937	1,242	3,179	2,066	1,422	3,488
Tillabery	954	797	1,751	1,024	797	1,821
Zinder	1,830	1,394	3,224	2,037	1,519	3,556
Total	17,222	14,317	31,539	18,430	15,296	33,726
Percentage	54.60	45.40	100	54.64	45.36	100

Source: Ministère de l'Education Nationale, de l'Enseignement Supérieur et de la Recherche 1993.

Table 7.2 Number of children attending primary school in rural areas of Niger, 1992–93 and 1993–94

Department	1992–93			1993–94		
	Boys	Girls	Total	Boys	Girls	Total
Agadez	496	232	728	548	293	841
Diffa	563	380	943	655	419	1,074
Dosso	5,244	2,149	7,393	6,273	2,699	8,972
Maradi	6,068	1,842	7,910	5,556	2,048	7,604
Niamey	–	–	–	–	–	–
Tahoua	6,076	1,951	8,027	6,585	2,282	8,867
Tillabery	5,371	3,896	9,267	5,987	6,487	12,474
Zinder	4,092	2,139	6,231	4,301	2,259	6,560
Total	27,910	12,589	40,499	29,905	16,487	46,392
Percentage	68.92	31.08	100	64.47	35.53	100

Source: Ministère de l'Education Nationale, de l'Enseignment Supérieur et de la Recherche 1993.

in the household. An urban primary school head teacher commented on differences between recruitment in rural and urban areas:

In town the parents understand the benefit of school so there is no problem [with recruitment]. We finish recruiting in one day. But in the villages the

Table 7.3 Percentage of children between the ages of seven and twelve attending school in Niger, 1992

	Urban	Rural	Total
Boys	54.8	16.8	23.1
Girls	44.7	7.1	13.5
Total	49.6	11.9	18.2

Source: Kourgueni et al. 1992.

parents don't understand the good side of school … I think it is because in the rural areas children are wanted more in the fields than somewhere else. They help their parents a lot – they fetch water and wood, pound millet … Parents think that these practical jobs have more benefit than wasting their children's time in school.

Because there is no reliable indicator of how many children are of school age, it is difficult to gauge what percentage are actually attending school. The 1992 Demographic and Health Survey (DHS) stated that, based on its own survey results, 18.2 per cent of children between the ages of seven and twelve were estimated to be attending school (Kourgueni et al. 1992: 23). Once again the differences between urban and rural areas are marked, as are differences between girls and boys (see Table 7.3).

Levels of attendance would no doubt be higher in urban areas if they were not limited by the number of places available in the schools. The double-shift scheme was introduced in 1992 in order to increase the capacity of the schools to educate more children. It is unpopular with parents, who feel that the quality of education is inferior.

Historical fear of schooling

During the post-colonial days of the early 1960s, the Nigerien government was anxious to establish a system of education quickly to produce the intellectual elite needed to support the newly independent country. In order to ensure sufficient numbers within the system, the army was sent to the villages to recruit children into school. Parents, terrified that their children would be forced into labour or killed, sent the children to hide in the bush until the army had left. A young father in the village of Madogo told us:

Before, our grandfathers hid our parents if someone came to recruit the children for school. They used to hide the children and say that they had no children.

The fear of school recruitment clearly continues today, and situations where parents will hide their children, lie or respond very aggressively towards the request that a child attend school seem to occur with regularity. Parents are willing to go to great lengths to avoid sending a child to school and, as will be seen below, after a few of these experiences head teachers recruit only those they know will come to school.

Primary school recruitment

The initial reason parents in rural areas tend to give for not sending their children to school, for both boys and girls, is that the children have not been recruited by the head teacher of the local school. The system of recruitment for primary school in rural Niger is largely ineffectual and relies on the motivation of local head teachers. There are many problems with the system, as the school inspector from one village described:

> We go to the birth registers. Every child's name should normally be on the village registrations, so we refer to that and take those of six, seven, or eight years of age and invite the parents to bring their children. But what has happened is that the parents know that if their children's names are on the village registration they will be recruited sooner or later, so now the parents don't declare their children. So now most of the time children's names don't even exist on paper.

The two rural head teachers I spoke to rarely travelled to villages outside their own to recruit. They cited lack of transport and the knowledge that villagers outside the school village would be unlikely to be interested in sending their children to school as reasons for not casting a wider recruitment net. The head teacher from Ngida told us:

> Yes, there are [no children attending this school] from these villages – they don't like school at all. It is their parents' fault. Parents in these areas are hostile ... Very often they have answers such as 'she got married', 'he or she is not living in this village', 'I sent him or her to another village', 'he or she died'; even when we know nothing has happened to the children!

While they were sympathetic to their rural peers' problems, those head teachers interviewed in the urban areas were far less likely to cite any type of difficulty in recruiting schoolchildren, boys or girls. In Niamey announcements are made on the radio and parents bring their children to the schools to enrol. Wilkey-Merritt found intense competition for places for their children among government employees in urban areas. Such families pay high fees for pre-school education for their children, which then advantages them in the selection for scarce primary school places (Wilkey-Merritt 1994: 23). In rural areas, it is once again the children of government employees working in the area who are recruited, along with some of the children in the immediate vicinity of the school. Of the girls who did attend the school in Ngida, all lived in the households of government employees. If additional children from outlying villages arrive asking to attend school, they are not turned away, but instances of children willing to walk several kilometres a day to attend school, without being recruited, are rare.

This cycle of reluctance on the part of parents, lack of access to schools and poor recruitment on the part of head teachers denies young village children even the initial opportunity to begin school. In the case of the village of Madogo, the head teacher had stopped putting any girls' names on the recruitment list at the request of the village elders. Because girls from the village had never 'succeeded', the elders felt it unnecessary to spend any more time trying. Neither the head teacher nor the school inspector from Danjouma seemed to think that this request was problematic or even out of the ordinary. When the inspector was asked to comment on the situation he responded:

> This is an arrangement between the teachers and the villagers. They live together and they make a kind of deal: 'We will send you boys but don't send invitations for the girls.' Here, as an inspector, if we try to do something we will lose everything, including the boys.

The concept of success

The notion of 'success', or absence of it, is a commonly cited reason for not sending girls to school. Success in this context means securing a position in the civil service upon completion of university or professional school. A young man in Ngida spoke quite frankly about the notion of 'success':

> the only reason [villagers] don't like [sending their children to school] is because most children have failed and didn't succeed. Parents don't have civil servant children to give them money at the end of every month. The mother has to sell things, the father has to work in the fields. There is no benefit.

Outside the civil service, there are few opportunities for paid employment: the economy is based, for the most part, in the informal sector, with little formal, private sector to speak of. As a senior school inspector in Zinder said: 'We have to solve many problems, like job opportunities. Everybody can't find jobs in the government offices!' Until 1991, when automatic recruitment into the civil service was stopped due to budgetary constraints, all students who completed professional school or university had been guaranteed a job with the civil service. Initially, completion of primary school was enough to qualify for a job with the government. Over the years the level of the qualification required has steadily increased, however, and now a professional qualification or degree is required. A young woman participating in the focus group in the Zongo district of Niamey commented:

> After six years of education you can't do anything. Even after ten years you can't get a job now. So people think that going to school is a waste of time.

Success in terms of passing through the school system is rare, and for girls it is even more elusive. In 1989, of the 2,760 students who performed well enough in the exam to move from the *collège* (junior secondary) level on to the *lycée* (senior secondary) level, only 23 per cent were girls and, of the 1,479 who passed the *baccalauréat* exam, only 22 per cent were girls (Ministère de l'Education Nationale, de l'Enseignement Supérieur et de la Recherche 1993). At the senior secondary school level, boys outnumber girls four to one, and at the university level, women make up only 1 per cent of the population.

Perceived value of schooling

This definition of success is central to understanding the crucial lack of accord between what the education system offers and what the population requires to improve its present economic and social situation. First, it demonstrates that the anticipated benefit from education is viewed primarily in terms of financial security derived from a job in the civil service. In essence, the school system is viewed as a system that trains individuals to be civil servants, conditioned to work in an urban office setting. In Niamey, those who fail their exams are referred to as 'school garbage' because they are often seen as unable, or unwilling, to do anything other than white-collar, office-based work.

While the salaries of the civil service have been inconsistent and unreliable in the past, it can be argued that the civil service position itself gives individuals access to a number of opportunities to increase their financial security, whether it is through strategic use of any power and influence resulting from this position or other means of income generation. The education system is viewed as being 'successful' only when a student graduates and secures the job that will take him or, rarely, her[1] out of the village with its traditional values and into the city with its modern lifestyle.

Infrequently, there is some recognition that, if a person learns to read and write, it is not a bad thing. An older man in the Madogo focus group commented:

> Even those who didn't succeed have a benefit from the little bit they got

with reading and writing. They can shoo away ignorance and they have a certain open-mindedness.

Despite this, however, even for those children currently in school, the parents continue to focus on the salaried position. During an interview, the husband of a woman who had been to primary school explained that he was not yet benefiting from his sons' education because they were still at the primary level:

> To speak of benefits, the children have to succeed and get a job. With the money they get from the job they can help their parents, themselves, their relatives.

For members of a closely knit community network, the coveted job represents increased economic security not just for the individual, but for the entire extended family, and perhaps even the village. One man in the older men's discussion group in Niamey commented:

> The first benefit [of schooling] is to succeed. If you succeed you can serve your country, you support yourself, you support your parents, your neighbours.

Expectations of success: perceived preferences

The definition of success directly affects initial enrolment rates. It is widely understood that few children will be able to advance beyond the primary level and parents see that, year after year, children who have gone to school fail the Primary School Certificate exam, if not earlier. Few have any expectation of their children succeeding. I heard many stories from disgruntled villagers who claimed that either their children or they themselves had been cheated out of a passing grade in the primary exam, asserting that the passing grades were sold to government employees' children. When I asked a focus group of younger women why girls from the village did not seem to do very well in the primary exams, they explained that even if the child did succeed, her name would be taken from the list of those who had passed the exam and replaced with the name of a government employee's child who had failed the exam. One older woman in the focus group in Madogo said:

> The teachers from [the neighbouring village school] are the ones who take their names off the list.
> *Question*: Why would they do that?
> It's wickedness. Because they don't want them to go forward in their studies. They say that we are villagers. Even in [the neighbouring village], no one from the village has succeeded. Of those who have succeeded, it is

the daughters of the civil servants, like the police chief's daughters and the teacher's daughters. But no girl from this village has succeeded!

Whether there is any truth to these accusations or not, the fact is villagers believe that their children's chances of succeeding are very slim indeed.

A document of December 1993 from the Ministry of Education uses the statistics of those who passed the Primary School Certificate exam in the 1988–89 school year as its most recent indicators: of the 11,857 who received the certificate, 8,620 were boys and 3,237, or 27 per cent, were girls (Ministère de l'Education Nationale, de l'Enseignement Supérieur et de la Recherche 1993). The report does not supply the number of children who actually sat the exam, and while in an interview a ministry official stated that those numbers were available, they were unattainable. The Nigerien Plan of Action resulting from the Jomtien Conference on Education for All also makes a fleeting reference to the poor performance of Nigerien students in the primary education years, stating that the success rates of the exams had noticeably decreased over ten years, with a drop-out rate of approximately 52 per cent over the six-year cycle (Ministère de l'Education Nationale et de la Recherche 1992). Once again no indication of the numbers of students attempting the exam was provided. The World Bank presents an equally bleak picture of opportunities for success in a recent report:

> The quality of education in Niger is poor as evidenced by low internal efficiency and low examination pass rates at all levels. Low quality is reflected in repetition rates of 3–16% in grades one through five, and 42% in grade six. More than 40% of pupils drop out prior to grade six, and the pass rate at the leaving examination averaged only 29% over the last five years (World Bank 1994).

The impact of girls' failure to 'succeed'

The distinction between boys and girls is important. Despite the high failure rates, there is always a story of at least one boy from the village who has 'succeeded'. Whether he is a teacher, nurse, policeman or customs officer, the role models are available for the boys. For the girls it is different – of those few girls who do succeed nationally, most are urban. This lack of role models in rural areas is used as further justification for not sending girls to school. In one village the husband of a woman with primary education explained the difference between the benefits of education for girls and boys:

> Only boys advance in their schooling. No girls advance. Among our women, none of them has a job in the city or has money to help her parents and herself. In our village there has been a school for many years. The difference

is, in our village, no girl has succeeded in school; no girl has got a job with the government. But everyone knows that boys have succeeded, they have money and are helping their parents and relatives. There is no female government employee from Ngida helping her parents and relatives with what she gained as a civil servant!

In fact, those rural women who have attended school for a few years are regarded as failures and are held up as examples of the fruitlessness of schooling for girls. This same man commented on his experience of being married to a woman who had been to school:

> I see no difference between my educated wife and the others' uneducated wives. I would have seen a difference if she had succeeded and had some money from her job. At that time the money would make the difference between her and other women. Now, she does nothing. She's always just sitting there … Here, no one calls her 'Madame' and she's not being paid by the government!

He went on to concede that her education was helpful because it had given her the ability to read a little bit, and because she took the children to the dispensary. Nevertheless, he had decided that he would 'never' send his girls to school.

Girls' schooling, sexuality and shame

Parents assume that, in addition to wasting their time, girls who go to school are exposed to 'modern ways' of living. These ways are not condemned outright – if an individual succeeds in school and can use the modern ways and modern life to support the family, then the ways are acceptable. They become problematic when the individual fails and tries to carry the new behaviours and opinions back into local life. The group of older men of Madogo used the example of the problem of pregnancies to explain their point:

> If the girl is not succeeding and having babies without a father [it is a problem]. But she can have her babies without the father if she is succeeding, because the job she will get later will help her support the baby without a father. But in the village it's a shame … It's worrying if the girl has a baby without a father and she comes back to the village!

For the most part, the 'modern ways' refer to the girls' behaviour and its potential effect on their fertility. Within Nigerien society, a woman's opportunities to gain status or achieve any kind of security are limited. Perhaps most important to a woman's ability to secure a future for herself is her fertility. As a girl enters puberty, this fertility must be guarded. The adolescent or pre-adolescent girl is at a difficult stage: she is too young to be trusted to behave appropriately, to keep her sexuality hidden and to avoid getting into trouble with the weak male who may fall victim to her charms. For the parents and family, the adolescent girl has the potential to bring a great deal of trouble to the family. When asked what happens when a girl gets pregnant at school, one younger man explained:

> Everyone laughs at her and insults her. They call her an imbecile. It's a problem for the whole family: father, mother, grandfather. Every time they try to talk to their friends, people will say: 'Don't listen to them, they are stupid. They let their daughter get pregnant and she's not married!'

Should she get pregnant before marriage, the girl will shame the family, be forced to have a child out of wedlock, and have a difficult time finding a man who will marry her, thereby remaining a burden upon her family for a longer period of time. In order to avoid such difficulties, in the average Hausa village girls are often married around the age of twelve.

Thus, one of the problems with primary education is that it not only 'holds' girls in school until they are 14, but is also believed to expose them to increased risk. It is interesting to note that, in both Ngida and Madogo, people were hard pressed to come up with more than one example of a girl who had become pregnant at school over the last 30 years. Nevertheless, once parents see that their daughters are getting near puberty, if the girls are in school, they will try to get them out. A young man from Madogo explains:

> Even if the girl is brilliant, the parents go and beg the teacher to allow the girl to be married. If the teacher agrees she can be married. But if he refuses, she continues in her studies ... Sometimes there are teachers who say no, but unfortunately the girls do not succeed anyway. Most of the time they fail the primary exam.

While attending school, the girls will be spending a great deal of time around boys who could take advantage of them. Perhaps more threatening, the girls will be under the responsibility of a male teacher who will have ample time to take advantage of his position of authority. The girls are at the same time learning modern ideas that conflict with the local belief system. While every village has a story of a boy who has succeeded, it also has a story of a girl who has come back from school pregnant. The following excerpt from an interview with a woman who went to primary school demonstrates that, despite the fact that the basic benefits of reading and writing are recognized, the risk of pregnancy is just too much for the parents, specifically the mothers, to take:

> School helps a lot because the girls know how to read and write and count. They can read their letters themselves, and no one can know their secrets.

Primary school gives them good manners ... At school you learn to analyse the situation and decide if it is good or bad.

Question: If school does all these things, why don't you want your daughters to go to school?

[She laughs] Yes, I know. I recognize that school has its benefits. School didn't harm me at all! But the fact is, I didn't get any school success, and I have never seen another woman from this village who has succeeded. We *can't* send our girls to school – no woman has ever succeeded – *we can't!*

Question: Who or what says you can't?

We mothers decided that our girls shouldn't go to school ...

Question: If your sons don't pass, is that a failure as well?

It's a failure for boys, but it's more of a failure for girls because they grow older and become pregnant. And yourself, you know that being pregnant without being married is a very bad thing. As for boys, everything is easier, because even if they fail they help their fathers in the farms and gardens. They are used to it; they do it in the three-month vacations. So if they fail, it's no problem.

The common perception is that, the longer the girl stays in school, the more she is at risk. Most parents are planning to get their daughters married about the time the girls should be sitting their primary school exams. Those who have managed to stay in school until that stage are strongly discouraged from passing the exam. For the most part it appears that it is the mothers who act upon the fears and insist on putting a stop to the girls' educational endeavours. The instructor of a local literacy group explained the difficulties:

The mothers are the ones who discourage them. They say 'Look at that one, she got pregnant and came back [from Danjouma]', or 'That one is going to get married', or 'That one is married'. They say 'How long have we had a school? Can you show me a girl who has succeeded? Come now and be married!' Sometimes, beginning at the third or fourth year of primary school, some mothers start allowing boys to start courting their daughters. The girls listen to their mothers and take it into account. Sometimes in an exam, girls will write nothing; they will just hand in a blank paper to the teacher. It is the mothers who put bad ideas in their heads, even before they write the exam.

Students are allowed to attempt the primary exam twice, in most cases first at the age of 12 or 13, and then again at 13 or 14. These primary exam years are a crucial turning point not just because of the age of the girls, but also because success at this level most often means that the girl will have to move to the district capital of Danjouma to continue in school. She will be away from her parents' watchful eyes, perhaps living with strangers, being exposed to even more modern ideas and at a greater risk of getting pregnant.

Marriage potential and schooling

While parents do not value the content of the curriculum, young men are beginning to think differently. A mini-survey was conducted among younger men to investigate what they are looking for in a wife. At least five men were interviewed in each village and in Niamey. When asked what they considered desirable qualities in a wife, many young men stated that they thought a few years of education were a good thing. One young man said:

> Girls who have been to school get married more easily. It helps a lot if men know that a girl has been to school. They will rush to her door because everyone wants her as a wife.
> *Question*: Even if she has failed her exams?
> Yes ... Because educated girls are clean. They take care of themselves.

One young male went so far as to say that 'a woman who has been to school has a voice which soothes her husband'. Women who had not been to school, on the other hand, were often described as dirtier, less well-behaved and less likely to use the health centres.

While most boys and girls have gone to Koranic schools at least long enough to learn how to pray, young men seemed to think that Koranic schools did not have the same effect as primary school in a girl's education and later desirability as a marriage partner:

> the girl who goes to primary school is more civilized than the one who only went to Koranic school. Among the girls, the one that went to Koranic school, it's not her concern to be clean, because when she goes to Koranic school the *marabout* won't scold her and tell her to go back home and take a bath. But the one who went to primary school, every morning before going to school, she takes a bath. If she goes to school dirty, the teacher will ask her, 'Why do you come to school dirty?'

It is important to note, however, that for their first marriage,[2] young men and women have very little say in whom or when they marry. Ultimately it is the parents and extended families who make the decision and, in the girl's case, her mother is arguably the most influential in the process.

These opinions contrasted with those of older men married to women who had been educated for several years. While they conceded that they perceived their wives as more hygienic than uneducated women, and their wives did seem to have healthier children for the most part, they still clearly felt that the time in school was a waste of effort. Most of these men stated that when their daughters were old enough to go to school, they would not be sending them. Their focus group in Niamey closely echoed the opinions voiced in the villages: 'We don't want our girls to be away in school. We want them to get married early. But boys can go as far in school as they want.'

Girls' schooling and the domestic division of labour

Women in rural Niger work from dawn until dusk throughout the year. Mothers' interest in keeping their daughters at home is illuminated further when the household labour situation is considered. In the words of one woman from the village of Madogo, 'Women work all the time. They work all year long. A day doesn't exist where they don't work.' The work is physical, unrelenting, and often a woman's only relief from the workload comes in the form of her daughter. From an early age girls take care of younger siblings, gather wood, pull water, pound millet, run errands and sell goods for their mothers. If a girl begins school at the age of seven and remains until she is fourteen, her mother's life is much more difficult.

Many Hausa women are secluded to varying degrees and forbidden to sell in the market. Their young daughters are their only means of income generation. The money is turned directly into the household to buy supplementary food, pots and household goods for the girl's future marriage. Girls typically begin hawking goods for their mothers around the age of seven – the age at which they should be starting school. These activities are problematic. Some girls get into trouble with men tricking, or trapping, them into trading sexual favours for extra money. Interestingly, the pregnancies that result from these activities were rarely discussed. Unusually a local government official from Danjouma had apparently been alerted to the problem and had issued a warning that men seen talking to young girls would be fined and put in jail. However, no one had heard of any male suffering the consequences of ignoring the warning.

Planning for change

In order to increase education for girls in Niger, the government has to deal with very complex issues. The position of women in Nigerien society means even very young girls are valued for their reproductive labour within the household. The potential gains of primary school education do not outweigh the potential social risks or the loss of labour. While World Bank studies suggest that increasing levels of girls' education may lead to lower levels of fertility, that cannot happen until education is viewed as useful enough to attract girls and their parents.

The Ministry of Education has introduced awareness-raising campaigns for teachers and parents. They are unlikely to change parents' opinions of education for girls or boys until the system is seen to offer immediate benefits. Until the school curriculum is able to respond more directly to the parents' perspective, it will continue to be viewed as a waste of time.

Whether the system should be changed to a more community-based applied learning system, or to a system that focuses on a more skills-oriented curriculum, is a question that requires further investigation.

In the short term, the government should raise awareness of the importance of education for girls among head teachers to highlight the wider social benefits in terms of increased health and nutrition. At present there are not enough school places to offer every child in the country the opportunity to attend school. Urban schools are overcrowded, while some schools in rural areas have spare capacity. Head teachers of such village schools could recruit local girls who do not have long distances to walk to fill empty seats.

Because of persistent salary arrears one of the constraints of the Nigerien situation is the reluctance of government employees, including teachers, to consider initiating the process of change incentives from the international community.

Conclusions

Over the years the donor community, and the World Bank in particular, have been criticized for their failure to extend their analysis of education to include broader social issues and constraints, particularly in under-standings of girls' education. The analysis of Niger as a case study shows that the donor community's templates for educational reform have not worked. By focusing heavily on increasing access, the World Bank approach to girls' education overlooks the constraints of underlying social structures. As a result, those structures remain unchallenged and unchanged.

This Nigerien case study shows that for an SDP to be successful it must be able to respond to communities' understandings of an effective, quality education for their sons and daughters. The Nigerien example is interesting because it demonstrates the significance of the wider context of cultural values within which communities' understandings of girls' schooling operate. In Niger and elsewhere, the challenge to increasing girls' schooling is not just getting girls into school, but keeping them there. The indications are that, even for those who have benefited from some education, its results are not valued. These findings have implications both for the assumption that girls' education will result in the improvement of social development indicators and for any future movement towards SDPs. Clearly, if social development indicators are going to improve as a result of increased levels of female schooling, the community must be supportive.

In those countries where education SDPs are currently being developed (Ghana, Uganda, Tanzania), the outcomes thus far indicate that the approach is successfully incorporating the broader social factors into education interventions. The communities' interpretations of what is valuable must be reflected in the education process, or parents will continue to view formal schooling as inadequate for their children's needs. The expertise to analyse issues of access and equity and the power to ensure that broad social recommendations are implemented are key to this success.

Whether or not the SDP approach fulfils expectations remains to be seen. Increased recognition of the complexity of the gender, education and development issues brings with it an increased risk of failure. The successful coordination of government, community and the donors places large demands on all involved and, at times, requires leaps of faith. Despite the risks, however, the SDP carries with it the potential to break free of the constraints of previous education and development paradigms and move towards an approach that greatly enhances the potential for girls and women, boys and men, to realize their right to a quality basic education and an improved quality of life.

Notes

1. In an interview, Madame Eugénie Salifou, former director of primary school education, stated that of the 42,840 civil servants, only 7,370 or 17 per cent are women.

2. The DHS survey states that 23 per cent of women between the ages of 20 and 24 have been married at least twice, and by the time they reach the 45–49 age group, 42 per cent have been married at least twice. This would indicate that, for many women, their first marriage is unlikely to be their only marriage.

Bibliography

Kourgueni, I. A., G. Bassirou and B. Barrere (eds) (1992) *Enquête Démographique et de Santé: Niger*, Macro International Inc.

Ministère du Développement Social, de la Population et de la Femme (1994) *Population et Développement au Niger: Un Appel à l'Action*, Niamey, Niger.

Ministère de l'Education Nationale, de l'Enseignement Supérieur et de la Recherche (1993) *Problématique de la Scolarisation des Filles au Niger*, Niamey, Niger.

Ministère de l'Education Nationale et de la Recherche (1992) *Education de Base Pour Tous – Plan d'Action*, Niamey, Niger.

Stromquist, N. (1995) *Gender and Basic Education in International Development Co-operation*, UNICEF, New York.

Wilkey-Merritt, M. (1994) *Advancing Education and Literacy in Niger: Observations, Reflections and Recommendations*, UNICEF, Niamey, Niger.

World Bank (1994) *Report and Recommendations for a Basic Education Sector Report*, Niamey, Niger.

CHAPTER 8

Promoting Education for Girls in Tanzania

Stella Bendera

States, aid donors, religious bodies, individuals and the business community all invest in education as a means of developing human capital. Although education can take many forms, more knowledge has been generated about the role of formal schooling because it is most amenable to policy and therefore of particular interest to governments. There is a widespread perception that women who have had a certain level of formal education are better in processing information and are able to use goods and services more effectively (Behrman and Kenan 1991; Hartnett and Hensveld 1993; Ainsworth 1994). Deolalikar's (1994) study of Tanzanian household data showed that, if income and parental schooling are controlled, male-headed households spend 66.2 per cent less on a child in primary schooling than female-headed households. A more recent study by Al-Samarrai and Peasgood (1997) on household characteristics in Tanzania showed that an educated mother is likely to improve her bargaining power within the household and her preference for educated children will play a larger role in the decision to send children to school. Despite these demonstrable benefits of educating girls and women, Tanzania is among the many developing countries where women have less education than men. Tanzania has conducted more research on issues around education for girls than most countries south of the Sahara, focusing on access, persistence and performance of girls in schools.

This chapter will demonstrate Tanzania's efforts in addressing issues affecting girls and women in education. To contextualize this problem three broad areas are examined. An analysis of current economic and social developments in Tanzania is made and their impact on education for girls and the status of women assessed. Second, the chapter looks at different initiatives taken by the government, non-governmental organizations and academic institutions on issues of gender and education. Finally, the degree to which women and girls have been partners in this process themselves as subjects rather than objects of study is considered.

Tanzania: general background

Tanzania is the largest state in east and central Africa, after the Republic of Congo (formerly Zaire). It is situated on the east coast of Africa and lies between one degree and eleven degrees south of the equator. Extremes of topographic relief are found within Tanzania. From the towering Mount Kilimanjaro, with its permanent ice-cap reaching 5,895 metres above sea level, the country stretches to the trough-like depression of Lake Tanganyika, the world's second-deepest lake (772.4 metres). The country rolls from its lush, forested mountains in the north and south, through the great central plateau of rich brown savanna grass and bush, down to the tropical coastline. Large rivers and lakes make up 10 per cent of the country's total area. Tanzania's location is strategic as an outlet to several land-locked countries such as Burundi, Malawi, Rwanda, Uganda, Zambia and Republic of Congo. Kiswahili, the national language, is the most widely spoken of all African languages, with more than 70 million people using it in the eastern and central African regions. English is widely spoken and is the official language and medium of instruction in schools.

Economic conditions Tanzania is classified by the UN agencies as a less developed country (LDC), with an estimated gross domestic product (GDP) per capita of about US$180 (at constant 1985 prices) in 1995, although household surveys show a value closer to US $200 (World Bank 1995). About 75 per cent of the 28 million ethnically diverse population live in rural areas, with inequities in terms of living standards between rural and urban areas. It is estimated that 43 per cent of the rural population and 19 per cent of the urban population live below the poverty line (World Bank 1995).

In socio-economic terms Tanzania is characterized by a large subsistence sector, with agriculture, fishing and livestock-keeping occupying the dominant position in the rural productive activities. Agriculture is the backbone of the economy, contributing 50 per cent to GDP (1992–94) and employing about 85 per cent of the labour force (90 per cent women and 78 per cent men). The traditional export crops (coffee, cotton, tea, sugar, cashew nuts, tobacco and sisal) contributed over 60 per cent of foreign exchange earnings until 1995; while the industrial sector contributed about 15 per cent, and the mining sector accounted for 7 per cent (Planning Commission 1996).

From the mid-1960s to the mid-1980s, the country pursued economic growth policies based on state control and investment in commercial concerns in all sectors of the economy. Strong government commitment to developing human resources resulted in social indicators rising between 1960 and 1986. Gross primary school enrolment increased from 33 per cent of boys and 16 per cent of girls in 1960 to 69 per cent for boys and

67 per cent for girls in 1986 (UNICEF 1996). Access to health services improved, resulting in increased life expectancy and reduced infant mortality.

During the 1970s and 1980s the economy was in continuous crisis. The spiral of large deficits, rapid monetary expansion, high rates of inflation, balance of payment deficits, declining real per capita income and erosion of the tax base accelerated from 1979. Since 1986 Tanzania has been attempting to reform the regime of restrictive state controls with assistance from the International Monetary Fund (IMF) and World Bank by means of a national economic survival programme (NESP), a structural adjustment programme (SAP) and an economic recovery programme (ERP). Strategies include demand management, price liberalization, trade liberalization, financial sector reform, parastatal sector reforms, higher economic growth and administrative reforms, civil service reforms and macroeconomic reforms in general. These adjustments impact differently on the urban rich and the rural poor and differently upon men, women and children within these groups.

The education sector Immediately after independence in 1961, education policy focused mainly on strengthening the secondary school level by training local experts to replace colonials. Under the socialist government the primary sector was planned to expand gradually, and the aim was to provide schooling for all and to make people self-reliant. A more agriculturally based primary school curriculum was introduced following the Arusha Declaration in 1967 and a new policy of Education for Self-Reliance (ESR) was introduced. Schools were encouraged to contribute to their own upkeep through income-generating activities. The Musoma Resolution of 1974 made primary education compulsory, universal and terminal for 95 per cent of the population, as secondary education did not expand. Universal primary education was achieved in 1977. The number of primary school pupils increased immediately after the Musoma Resolution, with enrolments increasing fourfold during the 1970s and continuing to rise until 1983 (see Table 8.1).

Enrolment increased between 1975 and 1995, and equity was attained in 1988. Considerable decline was recorded during 1980–85. Census data show that the school-age population between 1978 and 1988 increased by 37 per cent, but stagnant enrolments resulted in a decline of around 16 per cent in the gross enrolment ratio (MoEC/FAWE 1997).

While UPE has facilitated the realization of gender equality at the primary school level, budgetary constraints have undermined the government's capacity to sustain both UPE and gender equality. The central government's allocation to MoEC has been steadily declining: 11.7 per cent in 1980/81, 6.5 per cent in 1984/85, 5.8 per cent 1989/90, 2.5 per cent in 1995/96. Moreover, many of the policies of the 1960s have changed

Table 8.1 Primary school enrolment in Tanzania, 1965–95

Year	Number enrolled (Standards 1–7)
1965	710,200
1970	902,619
1975	1,874,367
1980	3,530,144
1985	3,180,146
1990	3,372,362
1995	3,872,473

Source: MoEC/FAWE 1997.

with economic liberalization. Thus the reintroduction of school fees and cost-sharing measures (see p. 124) at all levels of education has affected parents' ability to meet the costs of education, and children have had to supplement family incomes. It is common in both rural and urban areas to see children of school age selling a wide range of commodities. These activities are carried on during the day and night time, even if the children need to do homework or sleep early to prepare for school the next day. Although girls are more exposed to sexual harassment, especially at night, they also have to work to supplement their parents' income. The effects of childen's involvement in these activities on their primary education is demonstrated by three crucial indicators:

- Primary school enrolment rates have dropped.
- Drop-out rates at schools are high.
- Performance, particularly that of girls, is very low.

Whatever progress had been made towards realizing gender equality at the primary school level is being undermined by the ongoing socio-economic crisis and the respondent World Bank/IMF structural adjustment programmes (SAP). For example, in one district, Dodoma, in 1995, there were 71,401 school-age children but only 30,065 were actually registered, leaving 19,896 boys and 20,440 girls out of school (MoEC/UNICEF 1995). A recent study (MoEC 1996) shows that gross enrolment rates at primary school level declined from 98 per cent in 1980 to an indicative 74–78 per cent in 1994. The drop-out rate is alarming if the 1988–94 cohort is taken into account. Based on 1993–94 promotion and repetition figures, 37.6 per cent of boys and 34.4 per cent of girls will not complete primary school education. A major finding of this study is that poverty among parents leads to this high drop-out rate. As well as not being able to afford school expenses, parents need their children's labour at home.

At the secondary school level, Tanzania operates a very constricted education system with a steep selective hierarchy. The rapid expansion of primary schooling has never been matched by a similar expansion at secondary school level. Before 1984, the private secondary school operations were severely restricted by government. Even with government restrictions removed, only about 13.3 per cent of all primary school leavers go to private secondary schools, and only 4.8 per cent go to government secondary schools (MoEC 1996). A mere 11 per cent of those sitting for Ordinary Level examinations are selected to enter Advanced Level studies in Form 5. In 1995, there were only 6,021 students in the whole country of 28 million people sitting Advanced Level examinations (MoEC 1996). Enrolment rates in public secondary schools are shown in Table 8.2.

Table 8.2 Public secondary school enrolment in Tanzania, 1965–95

Year	Number enrolled (O level)
1965	22,980
1970	41,178
1975	52,260
1980	67,296
1985	83,098
1990	145,242
1995	196,375

Source: MoEC 1996.

Table 8.3 shows the gender division of enrolment in public and private secondary schools in 1991 and 1994.

Table 8.3 Public and private secondary school enrolment in Tanzania, by gender

	Form 1, 1991	Form 4, 1994
Public total	18,892	16,474
Girls	8,138	6,776
Boys	10,754	9,698
Private total	27,554	19,809
Girls	12,859	8,964
Boys	14,695	10,845

Source: MoEC 1995.

The expansion of private secondary schools has increased girls' participation in secondary education. The number of private secondary schools has increased more than that of public secondary schools. In 1996, there were 353 private schools and 303 public schools (MoEC 1998). In 1996, there were 47,499 male students in public secondary schools as against 41,299 female students, and 50,936 male students were in private secondary schools as against 45,382 female students.

Situation of girls and women Women in Tanzania are valued for their labour power and reproductive capacity. As childbearers, rearers and food provisioners they are the mainstay of Tanzanian village life. During the colonial period there was mass male labour migration to plantations and mines, leaving women to cope alone with the agricultural workload formerly shouldered by men. Thus male elders and colonial government officials had direct vested interests in putting rigid limits on women's occupational choices and mobility. Mbilinyi (1989) documented the nature of the problem in Rungwe, where women were forcibly made to stay in the countryside. During the 1940s, many court cases were disputes over 'ownership' of girls and widows (Bryceson 1995).

In the years before and after independence the legal position of women was reformed and they became citizens rather than objects of lineage authority, facilitating increased female urban migration in the 1960s and 1970s. The passage of the Marriage Act of 1971 was a landmark in Tanzanian gender relations, standardizing marriage legislation throughout the country. The minimum age of marriage for girls was established at 15 and that of boys at 18. A couple had to agree on whether a marriage was to be polygamous or monogamous. A woman who cohabited with a man for two years was taken to be a legal wife. In 1983, the issue of family was resolved, and the contribution of women's domestic and childcare services to matrimonial assets was recognized.

At present the key issue in women's legal rights is women's access to and control of land in rural areas. The 1992 Presidential Commission of Inquiry into Land Matters took a conservative position by recommending 'Village' land tenure, placing the distribution and control of rural land in the hands of village chiefs. Such an arrangement was influenced by customary principles and placed women at a disadvantage in access to and control of land (Bryceson 1995). Within many ethnic groups in Tanzania, land passes from the father to the eldest and younger sons as the prime inheritors, or to the father's brother if he has no sons.

The impact of the situation of women on girls' education For poor families in a patriarchal society, a number of factors determine whether girls are sent to school. For example, at the household level, cost could be a problem and preference could be given to boys. A girl's labour could be needed more than that of her brother, so that she is kept at home. In Tanzania, girls' educational opportunities are also influenced and differentiated by factors such as family background, location and religious belief. Movement is often more restricted for Muslim girls than for those of other faiths. Girls who live in rural areas are at a disadvantage compared with those in urban areas because of the burdens of domestic and agricultural work upon them and their mothers. The fact that mothers are overworked and have little time to prepare food for their children has a tremendous impact on the health of children and on their performance at school.

The centrality of marriage and childbearing is internalized very early in life by girls in Tanzania (Bendera 1994; Meena 1994; Peasgood et al. 1997). Parents view early marriage as a solution to problems that girls might encounter in adolescence. With few other opportunities, a girl will be married immediately after completion of primary school for fear of getting pregnant before marriage. Although the Marriage Act of 1971 set a minimum age of marriage (15 for girls and 18 for boys), a recent study showed that in Tarime girls aged between 13 and 15 years had registered at the ante-natal clinic (UNICEF 1996). Some of the girls were married at 13 years of age. Unsurprisingly, the fertility rate in Tanzania remains high, with an estimated average in 1990 of 7.1 children per woman (UNPP 1992). This compares with an average of 3.9 for all developing countries and 1.9 for industrial countries (Bryceson 1995: 46). The high fertility rate arises mainly from the fact that women's childbearing careers begin early. In rural areas many of the norms of correct female behaviour are embedded in the marriage customs of the community (Bryceson 1995). Schooling does not seem to have altered societal norms. Young girls are considered marriageable from their first menstruation, and undergo initiation rites that inform them of the roles they will perform as mature women. Their lives are quickly dominated by the needs of their children. Childbearing at such a young age obviously narrows the social and economic horizons of girls and women. The provision of universal primary education has not reduced the number of early marriages and hence reduced the fertility rate in Tanzania in the way the World Bank analysts projected.

The economic crisis and pressure on women The effects of the SAPs prescribed by the IMF and World Bank have been felt by both the agricultural and urban sectors. Each has increasingly been unable to provide a livelihood for most households. A serious element in the effect of the economic crisis on families is the introduction of cost-sharing for social services. This has placed a heavier burden on women attempting to ensure the provision of health and education services for their families and themselves. An increasing number of pregnant women have resorted to home delivery in very poor environments and at a risk of their lives since they cannot afford the costs of hospital delivery. Women are expected, on top of delivery fees, to go to maternity wards with latex gloves, cotton wool, razor blades, baby clothing and bed-sheets. The maternal mortality rate is high, at between 200 and 400 deaths per 100,000 births (Tanzania/ UNICEF 1990). Following the economic crisis the Tanzanian public health service is conspicuously underfunded in absolute terms, spending about US$3.50 per capita annually, well below what is normally acceptable (Levine et al. 1994). This has led to a deterioration in health provision, leading to increasing difficulties in the control of such conditions as malaria and diarrhoea. Moreover, as more people become sick and hence less able to fulfil their responsibilities to their families, it is women who fill the gap created and whose work expands as the country and its people become poorer.

The newly introduced cost-sharing measures for education have aggravated the problem, as women have had to work even harder to pay for their children's schooling. TADREG (1990) found that the average cost of primary school attendance is 12,912 shillings ($23) per child, not including books and uniforms. World Bank data indicate that parental contributions (which are fixed, not means-tested) amounted to 37 per cent of total primary school expenditures nationwide (World Bank 1997: 44). Boys and girls do casual jobs to support their schooling. Whereas previously they could contribute their free time to the family economy, now they have to look for paid jobs, leaving women to do all the domestic chores. A recent study demonstrated that in Bagamoyo, one of the study areas, 55 per cent of boys and 37.5 per cent of girls were contributing to schooling costs (MoEC/FAWE 1997).

Empowerment of women through participation in the informal sector The growing inability, as a result of SAPs, of the agricultural sector and wage sectors to meet basic human needs has forced an increasing number of both young and adult members of households to search for alternative employment opportunities. The informal sector is a particularly important source of employment for women. Estimates based on national surveys reveal that women account for 35.4 per cent of total informal sector employment in Tanzania's mainland, as against only 3 per cent employed in the formal sector (Bagachwa 1995).

In urban areas, the sector contributes about 90 per cent of most households' earnings (Koda 1995). In rural areas, about 90 per cent of women are involved in micro-enterprises, mainly in groups or as individual entrepreneurs (Mbughuni 1994). Activities carried out in the informal sector include local beer-brewing, food-processing and marketing, retail selling of petty commodities, furniture manufacture, vehicle repair, shoe-making and repair, gardening, dairy and poultry-keeping and food-vending, to mention only a few. Other female-dominated activities include operating small eating places (Mama Ntilie), pig-keeping, selling charcoal and fire-wood, and providing decorations for seasonal festivals.

Women of all social groups participate in the informal sector, but richer ones have more time and capital and so run relatively large enterprises. Female entrepreneurs have little access to credit due to the limited size of their ventures, lack of property rights and inability to generate savings. In order to obtain credit for running their businesses, women have created an informal credit system, *Upatu*, in which they lend each other money in turns so as to accumulate cash to start a business. An increasing number of women are also members of women's associations where business networking is promoted. Through informal women's groups, women are learning about their legal rights. Thus women are being empowered as they participate in these activities. In the early 1980s only one-third of women had a cash income, whereas in the 1990s about 70 per cent of adult female population have a cash income (Koda 1995). This trend is changing gender relations at the household level. Women are now seen as important partners in life, since their economic contribution is felt at both household and public levels. Women are building houses, paying school fees for their children and paying for health services. Women are now more knowledgeable about resource mobilization, allocation and control. Their success in this area could change societal attitudes and lead to better socialization of children, who need to grow up with different perceptions of women and men in Tanzanian society.

While there is a genuine cause for optimism about women's increasing economic empowerment, one should not ignore the fact that they have not been relieved of their ardous service-oriented roles. Women continue to provide most of the household services, caring for the old, sick, children and disabled. Contributing their services to mourning ceremonies has also increased due to deaths from AIDS.

Agencies addressing gender issues in education

In order to look at the interaction between gender, education and development as far as the provision of education for women is concerned one has to move beyond the World Bank's reductionist perspective, which focuses on access to and provision of girls' education.

In Tanzania issues of access have not been solved by the introduction and enforcement of compulsory school attendance. In recent years, as we have seen, enrolment rates have declined. Issues of education for girls have to be addressed in their totality by moving beyond the classroom to the educational practitioners, the civil society and girls themselves. The contemporary period has been marked by a number of initiatives to highlight and attempt to solve issues around girls' education in Tanzania.

MoEC initiatives addressing gender issues   Since 1994 the Ministry of Education and Culture (MoEC) has been associated with a number of

Table 8.4 Number of women holding senior positions in Tanzanian Ministry of Education and Culture

Level	Position	Men	Women	Total	Women (%)
Primary education	District education officers (DEO)	89	15	104	14.4
	Regional education officers (REO)	15	5	20	25.0
Secondary education	Heads of schools (public and private)	540	62	602	10.3
Teacher education	College principals	28	7	35	20.0
Inspectors	All levels	438	91	529	17.2
	Zonal	7	0	7	0.0
	Headquarters	5	6	11	54.5
Directors	Headquarters	6	1	7	14.3

Source: Compiled from MoEC 1997.

initiatives. Three seminars were held in 1994 to sensitize top officials at the MoEC to gender issues. A curriculum review is being carried out and a new package, including the introduction of family life education, is being prepared for early introduction in schools to teach life skills (*stadi za kazi*) to the students.

A gender coordinating unit (GCU) has been established within the MoEC to coordinate gender issues, monitor gender activities in schools and conduct research. The unit has collaborated with donors, including UNESCO and SIDA, in acquiring funds to operationalize some of its tasks. Critics of the GCU see it as a mere rubber stamp in the MoEC. The unit has no autonomy and no authority to criticize the MoEC's way of handling issues. In most cases, the unit is side-tracked even when issues pertaining to girls' education are being discussed. The GCU is weak due to structural problems and lack of initiatives from its leadership. It is not officially within the structure of the MoEC and is composed of ministry personnel who have other duties in their respective departments. The leadership is too bureaucratic and lacks dynamism and networking spirit. The weakness of the GCU is demonstrated by the fact that there are few women in positions of influence at the MoEC (see Table 8.4). While the prevailing Tanzanian political ideology endorses egalitarian ideals, social attitudes support a patriarchal value system of male superiority and female subordination. Male domination among policy-makers and practitioners is perpetuated by appointments from the 'old boy network'.

The role of NGOs in advocating education for girls   Certain NGOs have shown great determination in pursuing the cause of education for girls and women. The Tanzania Gender Networking Programme (TGNP) is a lobbying and advocacy group that organizes weekly seminars for an audience drawn from government departments, youth and women's groups. The principal secretary of the MoEC was petitioned to come out with a clear policy on the issue of re-admission to school of girls who get pregnant while in school. TGNP's direct contribution to girls' education has been its publications on problems faced by girls in Tanzania. Its most recent Swahili publication, *Kwangu Wapi* ('No Home is My Home'), is in the form of a dialogue between a teenage girl and her aunt, and highlights the oppressive elements girls have to face in society. Men monopolize decision-making positions in the family and communities, supported by a patriarchal system of property ownership and customary laws of marriage and inheritance. While TGNP addresses wider societal issues affecting girls and women, the Forum for African Women Educationalists (FAWE), launched in 1996, focuses specifically on the issue of education for girls. FAWE has held three workshops with a variety of participants including parliamentarians, educationalists, the donor community and religious bodies. A research report, 'Gender in primary schooling in Tanzania', has been produced. Among the issues considered are the school environment (physical and sexual harassment in schools), school drop-out due to pregnancy, and cost-sharing.

In Tanzania, domestic violence is sometimes seen as a family affair. As a result the issue is side-tracked, and women are harassed or even killed by their spouses. The Tanzania Media Women's Association (TAMWA) has been campaigning on three issues that affect girls' education: violence against girls and women, teenage pregnancy, and female genital mutilation (FGM), which unfortunately is practised in Singida, Dodoma, Arusha, Mara and a few parts of the Kilimanjaro region. TAMWA is lobbying to get special courts to deal with domestic violence. Research conducted by WIDAF–Tanzania in 1996 at the Tanzania High Court revealed that, between 1992 and 1996, 70 (known) women had been killed by their husbands (TAMWA 1977). The instability created in households affects children's schooling. TAMWA has set up a legal centre for counselling battered women, sexually abused schoolchildren and teenage mothers, and has been in close contact with schools. Schoolgirls have testified in parliament on the trauma caused by such experiences. They spoke for millions of other girls who have remained silent through fear of social stigma.

Women organizing around gender issues

The debate on education for girls has been spearheaded mainly by women academics. The women's groups at the University of Dar es Salaam

(UDSM) were formed after the UN Women's Conference in Mexico in 1975. Their objectives include research, documentation, publication, and the organization of seminars and workshops on issues of gender. Currently, most of these groups operate under the umbrella of the University of Dar es Salaam.

In 1990, the Teenage Reproductive Health Group (TRHG) was set up in collaboration with members of the IDS Women's Study Group. In the same year it undertook a research project concerning teenage pregnancy and other reproductive problems faced by adolescents. Eight studies were done, ranging from legal perspectives to dating and the kind of life a girl leads after dropping out of school. This project led to the publication of a book entitled *Chelewa, Chelewa: The Dilemma of Teenage Girls* (Tumbo-Masabo and Liljestroum 1994).

Women Education Development (WED) has concentrated mainly on research dealing with education for girls. Research projects and work documented include the following:

* Knowledge About and Attitudes Towards AIDS among Girls Aged Between 13–19 in Tanzania (1989);
* The Expectations of High Achieving Secondary School Girls Concerning Future Education and Jobs (1990);
* The Struggle for Education: School Fees and Girls' Education in Tanzania (1991);
* How to Improve the Situation in the Education Sector for Girls in Tanzania (n.d.);
* Gender and English Language Teaching (1992);
* Gender Streaming in Science and Arts (1994)
* Violence: its Form and Consequences for Primary School Pupils, a Gender Perspective (1997).

It was through its research projects that the group struggled towards ensuring that information was generated and disseminated, which raised awareness of the problem of education for girls. The group is about to produce a publication entitled *Gender and Education in Tanzanian Schools*.

Other projects undertaken by the Faculty of Education have given a voice to girls in secondary schools. A project aimed at strengthening girls' education in science and mathematics has given rise to three publications entitled Dare Booklets. It is anticipated that these booklets will act as a focus for discussion among girls and teachers and will help to popularize the study of mathematics and science. The booklets include writings by schoolgirls whose aim is to change the attitude of other girls towards studying science and mathematics.

Conclusion: levelling the ground

Any education system that has gross inequalities of any type – gender, class, ethnicity, or geographical zones – is inherently inefficient since it is not optimizing its investments in human resources. Since females constitute over 50 per cent of the population, it is leaving out some of the best potential contributors to the economy. Education increases girls' willingness and ability to join the labour force, reducing their statistical invisibility in the national economy, improving their productivity and leading to national development.

Any consideration of girls' education that has been dealt with by gender advocates has addressed the following:

- the labour market structure;
- employment signals;
- household division of labour;
- the issue of role models; and
- women's empowerment.

In addressing all these issues, a number of factors have been considered. These include individual characteristics, organizational policies, politics and practices, and broader social cultural norms and expectations. Making sure that girls have access to and persist and perform in school is necessary, but is not a sufficient precondition for better female representation in the development process. Problems of educating girls have to be seen in the context of the wider social environment rather than in terms of the education system alone.

With respect to the labour market, the 1997 curriculum review undertaken by the Tanzanian Institute of Education (TIE) and the MoEC is important because the aim is to introduce gender and family life education into the education system. Of even more importance has been the attempt to encourage girls to study the subjects that are most valuable in terms of employment opportunities. Previously, girls were being streamed to subjects with little relevance to the labour market. The collaborative efforts of NGOs and women's groups at UDSM and other institutions of higher learning in reaching out to girls through documentation, popular media and drama are commendable. They have created forces that have led to a raised awareness in society of the issue of girls' education.

In a classical case of the self-fulfilling prophecy, negative and indifferent attitudes and expectations of teachers and parents have led to girls' low self-esteem and failure. Insensitivity to specific problems encountered by girls at school has also led to reduced ambition. For example, puberty brings new problems for girls for which there are very few helping mechanisms within the school system. There is a lack of privacy due to inadequate provision of lavatories, a lack of facilities for menstruating girls and a lack of guidance from teachers. In Tanzania, open discussions of puberty are taboo and many girls receive little guidance from either parents or teachers on how to handle the physical changes of puberty and how to deal with menstruation while at school.

The importance of teachers' roles in shaping the future of pupils is critical. Teachers are the common role models for boys and girls, providing them with a sense of direction and encouraging them to work hard both at school and at home. This shows the need for more female teachers in all schools and the importance of including gender issues in the teacher training curriculum.

'Better schooling for girls', a module prepared for teachers by the Primary Education Programme (PEP) at the MoEC, has, though not published, been used in teachers' resource centres. This module contains useful training material and covers most of the aspects needed to enhance teachers' awareness of the important role of the school in the socialization process.

Parental and societal lack of enthusiasm for differential support for girls, poor household demand for higher education and unequal division of labour in the household are social cultural constraints that need to be addressed by the different actors interested in education for girls.

We have seen, however, that a dynamic interplay of factors is fostering more equal relations between men and women. Women's involvement in the informal sector has given them financial power, hence their increasing involvement in decisions about their children's education. Increasing socio-economic empowerment of women is leading to greater gender equality in both the household and public domains.

When household structures are holding together and stakeholders such as education practitioners, NGOs and donors have shown commitment, efforts towards education for girls should then be directed to local groups such as members of parliament, and students themselves. This will make education for girls a national issue. It will ensure that the whole society and the education system are convinced and therefore active in bringing about changes in classrooms, in the behaviour of pupils, teachers and inspectors, in the printed curriculum, in textbooks and most of all in the teacher training curriculum. In order to tackle the issue of girls' education effectively, therefore, it is necessary to address both school and societal aspects.

Bibliography

Ainsworth, M. (1994) *The Social Economic Determinants of Fertility in Sub-Saharan Africa*, Washington, DC.

Al-Samarrai, S. and T. Peasgood (1997) 'Educational attainments and household characteristics in Tanzania', IDS Working Paper No. 49, IDS, Sussex.

Bagachwa, M. S. D. (1995) 'The informal sector under adjustment in Tanzania', in L. A. Msambichaka et al. (eds), *Beyond Structural Adjustment Programmes in Tanzania, Success, Failures, and New Perspectives*, Economic Research Bureau, University of Dar es Salaam.

Behrman, J. R. and W. R. Kenan (1991) 'Investing in female education for development: women in development strategy for the 1990s in Asia and the Near East', unpublished paper, Williams College, Williamstown, MA.

Bendera, S. (1994) 'Training for improvement of girls' education in Tanzania', paper for meeting on Measurement and Evaluation, National Examinations Council, Dar es Salaam.

Bryceson, D. F. (1995) 'Gender relations in rural Tanzania: power politics or cultural concern?', in C. Creighton and C. K. Omari (eds), *Gender, Family and Household in Tanzania*, Avebury Ashgate, Hong Kong/Sydney.

Deolalikar, A. B. (1994) 'The demand for secondary schooling: quantity and quality in Tanzania', paper presented at World Bank conference 'Investing in Human Capital', Arusha, Tanzania, 15–20 April.

FAWE (Forum for African Women Educationalists) (1996) 'Launching the FAWE chapter', workshop for members of parliament, Dodoma, Tanzania.

Hartnett, T. and W. Hensveld (1993) *Statistical Indicators of Female Participation in Education in Sub-Sahara Africa*, World Bank, Washington, DC.

Koda, B. (1995) 'The economic organization of the household in contemporary Tanzania', in C. Creighton and C. K. Omari (eds), *Gender, Family and Household in Tanzania*, Avebury Ashgate, Hong Kong/Sydney.

Levine, R. et al. (1994) 'Health financing alternatives and legal and regulatory analysis for health', unpublished paper presented at World Bank conference 'Investing in Human Capital', Arusha, Tanzania, 15–20 April.

Masabo-Tumbo, Z. and Liljestroum (eds) (1994) *Chelewa, Chelewa: The Dilemma of Teenage Girls*, Scandinavian Institute of African Studies, Uppsala.

Mbilinyi, M. (1989) 'Women's resistance in "customary" marriage: Tanzania's runaway wives', in A. Zegeye and S. Ishemo (eds), *Forced Labour and Migration: Pattens of Movement within Africa*, Hans Zell Publishers, London.

Mbilinyi, M., P. Mbughuni, R. Meena and P. Ole Kambaine (1991) *Education in Tanzania with a Gender Perspective*, Education Division Documents No. 53, SIDA, Sweden.

Mbuguni, P. (1993) 'Country gender analysis for Tanzania', paper prepared for SIDA, Dar es Salaam.

— (1994) 'Gender poverty alleviation in Tanzania', unpublished paper presented at a workshop organized by Commission for Science and Technology (COSTECH), Economic Research Bureau (ERB) and Tanzania Development Research Group (TADREG), Dar es Salaam, 11–12 January.

Meena, R. (1994) 'Gender issues in the education process', paper presented at World Bank conference 'Investing in Human Capital', Arusha, Tanzania, 15–20 April.

MoEC (1990) *Basic Education Statistics in Tanzania (BEST) 1990*, Ministry of Education and Culture, Dar es Salaam.

— (1995) *Basic Education Statistics in Tanzania (BEST) 1990–1994*, Ministry of Education and Culture, Dar es Salaam.

— (1996) *Basic Education Statistics in Tanzania (BEST) 1992–1996*, Ministry of Education and Culture, Dar es Salaam.

— (1997) *Basic Education Statistics in Tanzania (BEST) 1996*, Ministry of Education and Culture, Dar es Salaam.

— (1998) *Basic Education Statistics in Tanzania (BEST) 1997*, Ministry of Education and Culture, Dar es Salaam.

MoEC/FAWE (1997) *Gender in Primary Schooling in Tanzania*, main report, MoEC/FAWE/IDS, Sussex.

MoEC/UNICEF (1995) *Declining Enrolment and Quality of Primary Education in Tanzania Mainland: An Analysis of Key Data and Documentation and Review of Explanatory Factors*, Dar es Salaam.

Peasgood, T., S. Bendera, M. Kisanga and N. Abrahams (1997) *Gender and Primary Schooling in Tanzania*, Research Report 33, IDS, Sussex.

Planning Commission (1996) *Hali ya Uchumi wa Taifa Katika Mwaka 1996*, Government Press, Dar es Salaam.

TADREG (Tanzania Development Research Group) (1990) *Girls' Educational Opportunities and Performance in Tanzania*, Research Report No. 2, TADREG, Dar es Salaam.

— (1997) 'Health and education: a brief situation analysis', paper presented at Tanzania Gender Networking Programme (TGNP) Annual Gender Studies Conference (AGSC), Dar es Salaam, 15–18 September.

TAMWA (Tanzania Media Women's Association) (1997) 'Everyone has the right to life and security', symposium, Dar es Salaam.

Tanzania/UNICEF, (1990), *Women and Children in Tanzania*, Dar es Salaam.

Tumbo-Masabo, Z. and R. Liljestroum (eds) (1994) *Chelewa Chelewa: The Dilemma of Teenage Girls*, Scandinavian Institute of African Studies, Uppsala.

UNDP (1992), *Human Development Report 1992*, Oxford University Press, New York.

UNICEF (1996) *Today's Girl, Tomorrow's Woman*, research report, Dar es Salaam.

WED (Women Education Development) (1991) *Women and Education in Tanzania*, twelve seminar papers, WED, Dar es Salaam.

World Bank (1995) *African Development Indicators*, World Bank, Washington, DC.

— (1997) *Social Sector Review*, World Bank, Washington, DC (May).

PART THREE

Middle Income Countries: Gender, Education and the Labour Market

CHAPTER 9

Gender Inequality: The Mauritian Experience

Sheila Bunwaree

The official discourse in Mauritius is one of educational gender equality, yet Mauritian schooling fails to translate this discourse into reality. Access to education in the form of free education masks both gender and class inequality. The schooling process and education-related decision-making at the household level remain undemocratic and highly gender-insensitive. The low Gender Empowerment Measure (GEM; see p. 138) that the country records has very little chance of improving, since schools contribute to disempowering girls and reinforcing their subordination in an already patriarchal context.

The chapter first locates Mauritius geographically and historically. It then explains the Mauritian success story and discusses briefly the structural adjustment programmes implemented in Mauritius. It argues that the country's refusal to abolish free education as a component of the IMF/ World Bank conditionalities had unintended benefits for girls. Outlining the history of girls' education in Mauritius, the chapter highlights the inclusion of girls in the post-colonial era but argues that complete inclusion, where girls have an equal share and are treated as full-fledged citizens, is far from being attained.

The second part of the chapter demonstrates the extent to which girls' inclusion is incomplete. The multiple 'voices' of the different stakeholders – teachers, parents and students – highlight the subtle mechanisms that contribute to the marginalization of girls. Textbooks remain heavily stereotyped. Very little gender training takes place for teachers, and parents continue to allocate differential resources to their sons and daughters. In short, girls are socialized into a society that continues to oppress the vast majority.

The third part of the chapter argues that although education is generally regarded as a means to empower the citizens of the country, girls' autonomy and empowerment is still problematic in Mauritius. This is reflected by the low female participation rate in the labour market – women are 'crowded' into low-status positions by the 'glass ceiling'. The heavy under-representation of girls in the technical and scientific fields does not seem to attract the attention of the authorities. In stark contrast to its silence on this issue, in 1983 the state expressed a clear and overt concern over the gender employment imbalance prevailing in the export-processing zone (EPZ). The gender-blind stance of the state perpetuates gender inequality.

The chapter concludes by drawing attention to the new challenges facing Mauritius in the post-GATT era. The labour market will shrink and be restructured. Unless a new educational order that reduces rather than reinforces gender segmentation in the labour market is established, the Mauritian development express runs the risk of derailing. A new gender order of education and society is needed for the country's future sustainable human development.

Mauritius: geography and history

Mauritius is a small island of 1,840 square kilometres, located in the southwestern Indian Ocean, about 880 kilometres to the east of its closest land mass, Madagascar. Mauritius has experienced successive waves of Dutch, French and British colonizers. Although the island was first settled by the Dutch, the latter deserted the island in 1710 and the French took control in 1715. The French have played a most significant part, first as colonizers and then as a local dominating group. The French lost their political power to the British in 1810, but their economic and cultural power remained for a much longer period.

The French contributed to the development and expansion of sugar cultivation, which was introduced by the Dutch. Slaves were brought from different parts of Africa to work in the sugarcane fields. After the abolition of slavery in 1835, the British turned towards India to import indentured labour. The ethnic composition of Mauritius is made up of whites (of French and English descent), Indo-Mauritians (Hindu and Muslim), and people of African descent, commonly known as the 'Creoles' in Mauritius. There is also a small Chinese community who began to settle on the island in the 1830s. Mauritius became independent in 1968 and is now a multi-ethnic and poly-lingual society.

The Mauritian success story and structural adjustment

The economic situation prevailing in Mauritius in the immediate post-independence period was one bordering on disaster. The country had to struggle with a stagnating monocrop economy, heavy unemployment, a huge balance of payments deficit, a heavy budget deficit and an exploding population. However, it has successfully avoided a Malthusian nightmare and has been able to diversify its economy with a strong tourist industry and the creation of an export-processing zone (EPZ), concentrating mostly on textiles. In an effort to grapple with its multiple problems, in 1979 the government embarked on a stabilization and structural adjustment programme.

In May 1981, the World Bank (WB) approved a loan of £15 million to support a structural adjustment programme. The major purpose of the programme was to boost the economy by encouraging private enterprises and improving agricultural productivity. The programme complemented the International Monetary Fund (IMF) stabilization requirements, which had been developed between 1979 and December 1981.

As part of the stabilization requirements, Mauritius had to devalue its currency in 1979 and again in 1981. The devaluations were widely seen as symptoms of the government's bankrupt economic policies, which had their political outcome in the 1982 election with a landslide victory of the Mouvement Militant Mauricien (MMM) – a rather radical political party. The government was also very concerned to reduce its fiscal deficit. Reduction in consumer subsidies and an increase in indirect taxation were used as measures to reduce the deficit. The MMM's victory ushered in a new era as far as the elaboration and the implementation of the SAP was concerned. The 1982 budget speech highlights the philosophy of dialogue and proximity adopted by the new government:

> In our approach to administration, the government has broken decisively with the leisurely, inefficient and secretive practices of the past. The scale of adjustment effort proposed by the IMF is enormous. Only a mature and informed nation could be confident of achieving it. Underlying the search for a 'national consensus' is a willingness to share the burden of adjustment fairly … Government is determined to shelter the weaker sections of our society, the low income family, the sick and the elderly.

The 'national consensus', however, is often male-dominated and hardly takes into account the best interests of women, especially 'disadvantaged' women whose 'voices' are often unheard.

According to Bheenick (1991), the government was committed to reform but maintained an 'intensive policy dialogue' with the Bank, which meant that the structural adjustment loan was bank-supported, rather than dictated. The main features of the structural adjustment loans were cuts in expenditure on construction works and education, the reduction of the Public Sector Investment Programme, policy reforms regarding taxes and interest rates, a focus on the supply-side measures for export-led industrialization, the restructuring of the sugar sector and tourism development. Twenty so-called 'private' schools were closed. In contrast to many other countries, 'private' schools in Mauritius are funded by the government and are non-fee-paying. They are poorly resourced schools whose student population come from poor socio-economic backgrounds.

Because the general standard of living has continued to rise, no attention has been paid to the impact of SAPs on the vulnerable groups of Mauritian society. Gulhati and Nallari (1990) are among the very few who draw attention to the plight of the underprivileged:

> The macroeconomic stabilisation, mainly through curtailment of aggregate demand, involved quite a painful adjustment, consisting of rising unemployment, declining real wages and disciplined austerity. The government persevered with reforms even though it meant a considerable loss in momentum of economic growth and a perceptible setback in the welfare of low income groups. Very little was done to 'sweeten the pill' for underprivileged social groups.

The underprivileged groups certainly include many women, but no gendered analysis of SAPs and their impact has been undertaken.

Within two decades, Mauritius had succeeded in mitigating many of its economic problems. It was also successful in bringing about a decline in fertility rates, thus getting rid of the fear of a Malthusian nightmare. While high health standards, relatively high literacy rates among women and successful family planning programmes are often put forward as explanations for fertility decline in Mauritius, one can argue that the disastrous economic conditions and abortion (still illegal in Mauritius) may have also contributed to the decline in fertility. Women had to control their fertility to ensure their participation in the labour market, especially at a time when economic conditions were difficult and social aspirations were rising. This seems to confirm Jeffery and Basu's (1996) argument that drawing conclusions on the links between education, women's autonomy and fertility from simple indicators of female education, such as years in school and school enrolments, is simplistic.

Mauritius managed to diversify its economy so successfully in the 1980s that it may be seen as an economic 'miracle'. The international press referred to it as the 'tiger' of the Indian Ocean, comparable to the East Asian tigers. It developed a relatively strong welfare state, a factor contributing to its relatively high development index (HDI). It ranks sixty-first among the high-income developing group of countries. However, the women of Mauritius have not fared very well within the overall development context, and the country has a low Gender Empowerment Measure (a measure defined as follows in the 1995 United Nations Human Development Report: 'While the Gender Development Index (GDI) focuses on expansion of capabilities, the GEM is concerned with the use of those capabilities to take advantage of the opportunities of life.')

Some Mauritian women do not have the 'capabilities', and many who do are barred from significant opportunities in the labour market and political spheres. Mauritian society remains patriarchal, and various subtle mechanisms continue to work against women.

Girls' education and the effect of SAPs

The history of girls' education in Mauritius is one of exclusion. It was not a priority under colonial rule: women were considered a subordinate group, and they were excluded from positions of power in the administration of the colony. Women's production was 'invisible' and their economic potential disregarded. Their education was regarded as insignificant to the economic development of the colony, and they were kept at home to learn domestic skills. When schools for girls were established, the curriculum was heavily sex-stereotyped, socializing girls for roles regarded as 'feminine'. They were taught how to look more graceful and agreeable to their companions. Music, drawing and sewing were also taught, as they were considered useful for the housewife (Milbert 1812).

Schools for girls were established in Mauritius from the early nineteenth century under the French and later the British colonial administrations. Girls of African descent were denied access to these schools under strong pressure from white parents, who threatened to withdraw their daughters if girls from other racial groups were admitted. The education of 'coloured' girls received a further setback when the colonial government issued a statement in 1851 that the 'Indians are aliens, a race apart' (Tinker 1974: 125). The education of girls received more attention only in the 1950s. With the passing of political power into the hands of the local Indians, education took a new direction. Many more children from different socio-economic and racial groups gained access to education with the expansion of schools in the 1950s and 1960s. Girls' education started developing, and after independence this development continued. Literacy among women increased and it became possible for some women to pursue professional careers. But in spite of these efforts, more than twenty years after independence, very few women occupy top positions in either the public or private sector.

Mauritius has achieved universal primary education. The enrolment of boys and girls in primary education is similar. While there are no disparities between rural and urban areas in terms of access to primary school, quality of schools varies across the island. The official national literacy rate for adults was approximately 90 per cent in 1990, with that of women only 65 per cent, a highly significant gender gap. Although there is an almost 100 per cent enrolment at primary level, there is a sharp drop at secondary level. The secondary enrolment rate is about 52 per cent and there is no gender disparity. Despite free education, equality of opportunity remains a myth in Mauritius. Fierce competition exists at the end of the primary cycle, when an examination selects children at the age of ten-plus. The better performers go to the best schools, leaving the weakest with very poor-quality schools.

The system is elitist, privileging children from better socio-economic backgrounds. The vast majority of children attending the better-resourced schools are from upper- and middle-class homes. Approximately 40 per cent of children fail the examination at the end of the primary cycle and leave the education system completely. Not much is known about what becomes of them after they leave school. However, even if more children did pass there would not be enough school places, since there was a massive freezing of school expansion during the structural adjustment programme. The cuts in educational expenditure brought about by the SAP caused a severe shortage of schools in the country. Many people regard the shortage of secondary schools as the major problem faced by the education sector in Mauritius. It also faces a number of other problems.

In spite of a substantial reduction in capital expenditure for education and restraints on the recurrent expenditure, the commitment to free public provision of primary and secondary education was not revised. Within the overall philosophy of the SAP regarding public expenditure on social services, the government's educational policy became problematic. The World Bank and IMF pressurized the country to abolish free education, but it refused to do so. This had unintended benefits for girls. Free education has contributed to giving more girls access to education. According to the census, in 1972 the enrolment rate for girls was 28 per cent, while that for boys was 40 per cent. In 1983, enrolment for girls was 42 per cent and that for boys 46 per cent.

The contribution of free education to the reduction of the gender gap is confirmed by the views of a range of stakeholders. Free education was introduced in 1976 by the Labour Party of the time, and it is generally argued that it was largely a political bait – it was the last card that the increasingly unpopular Labour government could play. When the MMM swept into office in 1982 with a landslide victory of 60/0, they could not touch free education since many MMM members themselves promoted and demanded free education in the 1970s. Moreover, abolishing it would have caused the newly elected government to lose its popularity very quickly. Although the post-colonial era has had a more inclusive policy as compared to the colonial period, girls continue to be discriminated against. The 'voices' of the different stakeholders that we now turn to emphasize this point. Various processes, in and out of school, contribute to disempowering girls.

Stakeholders' voices

The data used here come from a United Nations Development Programme (UNDP) consultancy by the author on gender and education (Bunwaree 1997b) and a study on the problem of exclusion in Mauritius (Bunwaree 1997a). Qualitative data were privileged over quantitative data in both studies, since the former illuminate the complexity of social relations more fully, indicating the simultaneous influences of gender, class and ethnicity. Feminist methodology of this kind helps researchers to be more sensitive to social interaction, discourse, silence and ideology, all of which call for more probing and naturalistic methodologies to examine the unfolding subjectivity of the individuals being investigated.

As part of the methodology, a 'voice' was given to the various actors (girl students, parents, teachers, policy-makers, educational administrators and career advisers) in an attempt to understand the various mechanisms/ processes that contribute to the marginalization of girls/women. Participant observation as well as structured and unstructured interviews were carried out in Creole, the mother tongue of the participants, and then translated. The interviews were taped and the multiplicity of 'voices' emerging out of the transcriptions reflect the extent to which the microrealities and life worlds of girls and women often elude quantitative data study and are ignored by institutions such as the World Bank.

Processes working towards the marginalization of girls

Sangeeta is 15 and in Form 3 at a poorly resourced school. She speaks only Creole. She does not like school, but prefers it to staying at home so as to escape the heavy household work:

> I don't like school, teachers are sarcastic, I don't know how to do my homework, my parents cannot help me, they themselves do not know, they have not had much schooling. My father wanted me to leave school to help with the household work. My mother told him to allow me to continue since there are no school fees to be paid. My mother works in a factory. There are days when I am forced to absent myself from school, I need to fetch the water, clean the house, look after my younger brother when my grandmother has to go out and cannot keep him. There is a lot of work when I stay home so I prefer to come to school. My eldest brother takes tuition, he does not have time. Moreover, my parents never ask him to do household work, they always say it is a girl's job.

Sangeeta's parents were also interviewed. Here is what Sangeeta's father had to say :

> I have three children, we are not very rich. I am a mason, sometimes there is work and sometimes not. My wife works in a factory, and we both get very tired. I've told my wife that we could make Sangeeta leave school – she is not all that brilliant, and moreover we will be marrying her off in one or two years, but she says we should let her do up to Form 5, schooling is free. But there are expenses, my eldest son takes private tuition, I would like him to get a good job and stand on his own feet. School is free, yes, but we need to find the children's uniforms, copy-books and books, etc.

Patterns of differential allocation of resources are clear in this household. Sangeeta has to do more housework than her brother, does not take tuition and is regarded as somebody who needs to be subordinate and dependent. She will be 'married off', whereas the brother needs to 'stand on his own feet'. If school were fee-paying, Sangeeta would probably have left earlier.

Similar views were expressed by other parents. Mrs X has two children, Deepak and Rita. Her husband died recently, and Mrs X is now the breadwinner. Rita has left school to ensure that her younger brother has the chance to continue his schooling. Mrs X is illiterate, but thinks that schooling is important for boys. She sees her daughter as having to go 'to somebody else's home' one day, implying that she will be dependent and subordinate. The importance of free schooling is emphasized once more, but free schooling on its own is not enough to empower girls in Mauritius. Mrs X:

> When we were young, we simply did not have the same chance that children have today. We only knew the hard work in the sugarcane fields. Now schooling is free but since the children's father has died, I have much more difficulty. Rita has had to leave school. I am putting in some more efforts to allow Deepak to continue his schooling. Rita is a girl, one day she'll get married and go to somebody else's home. I am thinking of taking an additional job to pay for some tuition for Deepak. If he has good grades, he'll be able to get a good job and one day he'll look after us.

In times of financial constraint parents tend to privilege boys. Deepak's mother tries to find another job to pay for the private extra tuition so necessary to success in the competitive examination at the end of the primary cycle. In contrast, Deepak's sister has had to leave school. An analysis of private tuition in Mauritius seems to highlight the overlapping of class and gender. Although the University of Mauritius study on private tuition (1989) does not mention the gender issue, it is clear that inequalities facing girls are compounded. Girls from disadvantaged backgrounds, as in the two households discussed above, do not obtain the same share of resources. Summarizing the University of Mauritius study on private tuition, the Ramdoyal Report (Ministry of Education 1990: 28) points out that:

> There was a general tendency for students from better-off families to take more tuition than students from poor families. Private tuition thus constitutes a source of inequity in the system. The White Paper (1984) also pointed to the inequity emerging from private tuition. Competitive pressures work against two groups of children – those whose families are too poor to pay for private tuition, and the slow learners who are considered by their teachers to have little chance in the CPE and who are therefore neglected.

The gender-blind stance of the state is striking. The authorities often use the argument that girls do better than boys to quieten down the few feminists who attempt to raise the inequality issue. Neither disaggregated nor qualitative data are collected by the authorities. In fact, when data are disaggregated, one finds that it is only girls from higher socio-economic backgrounds attending the 'star' schools who perform better than boys (Bunwaree 1997).

A girl of ten who has had to leave school tells her story:

> My father and mother separated a year ago. My mother now has to go to work. I am the eldest, my mother has made me leave school to look after my youngest brother and sister. My other brother is in Standard IV. It is I myself who do most of the household work, I wash, clean and iron. When my mother comes back from work, she is tired but she still does some work, she cooks the food.

This little girl has poor prospects, as she has had to leave school without acquiring literacy and numeracy. She talks of her brother in Standard IV in whom her mother places all her hopes:

> My mother says that when my brother grows up, he will work and look after us. My mother won't go back to my father because he beats her up too often.

She is only one and a half years older than the brother, but her mother has chosen to make her leave school. The brother is seen as the future breadwinner, just like Deepak, whose mother we met above. The boy is regarded as a potential worker who will be able to look after them. This little girl has also internalized the fact that males are stronger and that women and girls have to be looked after. Her own contribution in the home is disregarded, and remains 'invisible' and 'unpaid'.

A drop-out girl who is desperate to find a job argues:

> When I was at school, I didn't like it, I was scolded all the time by a teacher, he always used to ask me to leave school and enrol in sewing classes or get married. Finally, I've left school. When I went to look for a job the boss laughed and said, 'We don't take your sort of people.' First I'd failed Form 3 and what's more, there they employ people with straight hair that's lighter in colour.

After leaving school, this girl was excluded from the labour market not only because of her poor qualifications but also on racial grounds. An analysis of some of the girls' lives indicated a frequent intersecting of class, gender and ethnicity. Girls coming from a deprived, working-class 'Creole' background often spoke of the ethnic discrimination they experienced. Some referred to sexual harassment at school and the feeling of revolt they developed as a consequence.

Expressing her views about school, a 12-year-old girl who failed CPE (Certificate of Primary Education) said:

> I was fed up with school, very often teachers called us names of all sorts. Also, they used to call me 'ti cheveux', 'mazambique'. I never used to understand much in class. I wanted to leave but then I failed and had to leave. But now I don't know what to do, I'm fed up at home, it gets boring.

A 14-year-old living in one of the deprived areas of Mauritius, who has dropped out:

> I didn't like school, when I failed sixth standard, I wanted to leave. My mother forced me to stay on and repeat. I was fed up. There was a teacher who used to do things that shouldn't be done to the girls. He used to force us to stay, otherwise he would punish us. I didn't know what to do, I felt embarrassed and frightened.

When questioned further, this girl made it clear she and her friends were sexually harassed by the teacher.

Another 15-year-old dropped out of school because she became pregnant:

> I felt sad that I had to leave school, I had become pregnant, the school came to know about it. I was expelled. I would have had to leave anyway, people would have started talking about it. I then decided to have an abortion. I still see my boyfriend – he's still at school. I think of getting married one day, but Jean is not happy when I talk about marriage to him. I'm scared that he might leave and go.

This young girl is out of school and living a rather uncertain life. She sees marriage as a possibility. She is strongly socialized into being a housewife who is both subordinate and dependent.

The high enrolment levels for both boys and girls at primary school and the absence of a gender gap at secondary level demonstrate that access is not a problem. However, there are many subtle mechanisms at work that push disadvantaged girls to the fringes of society. Exclusion from the labour market is a wider problem, affecting not only girls from disadvantaged backgrounds. Girls from middle-class backgrounds who succeed are also marginalized in the labour market, for different reasons. The curriculum and labour market are seen as strongly gender-segmented by key stake-holders. An official of the Ministry of Education working as a careers adviser spoke to one middle-class parent about the choice of subjects for his daughter, who is quite good at science:

> I am telling you, it is much better to let her do economics and accounting. Let us say she does sciences and becomes an engineer, there is no scope

for her on the labour market. Look at Miss X, she went to QEC, then studied engineering in the UK and now works as public relations officer in a firm. She had applied for an engineering position. I knew the employer, I pleaded in her favour, but this is what he said: 'I would have to pay for maternity leave and all the rest, would you pay for that? All this is very nice, she is well qualified, but will she be able to wear a helmet and climb scaffolding when there is a need to?'

Perceptions of male employers contribute largely to driving girls and women away from scientific and technological careers. A young woman engineer tells her story :

I was interviewed for the post of civil engineer – I have a higher degree in this field. The questions that were asked at the interview had nothing to do with my qualifications or studies or the job. Instead, they asked me whether I was planning to get married and how many children I was hoping to have. Having heard stories about employers being irritated about women going on maternity leave, I told them I was hoping to have only one child but not in the next few years. Even then I didn't get the job. I happen to know the man who got it.

Discrimination against women scientists, particularly engineers, seems to be quite pronounced. Women engineers are regarded as not being able to perform outdoor work. However, prejudices and discrimination are not restricted to employers. Often parents themselves discriminate between their sons and daughters, as exemplified by the parents encountered above. Even parents from higher socio-economic backgrounds spoke of privileging their son's education in times of financial constraints. A father of three (two sons and a daughter), working as a primary schoolteacher, argues:

It is important for my children to be educated, but education in Mauritius is not really free when we think of private tuition fees. It will not be possible for me to send all three children to university – perhaps my daughter will stop after HSC [Higher School Certificate] and get married.

Although this particular father does not spell out the fact that he sees the future of his daughter more in terms of being somebody's wife and dependent, some other parents from poorer socio-economic backgrounds made the point that men need to cater for their families whereas women can be dependent on their husbands.

I'll make sure that my daughter has some education, but my son will have to stand on his own feet, be somebody and manage in life. He will have to make a family live, my daughter will be married off and sent to somebody's home. There will be someone to look after her.

A complex interplay of factors impacts upon girls' and women's subjectivities. The lack of democracy and gender insensitivity in the home illustrated by the parents' views is compounded by teachers' attitudes as well as by schoolbooks. Teachers have hardly any gender training and continue to socialize girls towards things feminine. Explaining how to write an essay on one's hobby, one teacher in a mixed class said:

> Well, you girls, you can explain what a hobby is, then take the example of sewing, embroidery, cooking or music as your hobbies, and the boys could choose from things such as football, cycling, fishing, anything boys usually do.

Girls in many schools and homes are encouraged to engage in pursuits usually associated with female roles within the four walls of the home, whereas boys are directed towards outdoor activities.

One male teacher teaching a mathematics class in a poorly resourced school said:

> It's hard enough to teach students in this school since they are rather slow, but trying to get the girls to do maths is even harder. They don't have the brains for it, that's why you see them fiddling around and not interested.

This was his explanation for the girls' lack of interest in maths. Another teacher claimed:

> Anyway, girls don't have a scientific mind, it's better to offer them subjects for which they are geared. Moreover, society needs more women who can look after their families well.

Many of the teachers expressed similar views. The availability of girls as a negative reference group often helped boys learn and practise the masculine identity through which each generation re-creates the patriarchal relations of adult society. Classroom interaction and learning materials, especially textbooks, reinforce gender differences. School textbooks are major instruments through which children learn about the social values and norms of the period in which they live. The sexism propagated at school becomes even more apparent when the text and illustrations in school textbooks are analysed. An analysis of the ideologies embedded in Mauritian textbooks and the visual and literary resources teachers use shows a large degree of gender inequality (Bunwaree 1997a). Gender stereotyping is so strong that girls tend to internalize the roles assigned to them. Many girls attending the poorer-resourced secondary schools did not envisage a career, but projected a future for themselves similar to their working-class mothers' experience. They also spoke of being house-wives without paid work, and referred to the need to be subordinate to their husbands' wishes. Françoise is 16 and wants to leave school after her 'O' levels:

I'm not sure whether I'll work when I leave school, when I get married if my husband asks me not to work, I'll have to do what he says.

This notion is reflected in what Mariam says:

We have to learn to listen to what our husbands say, they are the heads of households and to help hold a family together, one has to be obedient and not to argue over things.

These young girls seem to be imbued with the ideology that men are and should be in control. Their schooling has certainly not helped them to realize that each human being, irrespective of sex, belongs to a democratic space where the principle of equality should prevail. The formal and informal curricula to which girls are exposed, as well as the decision-making at the household level, legitimize inequalities and contribute to their marginalization.

Girls' education and their position in the labour market

Education has certainly contributed to more women participating in the labour market, but it is still heavily tilted in favour of males. Female participation rates amount to 40.5 per cent but this is still below the National Development Plan 1988–90 target of 44 per cent for the 1990s and well below the male participation rate of approximately 80 per cent. An analysis of employment patterns indicates that women still cluster around the lower segment of the labour market in low-paid, low-skilled and low-status jobs, as illustrated in Table 9.1.

A complex range of supply and demand factors explains the predominance of women in the EPZ sector. Technical division of labour, which enables the separation of labour assembly operations, is a common feature of EPZs with product sectors such as clothing and electronics. The jobs are considered women's jobs because of what are considered their 'natural' attributes: docility and dexterity; ability to withstand routine, sedentary activities; acceptance of lower pay because of their subordinate position in society and in the family. The few women who do succeed in reaching middle management positions in some sectors often experience a 'glass ceiling' preventing any further promotion (Ministry of Education and Human Resource Development 1995: 35).

Employment patterns – the state breaks its silence in favour of males

Interestingly, the sudden large absorption of women into the EPZ provoked some reaction by the state, which had always been silent about the gender imbalance in the labour market. The poor female participation rate

Table 9.1 Mauritius: employment in large establishments, by gender, March 1993 and 1994

Industrial group	March 1993			March 1994		
	Male	Female	Both sexes	Male	Female	Both sexes
Agriculture and fishing	31,610	11,315	42,925	29,961	11,653	41,614
Sugar	28,517	9,843	38,360	26,737	10,259	36,996
Tea	1,045	595	1,640	901	403	1,304
Tobacco	124	252	376	123	271	394
Other	1,924	625	2,549	2,200	720	2,920
Mining and quarrying	81	88	169	79	86	165
Manufacturing	42,170	64,836	107,006	1,940	62,774	104,714
EPZ	24,994	59,936	84,930	4,045	57,661	81,706
Other	17,176	4,900	22,076	7,895	5,113	23,008
Electricity and water	3,465	137	3,602	384	147	3,531
Construction	13,730	222	13,952	3,161	216	13,377
Wholesale, retail trade, restaurants, hotels	15,581	5,040	20,621	17,658	5,685	23,343
Transport, storage and communication	12,191	1,620	13,811	12,492	1,704	14,196
Financing, insurance, real estate and business services	7,431	3,097	10,528	8,143	3,352	11,495
Community, social and personal services	57,375	17,111	74,486	58,708	18,076	76,784
Activities not elsewhere specified	2,891	89	2,980	3,083	75	3,158
Total	186,525	103,555	290,080	188,609	103,768	292,377

Source: Ministry of Women's Rights 1995.

and the marginal positions of women in the labour market never attracted government attention until the 1983 census indicated the heavy representation of women in that sector (see Table 9.2), when it saw a need for a 'more equitable sex-wise distribution of jobs in the manufacturing sector'.

The state saw the abolition of differential wages for men and women in the EPZ as enhancing the chances of male employment in textile industries and as reducing the 'inequity' in the distribution of jobs.

The government believed that the abolition of differential wages for men and women in the EPZ would enhance the chances of male employment in textile industries and reduce the 'inequity' in the distribution of jobs. The government's concern for 'equity' seems, however, to be male-biased. Now that the country faces a number of challenges in the post-GATT era, women may be marginalized further. A number of industries

Table 9.2 Gender distribution of employment in large establishments, sectoral distribution of earnings, Mauritius, 1988

Sector	Women (%)	Rank*	Average earnings**	Rank*
EPZ, clothing	68.5	1	45	9
Other EPZ	62	2	53	7
Services	36.8	3	53	7
EPZ, textile	33.4	4	47	8
EPZ, wood, furniture	31.7	5	69	4
Finance, real estate and business services	29.6	6	79	2
EPZ, jewellery	27.4	7	63	5
Agriculture	26.1	8	69	4
Wholesale, retail	21.6	9	59	6
Central government	19.9	10	61	5
Transport	8.6	11	79	2
Electricity/water	3.6	12	119	1
Construction, all sectors	1.5	13	76	3
All sectors			57	

Note: * From highest to lowest.   ** Daily earnings in rupees.
Source: compiled from Ministry of Employment 1988.

have closed down. Unemployment among women is rising in this sector, but the state is silent on all these issues.

The post-GATT challenges and the gender blindness of the state

The success story of Mauritius is well known to the world, but few appreciate that this success largely finds its sustenance in the expansion of the sugar and textile industries. Both are heavily dependent on preferential trade agreements with the European Union and the USA, which are gradually becoming redundant as a result of the conclusion of the GATT Uruguay round. Mauritius now faces the challenge of ensuring the sustainability of its success within an increasingly unstable global context. Given the present level of wages, it is vulnerable to competition from lower-wage countries such as Vietnam and China. Both the economy's prospective fragility and the unequal spread of its benefits derive from the uneven capacity of existing human resources to adapt to the job market's evolving demands. While there are highly skilled professionals, there are also pockets of people who are not equipped to deal with the higher levels of technology that the emerging sectors of the economy will need. The Master Plan for Education (Ministry of Education 1991) states:

Table 9.3 Mauritius: enrolments in higher education, by faculty and gender, 1992–95

Year	1992/93		1993/94		1994/95	
	Male	Female	Male	Female	Male	Female
Faculty of Engineering						
Degree course	23	1	39	10	23	2
Diploma course	66	16	37	4	66	11
Faculty of Law and Management						
Degree course	42	44	31	45	32	28
Diploma course	103	23	93	48	104	57
Faculty of Science						
Degree course	21	32	31	13	44	31
Diploma course	13	2	–	–	–	–
Faculty of Agriculture						
Degree course	–	–	9	5	–	–
Diploma course	15	11	27	15	19	18
Faculty of Social Studies and Humanities						
Degree course	22	46	37	88	45	106
Diploma course	55	17	55	45	44	39

Source: University of Mauritius Statistics.

A major achievement of the system has been that it has provided the greater part of the manpower required for the first stage of Mauritian industrialisation. The education system will now be called increasingly to provide the managers, the professionals and the technicians who will be required for the second phase of industrial development.

However, the Master Plan ignores the gender dimension of human capital. It recognizes that the labour market will be dominated by science and technology, but no attention is paid to the disparity that exists between male and female representation in the scientific and technical fields. Enrolments at university reflect the entrenched gender stereotyping prevailing within the system. Table 9.3 indicates that fewer women than men enter tertiary education, and that those who do enrol mainly study traditionally 'feminine' disciplines.

Bearing in mind that the economy is likely to shift to an information-based one, it is vital that girls/women are encouraged to enter the disciplines or fields of study that lend themselves to the new emerging sectors. Many documents, such as Vision 2020, Master Plan 1991 and the World Bank's *Technology Strategy for Competitiveness*, speak about the need to have a greater focus on scientific and technical projects, but they all seem

Table 9.4 Subjects chosen by boys and girls at SC level, Mauritius, 1993 and 1994

Subject	1993		1994	
	Boys	Girls	Boys	Girls
Add. maths	3,681	2,895	3,615	2,912
Chemistry	2,039	1,271	2,183	1,547
Commercial studies	15	221	20	217
Computer studies	440	192	415	238
Design and technology	119	–	205	–
Design and communication	153	3	327	2
Electronics	51	2	49	4
Fashion and fabrics	–	215	–	213
Food and nutrition	6	295	–	213
Geometrical and mechanical drawing	531	3	341	–
Physics	1,709	484	1,770	593
Statistics	190	28	196	38

Source: Mauritius Examinations Syndicate.

Table 9.5 Subjects chosen by boys and girls at HSC level, Mauritius, 1993 and 1994

Subject	1993		1994	
	Boys	Girls	Boys	Girls
Maths syllabus C	2,026	1,591	2,024	1,695
Geometrical and mechanical drawing	193	–	197	1
Chemistry	898	469	920	490
Food studies	–	46	–	43
Physics	787	156	791	186
Design and technology	9	–	21	–

Source: Mauritius Examinations Syndicate.

to ignore the gender gap in the scientific and technical fields. The government is selective in addressing gender imbalances. The official document's silence on the gender gap in science and technology is in stark contrast to its reaction to the EPZ's privileging female employment.

The World Bank document (1994) states: 'Mauritian authorities need to ensure that rapid expansion of tertiary enrolment does not increase the existing bias towards liberal arts but reduces it.' Addressing the feminization of the liberal arts may well benefit an economy increasingly dominated by science and technology. Reducing the bias without introducing other

Table 9.5 Subjects chosen by boys and girls in vocational and training sector, Mauritius, 1994

Courses	Male	Female
Pre-vocational training (PVT)	909	320
PVT, third year	227	60
Training in maintenance of industrial machinery	14	–
Training course for clothing merchandizers	30	31
Le Chou Training Centre		
Motor vehicle mechanics	20	–
Cabinet-making	20	–
Electrical installation	20	–
Welding and metal fabrication	20	–
Hydraulics and Pneumatics Training Centre		
Hydraulics	175	–
Pneumatics	125	
Bel Air Training Centre		
Welding	18	–
Mechanical engineering	20	–
Mont Ida Training Centre		
Automechanics	20	–
Electrical installation	20	–
Training in printing (NTC 3)	23	4

Source: Industrial and Vocational Training Board Statistics 1995.

policies to protect women in the liberal arts and encouraging more girls and women to go into traditionally 'male' subjects may contribute to a feminization of poverty in the present context of shrinking labour markets.

Jaddoo (1997) also draws attention to the 'scientifically' and 'technologically' poor human capital in Mauritius. He writes: 'At the operator level, two workers out of every three have only had primary schooling. At higher levels, the employees do not have a science background and this prompts me to say that we are still scientifically and technologically illiterate.' Jaddoo ignores the gender issue. The gender gap prevailing in the science and technical fields and the lost female economic potential do not seem to be of concern to planners and policy-makers. The consequences of this for the sustainable livelihoods of women in a declining labour market seem to be of even less concern.

The fact that girls' enrolments in traditionally 'male' subjects such as engineering, design and technology, computer studies and other science subjects remains rather low has serious implications not only for the future development of the country but also for the girls' own development, autonomy and empowerment. Tables 9.4, 9.5 and 9.6, showing choice of subjects by students at school, indicate the extent to which girls continue to opt for subjects regarded as 'traditionally feminine'. The small numbers or total absence of girls in subjects such as computer studies, physics, geometric and mechanical drawing, as well as in the vocational and training sector, call for an urgent review of policy.

As the economy of Mauritius becomes more vulnerable in the post-GATT era, government policies to prevent girls and women from being further disadvantaged are needed, for in difficult economic conditions they tend to be the first and worst hit. Mauritius, like many countries, is a signatory of the Convention on the Elimination of All Forms of Discrimination against Women (CEDAW), yet it has a long way to go before it actually eliminates the various discriminations that women are subjected to. Efforts need to be intensified and multiplied by all quarters. NGOs, the business world, academia and the government have an important role to play in making Mauritius a more just society. If the inequalities that girls/women face in the educational sector remain unaddressed, not only will the women be marginalized further but the country as a whole will lose out since a large part of its economic female potential will remain untapped.

Bibliography

Alladin, I. (1993) *Economic Miracle in the Indian Ocean*, Editions de l'Océan Indien, Mauritius.

Bheenick, R. (1991) 'Beyond structural adjustment', paper presented to seminar on 'Deficit Financing and Economic Management', University of Mauritius.

Bunwaree, S. (1994) *Mauritian Education in a Global Economy*, Editions de l'Océan Indien, Mauritius.

— (1997a) 'Education and exclusion', in *Etude pluridisciplinaire sur l'exclusion a Maurice*, Government Printing Press, Mauritius.

— (1997b) *Gender, Education and Development*, UNDP Discussion Paper No. 1.

Chinapah, V. (1983) *Participation and Performance in Primary Schooling: A Study of Equality of Educational Opportunity in Mauritius*, Institute of International Education, University of Stockholm, Stockholm.

Gulhati, R. and R. Nallari (1990) *Successful Stabilisation and Recovery in Mauritius*, EDI, Policy Cast Series, World Bank, Washington, DC.

Industrial and Vocational Training Board (1995) *Statistics Handbook*, Reduit, Mauritius.

Jaddoo, R. (1997) *Gaining a Competitive Edge*, Quad Printers, Mauritius.

Jeffery, R. and A. Basu (1996) *Girls' Schooling, Women's Autonomy and Fertility Change in South Asia*, Sage, New Delhi.

Jones, H. (1989) 'Fertility decline in Mauritius: the role of Malthusian population pressure', *Geoforum*, 30 (3): 323–7.

Khotari, U. and V. Nababsing (1996) *Gender and Industrialisation*, Editions de l'Océan Indien, Mauritius.

Mauritius Examinations Syndicate (1995) *Statistics Handbook*, Reduit, Mauritius.

Milbert, J. G. (1812) *Voyage pittoresque a l'Ile de France, au Cap de Bonne Espérance et l'Ile de Tenneriffe*, 2 vols, A. Nepveu, Paris.

Ministry of Economic Planning and Development (1995) *Vision 2020: National Long Term Perspective Study*, Ministry of Economic Planning and Development, Mauritius.

Ministry of Education (1990) *The Education System of Mauritius: Proposal for Structural Reform* (Ramdoyal Report), Ministry of Education, Mauritius.

— (1991) *Master Plan for Education*, Ministry of Education, Mauritius.

— (1995) White Paper on Education, Ministry of Education and Human Resource Development, Mauritius.

Ministry of Employment (1988) *Bi-Annual Survey of Employment and Earnings*, Ministry of Employment, Mauritius.

Ministry of Women's Rights (1995), *Women in Figures*, Ministry of Women's Rights, Mauritius.

Tinker, H. (1974) *A New System of Slavery: The Export of Indian Labour Overseas, 1830–1920*, Oxford University Press, Oxford.

UNDP (1995) *Human Development Report 1995*, Oxford University Press, New York.

University of Mauritius (1989) *The Private Costs of Education/Private Tuition*, Government Printers, Mauritius.

World Bank (1994) *Technology Strategy for Competitiveness*, World Bank, Washington, DC.

CHAPTER 10

Gender Inequality in Educational Attainment in Peninsular Malaysia

Suet-ling Pong

During the 1990s, international agencies adopted the active promotion of girls' access to education as a development strategy. Since 1987, the World Bank has intensified its efforts to enhance the role of women in development (WID) through its lending, sectoral analysis, and research in the area of education and training, as well as in health and family planning (DaVanzo and Haaga 1991). The 1994 International Conference on Population and Development (ICPD) and the 1995 women's summit in Beijing, both held under the auspices of the United Nations, identified the urgency of improving women's access to education as a means to development. According to the Commission on the Status of Women, '[i]nvesting in educational opportunities for girls yields perhaps the best returns of all investments in developing countries'. One of their recommendations is that a 'substantial increase be advocated in donor agencies' allocations for narrowing the *gender gap* in education and training' (United Nations 1995; emphasis added).

The call for reducing the gender gap in education has empirical justifications. The gap has been found to be negatively related to the economic growth and social well-being of a country. A 1993 study showed that the narrower the gender differential in education, the higher a country's GNP per capita and the longer the male life expectancy. A smaller gender gap also lowers the infant mortality rate and the total fertility rate (King and Hill 1993). Despite such evidence from quantitative analysis, the theoretical bases for the effects of educational gender gaps on development are weak and *ad hoc*. Nevertheless, the World Bank and other funding agencies, such as the Rockefeller Foundation, continue to support the use of the gender gap as a development indicator or definition of women's status (Mason 1985).

John Knodel and Gavin Jones (1996) have contended that the international population policy that emphasizes the gender gap in education as a means to achieve sustainable development has missed the mark. They argue, using evidence from Thailand and Vietnam, that the gender gap in educational attainment is narrowing everywhere, and that in some developing countries it is non-existent. In the countries studied by Knodel and Jones, educational differentials are much more pronounced between different socio-economic groups than between boys and girls.

This chapter examines that claim by studying the gender gap in educational attainment in Peninsular Malaysia. I first present a brief history of Malaysia, emphasizing the fact that Malaysia is a multi-ethnic society, with its development closely tied to the social, economic and cultural development of its three ethnic communities. Second, I present the development of girls' education in both the colonial and post-colonial periods. I then use data from the Malaysian Family Life Survey to argue that the focus on gender equality in educational attainment often masks educational inequality by social class and ethnicity. Finally, I discuss the disappearing gender gap in education in the larger historical and political context of Malaysia.

Peninsular Malaysia: its history and people

Historians tend to begin the history of Malaysia by referring to the rise of a great entrepôt, Melaka (Malacca), on the east coast of today's Peninsular Malaysia in around 1400. Peninsular Malaysia was then part of the Malay archipelago, and participated in a complex trading network stretching from Africa to China. At that time, the inhabitants in the coastal regions of the Malay Peninsula were descendants of Proto-Malays from the neighbouring Thai and Indonesian Islands. Malaysia's colonial period began in 1511, when Malacca was conquered by the Portuguese, who were replaced by the Dutch in 1641. The year 1786 marked the beginning of the British colonial period, when a British force occupied Penang and made it the outpost for the British along the Straits of Malacca for the purpose of trade and use as a military base (Andaya and Andaya 1982; Ariffin 1992).

To maintain a stable colonial rule, the British adopted a non-interference policy, aimed at minimum Westernization of the Malay population. The Malay sultans were granted special status over their land and subjects. Concurrently, the colonial government adopted an open immigration policy aimed at attracting foreign labour to participate in the flourishing European trade and commerce. Partly attracted by work opportunities, and partly to escape political turmoil at home, peasants and merchants from southern China began to migrate in large number to Malaya. Most immigrants came as merchants or as labourers working in tin mines. Labourers were also imported as field-hands from Madras and Southern India by British plantation owners after a rubber boom in 1910. It was not until 1929 that the British began to control immigration (Waston 1980). By that time the Chinese and Indian immigrants already formed two distinct minorities.

For convenience of administration, the British adopted a divide-and-rule strategy by confining these three culturally diverse populations to distinct geographical areas, allowing little chance of interaction and assimilation (Takei, Bock and Saunders 1973).

The year 1957 marked the independence of the Federation of Malaya, and the implementation of the Merdeka Independence Constitution, which affirmed the citizenship and the special privileged status of Malays. In return for recognizing the special position of Malays, Chinese and Indians were granted citizenship as long as they were born in Malaysia or had lived in Malaysia for a specified length of time (Govindasamy 1991).

Peninsular Malaysia today is a multi-ethnic society in which 59 per cent are of Malay ethnicity. The Chinese and Indian minorities make up about 31 per cent and 10 per cent, respectively (Department of Statistics 1992). The British policies resulted in the demarcation of Peninsular Malaysia's three ethnic groups, which continue to differ by language, religion and culture. Malays are largely Muslims; the Indians are predominantly Hindu; the Chinese include Taoists, Christians and Buddhists. Intermarriage is rare. A non-Muslim must convert to Islam in order to marry a Malay, and a Malay woman marrying into a non-Muslim family risks disinheritance.

Female education in colonial Malaysia

It was the British colonial government that first introduced a formal system of secular Malay education. Prior to the introduction of secular schools, schooling for Malay boys meant attendance at Koran classes in the local mosque or becoming a resident pupil in the house of a recognized religious leader (Loh 1975). The first Malay boys' school was established in 1835. There was no formal schooling for girls at that time. Forty-eight years later, in 1883, the first Malay girls' school was established in Johore, followed by another one in Penang in 1884. These were started as Koranic schools for the purpose of teaching prayers in Arabic. At the same time, European missionary schools opened their doors to girls. However, partly because these schools were located in urban areas where few Malays resided, and partly because Malay parents were sceptical about Christian education, few sent their daughters to missionary schools, where the medium of instruction was English. Education of girls in English did not occur until 1907, when the first Malay girl, Sofiah binti Abdullah, entered Bukit Nanas Convent School in Kuala Lumpur (Dancz 1987).

By the end of the 1930s, literacy figures suggested that Malay parents had begun to send their daughters to school, especially to government-assisted primary schools, which used the Malay language as a medium of instruction. In 1938, 56,904 Malay children attended government-assisted primary schools, and about 27 per cent of them were girls. There were 662 vernacular schools for Malay boys but only 126 such schools for

Malay girls. Attrition rates over the six years of primary school were greater for girls than for boys. In 1938, only 24 Malay girls but 479 boys were enrolled in the final year of primary school (Dancz 1987; Ariffin 1992). This gender gap remained substantial throughout the colonial period.

Almost without exception, educated Malay women became teachers, and female teachers were the driving force for increasing education opportunities for Malay girls. The year 1929 saw the first teachers' union organized by women teachers under the leadership of Ibu Zain. During the 1930s, its members travelled throughout Malay villages to urge parents to send their daughters to school. Prior to 1935, no education for girls was provided in the Malay language beyond the primary level. With efforts from this group of women teachers, the Malay Women's Training College (MWTC) was established in Malacca in 1935, providing two years of schooling beyond the primary level. The call to educate Malay girls, led by a group of teachers, was the major women's issue before the Second World War (Dancz 1987).

As for non-Malay immigrants' education, the colonial government adopted a *laisser-faire* policy. During the early colonial period, the Christian missionaries were active in providing formal education to the European community residing in Malaysia. Chinese and Indian boys patronized missionary schools, which were established in urban areas where these two ethnic groups were concentrated. However, for the majority of Chinese and Indian girls, formal education proceeded very slowly.

For Chinese girls, education was provided by the Chinese vernacular schools, English-medium private schools, the Singapore Chinese Girls' School and the missionary schools. The first Chinese girls' primary school was the Kuen Cheng Girls' School in Kuala Lumpur, which began admitting students in 1908 (Loh 1975). Like parents of other ethnic groups, Chinese parents held a traditional view about a woman's place. They saw no benefit in educating their daughters, and therefore did not take advantage of girls' education. After the Chinese Revolution in 1911, Chinese education in Malaysia extended somewhat and clearly broke from its traditional practice to educate girls. Nevertheless, the Chinese gender gap in literacy rates was high in 1931. Fewer than 112 Chinese females per 1,000 were literate, compared to 408 Chinese males. These rates were slightly more favourable than the overall literacy rate: 76 per 1,000 for women and 355 per 1,000 for men (Dancz 1987).

Indians relied largely on the patronage of the British rubber plantation owners, who provided them with primary education in Tamil. However, Indian parents seldom sent their daughters to those schools. Not only were there fewer Indian girls in Tamil schools, they were also more likely than boys to drop out from the upper primary classes.

By the time of the Second World War, primary vernacular schools (first to sixth grades) were available in four languages: Malay, English,

Table 10.1 Female enrolment rates, Malaysia, 1938–67

Medium of instruction	1938	1947	1957	1967
Assisted primary schools				
Malay	28.63	28.25	38.07	49.62
English	32.35	34.89	38.85	41.01
Chinese	29.01	28.65	39.87	47.40
Tamil	31.71	38.64	48.48	51.98
Assisted secondary schools				
Malay	n.a.	n.a.	27.69	40.30
English	27.10	25.68	35.36	40.08
Chinese	33.16	27.45	30.77	n.a.
Tamil	40.00	9.68	28.64	n.a.

Note: n.a. = not available.
Source: Rates are calculated from figures in Ariffin 1992.

Chinese and Tamil. Secondary education (seventh to eleventh grades) was available in only English and Chinese, while post-secondary education was available only in English (Waston 1980). Schooling beyond the primary level was unavailable to most Malays, who were educated only in the Malay language. For religious reasons, Malays' participation in English schools was very low. This not only limited their educational opportunities at the higher level, but also prevented them from climbing the occupational ladder, which was closely associated with European trade and commerce.

These developments left Malay girls at a great disadvantage. At the time of independence, in 1957, Malays had fewer years of schooling than Chinese and Indians, regardless of age and gender (Hirschman 1975). Malay girls received less schooling than any other ethnic group. From a historical perspective, however, the gender gap in educational attainment had improved over time from 1938 to the end of the colonial rule (see Table 10.1). In 1957, girls' primary school enrolment reached almost 40 per cent for Malays and Chinese, and well over that figure for Indians. The gender gap in secondary school attainment narrowed somewhat over time, reaching around 28–31 per cent. However, the gap was quite substantial for all groups at the time of independence, and was more so among Malays than any other ethnic group.

Education in the post-independence era

Ethnic politics dominated Malaysia's post-independence education policies. The Malays, who gained political power after independence, tried to improve their education as a legitimate means of attaining upward mobility in order to improve their depressed social and economic position.

Preferential policies in education favouring Malays were implemented. They included educational subsidies and loans, quotas, exclusive admission to certain institutions, use of the Malay language in classroom instruction, and guaranteed employment for Malays with appropriate credentials (Pong 1993, 1995). The Chinese and Indian minorities, on the other hand, feared that their culture and language would be suppressed, and that their economic advantage would disappear as they became less advantaged in education. Ethnic conflict and distrust built up soon after independence, and culminated in the 1969 race riots (Liang 1987).

After the riots, Malays gained further dominance of the ruling party. Preferential policies began to accelerate in response to Malay demands and aspirations. In 1971, the New Economic Policy was implemented. After 20 years of implementation, the premise of the New Economic Policy was extended for another 20 years under the title 'New Development Policy'.

The competition among the three ethnic groups has ramifications for gender equality. As noted above, Malay girls were the most educationally disadvantaged at the time of independence. They naturally became the primary beneficiaries of preferential policies favouring Malays. In fact, by 1967, Malay girls' enrolment rates exceeded those of Chinese girls at the primary level, and were on a par with those of Malay boys. Girls' enrolment rates at the secondary level were the same for both Malays and Chinese (see Table 10.1). Studies of Malaysian education have shown that by the 1980s, the gender gap in educational attainment had virtually disappeared among Malays (Lillard and Willis 1994). The remaining gender gap among non-Malays was small and is largely at the secondary and post-secondary levels (Pong 1993, 1995).

Forms of educational inequality in Malaysia

As the gender gap has virtually disappeared at the primary level and has been substantially reduced at the secondary and post-secondary levels, Malaysia's situation illustrates the validity of Knodel and Jones's contention that the call for gender equality in education misses the mark of a sound development policy. What remains to be seen is whether socio-economic inequality in education is more pronounced than gender inequality, as Knodel and Jones also argued. In this section, I use data from the Second Malaysia Family Life Survey (MFLS-2) to examine gender inequality in education, as compared to other forms of socio-economic inequality.

Most of my analysis in this study is based on children from the main female respondents – the 'Child sample'. Additional data come from the main female respondents and spouses themselves, and I refer to this data source as the 'Adult sample'. The Adult sample includes older individuals aged 40–48, while the Child sample includes young people aged 13–24.

Table 10.2 Percentage of respondents attaining at least the stated level of schooling, Malaysia, 1988

Level of schooling	All	Male	Female	Difference (male–female)
Adult sample (age 40–48, n = 1,338)				
Some primary	84.23	95.00	73.10	21.90
Some secondary	28.84	38.98	18.38	20.60
Upper-secondary	16.66	22.80	10.33	12.47
Child sample[a]				
Some primary	99.28	99.43	99.12	0.31
Some secondary	83.54	85.64	81.33	4.31
Upper-secondary	41.52	42.16	40.83	1.33

Note: [a] Calculation of the completion of primary school is based on a sample of 13–24-year-olds (n = 3,471); completion of lower-secondary school is based on the 16–24-year-olds (n = 2 ,389); completion of upper-secondary school is based on the 18–24-year-olds (n = 1,768).
Source: Second Malaysian Family Life Survey 1988.

Analysis of both of these samples enables us to cover a broad range of birth cohorts.

The diminishing gender gap in education I first examined the percentages of men/boys and women/girls who have attained at least some primary education, some lower-secondary education, and some upper-secondary education. Table 10.2 shows the percentages for both the Child and Adult samples. It is clear that gender differences in educational attainment are more pronounced among the older group than among the younger group. Among the Adult group aged 40–48, only 73.1 per cent of women had some formal schooling, meaning that 26.9 per cent of women never attended school. By contrast, the figure for adult men without formal schooling is only 5 per cent. If we can assume that illiteracy is an indicator for having no formal education, the gender difference in illiteracy rate would be about 22 per cent, large enough to warrant a strong policy to promote gender equality in education.

However, as Knodel and Jones have pointed out, it is often misleading to use adult illiteracy rates to illustrate the status of gender inequality in education, as the rates reflect education situations in the past. What is more appropriate is to examine cohorts of individuals who would have recently completed a stated level of education. Following this line of argument, we need to focus on the attainment rates based on the younger cohorts in the Child sample. In Table 10.2 we can see that the gender gap is very small among the younger cohort: less than half of 1 per cent at the primary level, about 4 per cent at the lower-secondary level, and slightly more than 1 per cent at the upper-secondary level. Compared to the figures of 21.9 per cent, 20.6 per cent, and 12.47 per cent for the respective levels of education among the older cohort, we can conclude that the overall gender gap in educational attainment is disappearing with time in Malaysia.

It is noteworthy that MFLS-2 was fielded ten years ago. Even then, virtually every child (over 99 per cent) aged 13–24 had some formal schooling, and over 80 per cent of the 16–24-year-olds had some lower-secondary education. Upper-secondary education was more limited, but both gender groups appear to have equal chances (see Table 10.2).

Inequality by socio-economic status   While the percentages of girls attaining a stated school level did not differ by gender, they *were* clearly linked to socio-economic status. I illustrate this socio-economic inequality in Figures 10.1 and 10.2, using two indicators: the highest parental education level and family income. Family income is measured by both father's and mother's earned and unearned incomes. Income categories are grouped in quintiles. Primary school attainment is not analysed because virtually everyone in the Child sample attained at least that level.

Figure 10.1 shows that, within each level of parental education, there are few gender differences in lower or upper-secondary school attainment. The largest gender gap is among children whose parents had post-secondary education. Among these individuals, the chance of attaining upper-secondary level is about 9 per cent less for women than that for their male counterparts. Even this gender gap is small when compared to educational inequality by parental education. Figure 10.1 illustrates that a child of either sex whose parent had post-secondary education had a 100 per cent chance of attaining lower-secondary level. A girl whose parent had no schooling had only a 70 per cent chance of attending lower-secondary school. Such socio-economic differences at the upper-secondary level are even more pronounced. Daughters of highly educated parents were more than twice as likely to have attained upper-secondary education as compared with girls with illiterate parents. The educational opportunity of a child is more strongly related to his/her parents' education level than to his/her gender.

Figure 10.2 shows the relationship between children's educational attainment and the other socio-economic status measure, family income. This relationship appears to be curvilinear: children whose families had medium income attained less education than other income groups. This unexpected result may be due to chance: the dispersion of the percentage of children attaining the stated level of schooling is large among children who had a medium family income. Putting this aside, a linear relationship is evident between family income and children's secondary school attainment. Here

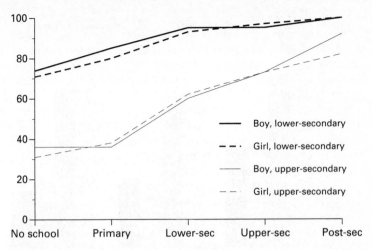

Figure 10.1 Educational attainment by gender and level of schooling as related to parental education (*Source*: Second Malaysian Family Life Survey 1988)

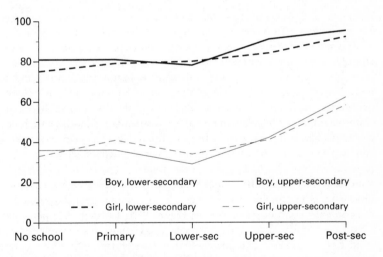

Figure 10.2 Educational attainment by gender and level of schooling as related to family income (*Source*: Second Malaysian Family Life Survey 1988)

again, educational inequality by family income is more pronounced with respect to upper-secondary school attainment than to lower-secondary school attainment.

Both socio-economic indicators presented in Figures 10.1 and 10.2

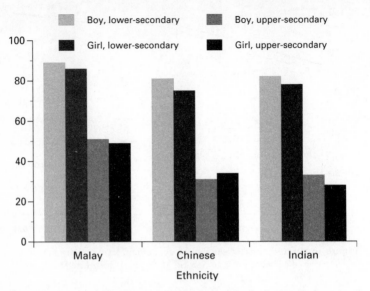

Figure 10.3 Educational attainment by gender and level of schooling as related to ethnic background (*Source*: Second Malaysian Family Life Survey 1988)

highlight the importance of socio-economic status as a correlate with a child's opportunity to attend secondary school. Gender within each socio-economic status appears to be relatively unimportant. These findings resemble those for Thailand and Vietnam in Knodel and Jones's study, despite very different social and political environments in these three Asian countries. The findings in this chapter substantiate Knodel and Jones's claim that, for some countries, the call for reducing gender inequality in education as a tool for development is a misguided policy.

Inequality by ethnicity Since Malaysia's education policies are closely tied to its ethnic politics, it is necessary to examine gender inequality in the context of ethnic inequality. In Figure 10.3, I present the percentage of youth attaining lower and upper-secondary school respectively for each gender. It is evident that Malays entered secondary education in both lower-secondary and upper-secondary levels in greater numbers than Chinese or Indians. About 95 per cent of Malay girls aged 16–24 completed lower-secondary education, and almost 50 per cent of Malay girls aged 18–24 had upper-secondary education. Both percentages are higher than the overall average of 81 per cent and 41 per cent (see Table 10.2). Malay boys have slightly higher rates, but they are not statistically different from those of Malay girls. From Figure 10.3 we can see that the gender gap in lower-secondary education appears to be larger among Chinese and Indians than among Malays. However, even the largest within-ethnicity gender gap is not as large as the gap between ethnic groups. For instance, the gender gap in lower-secondary school attainment is about 5 per cent within the Chinese population. However, the gap between Malay and Chinese boys for lower-secondary is around 8 per cent, and the gap between Malay and Chinese girls is over 10 per cent.

Similarly, the gender gap in attaining upper-secondary school within each ethnic group is relatively small compared with the ethnic gap. While the gender gap is generally less than 5 per cent within ethnic groups, inequality between Malay and Indian girls is almost 20 per cent. Ethnic inequality among boys is smaller, around 17–18 per cent.

Women and development in Malaysia: an anomaly?

The case of Malaysia is particularly intriguing, not only because it is a Muslim country, but because the gender gap closed most rapidly among its Muslim population. The evidence given above suggests that, today, Malay girls attain about the same amount of formal schooling as Malay boys and more than Chinese or Indian girls. Although the disappearing gender gap is not unusual among Southeast Asian countries, such as the former British colony of Hong Kong, South Korea, Taiwan, or Thailand (Post 1994; Knodel 1994), it is rare among Muslim countries. I argue that the dramatic improvement of Malay girls' education is unique in its own right. To understand the forces that dramatically narrowed this gender gap, one needs to examine the status of Malay women from a historical perspective, and to link women's issues to the larger context of government's nation-building policies.

As distinct from the case in Arab countries, Malaysia's Islamic religion did not originate within Malaysia. Muslim Indians spread their religion in the thirteenth century to Southeast Asia through trading in the Malay-Indonesian archipelago (Andaya and Andaya 1982). The import of Islam was characterized by considerable individual variation in piety and religious interest. Purdah, the Islamic custom of secluding women to ensure compliance with social standards of modesty and morality, was not practised until recently. In fact, the Malay traditional custom of *adat* regulated Malay social life more than Islamic influences. At the same time, Islamic law was interpreted in ways to accommodate Malay customs (Dancz 1987). In the state of Kelantan, where the influence of Islam is markedly stronger, various cultural rituals are questioned or condemned by orthodox followers (Winzeler 1985).

In many ways, Malays have a liberal attitude towards gender relations, and Malay women often have at least as much domestic power as their husbands. Malays did not have a patriarchal tradition. Most Malays maintain a bilateral kinship system, and Malays in the state of Negri Sembilan have a matrilineal system. The more common bilateral kinship system attaches equal importance to the mother's and father's kin. Malay descent is traced through both spouses' parents and children do not carry their fathers' surnames in order to continue the family line. Traditionally, landholding was associated almost equally with females and males. Thus Malay parents do not have a strong preference for sons. In fact, sometimes girls are preferred to boys because girls are believed to be more reliable in providing healthcare and security during their parents' old age. This may be why elderly Malay parents tend to live with their daughters rather than sons (DaVanzo and Chan 1994). A married Malay woman, once of childbearing age, is almost of equal status to men. In the northeastern fishing villages, businesswomen frequently control their family budget and make the most important decisions. Divorce was not frowned upon traditionally, and was very high among the Malay population. Shortly after the Second World War, for example, 67 out of every 100 Malay marriages ended in divorce.

This tradition of relatively equal gender relations was a crucial pre-condition for narrowing the gender gap in education among the Muslim Malays. The second precondition was the ethnic diversity in Malaysia and the competition among ethnic groups, which indirectly promoted Malay girls' education. Since 1971 the Malaysian government, which is largely controlled by Malays, has sought to promote the socio-economic status of the majority Malay population. From 1971 to 1991, Malaysia adopted the New Economic Policy, which had two goals: eradicating poverty and 'restructuring' society. The aim of restructuring society is to 'eliminate the identification of race with economic function and geographical location' (*Fifth Malaysian Plan 1986–1990*). To achieve this goal, the Malaysian government has used formal schooling as a legitimate channel for Malays' upward mobility. This is why the school language policy and university admissions became a battleground among ethnic groups. While gender equality was not a goal in the New Economic Policy, the drive for ethnic equality in education nevertheless benefited Malay women the most because they were the most educationally disadvantaged at the time of independence. The competition among ethnic groups tended to outweigh gender differences within groups. In the government's eyes, it was important that all Malays, regardless of gender, had, at the least, as many educational opportunities as other groups. Malay girls are not competing with Malay boys for educational success: they are competing with Chinese and Indian girls. It was ethnic group solidarity that made gender equality so readily acceptable to Malays as a group.

These preconditions – Malay tradition and ethnic competition – became a catalyst for foreign influence. Although Malaysia has been opposed to Western concepts of development, in many instances it is not free from foreign influences. The international call for integrating women in develop-ment, originating from the United Nations, has prompted Malaysia to set up a number of institutions to coordinate programmes and share information about women in development. In 1976, the National Advisory Council on the Integration of Women in Development (NACIWID) was established in the Prime Minister's Department to translate the world plan on women in development in Malaysia. In 1981, Malaysia joined other countries at the first ASEAN Women's Programme meeting held in Jakarta. Subsequently, in 1983, Malaysia set up the National Clearinghouse on Women and Development (NCWD) at the National Population and Family Development Board in the Prime Minister's Department. The NCWD received funding from the United Nations Fund for Population Activities (UNFPA) for three years from 1987 to 1989 to 'enhance awareness on [sic] the role and need of women in the overall development process' (National Clearinghouse on Women in Development, n.d.). Also in 1983, a Secretariat for Women's Affairs (HAWA) was established and placed under the Prime Minister's Department to act as the executive body of NCWD.

Finally, the Malaysia government formulated the National Policy for Women (NPW) in 1989. This national policy, included in the Sixth Malaysian Plan, has the objectives of ensuring equal opportunity by gender of access to resources and information, and of integrating women in all sectors of national development (*Sixth Malaysian Plan 1991–95*). Thus, like other Islamic countries, where the role of women is highly politicized, in Malaysia women's issues also have important symbolic connotations for the state.

Conclusion and discussion

This study presents a historical account of girls' education in Malaysia, and shows the dramatic increase over time in educational attainment in this century, with the disappearance of gender differentials by the time MFLS-2 was fielded in 1988. By that time, virtually every child aged 13–24 completed primary school. Over 80 per cent made the transition to secondary school. These female secondary enrolment rates are higher than the average rates in upper-middle-income countries, which were 25–70 percent in 1988 (King and Hill 1993).

The analysis of MFLS-2 suggests that the focus on gender equality in education masks inequality in access to education by groups of different ethnicity and socio-economic status. The majority group in Malaysia, the Malays, has achieved in promoting girls' education on a par with that of boys, but this is not the case for the minority groups. Even where a gender gap exists among minority groups, it is clearly smaller than the gap between the majority and minority groups, regardless of their gender. Also, gender differences are similar among the wealthy and the poor. However, the poor, boys and girls alike, clearly suffer from lower educational opportunities.

The disappearing gender inequality in education among the Muslim Malays can be explained by their traditional practices, as well as by the fact that Malays as a group were often in competition with other ethnic minority groups. It is the interrelationship between gender and ethnicity in Malaysia that provided the necessary precondition for international influence. The Malaysian government's national policy on women did not occur in a vacuum.

To the extent that education leads to economic power, one would expect that the diminishing gender gap in education reduces the unbalanced economic power between men and women. As elsewhere, Malaysian female workers earn less, on average, than their male counterparts. The female–male earnings ratio was 0.52 in 1988 among the older cohort aged 45–54. In other words, female workers were paid about half that paid to male workers. However, the female–male earnings ratio increased with workers' age, and was about 0.83 among the cohort aged 25–34. If the comparison of female–male wages is restricted to full-time employment in the non-farm sector, the earnings ratio among the cohort aged 25–34 is quite high, around 0.95 (Banerji, Mehotra and Parish 1993). Apparently, the evidence of a diminishing gender gap in education is associated with a diminishing gender gap in wages.

However, the female–male earnings gap differed by ethnicity. Even among young men and women aged 25–34, Chinese female workers' earnings were only 58 per cent of Chinese men's, while Malay women earned exactly the same as Malay men (Banerji, Mehotra and Parish 1993). The small Chinese gender gap in education presented above was unlikely to be a major cause of the pronounced gender earnings inequality among Chinese. The nature of the forces that produced different female–male earnings differentials for different ethnic groups is not completely clear. One explanation is that the patriarchal norms embedded in the family and the workplace are much stronger for Chinese than for Malays. Thus in the private sector, Chinese employers are more likely to discriminate against female workers than are Malay employers. Also, Chinese parents are less willing than Malay parents to transfer family resources to help their daughters set up private businesses.

Another, more plausible, explanation lies in the political economy of the state. Because of the government's preferential policies, educated Malay women are able to move quickly into professional and managerial occupations, most of which are provided in the public sector. Earnings in the public sector are higher than those in the private sector, based on educational credentials and seniority. As Malay women enjoy equal education with Malay men, their education also leads to equal earning power. All in all, the unequal access to education and public sector occupations by Malaysia's minority groups produce what Banerji, Mehrotra and Parish call 'a double disadvantage' facing Chinese women in Malaysia (Banerji,

Mehotra and Parish 1993: 19). In the wage sector, Chinese women did not have the preferential policies edge enjoyed by Malay women, and in the non-wage sector they are disadvantaged relative to Chinese men in their access to family resources. My analysis here suggests that gender inequality in Malaysia is a complex issue embedded in a larger political, economic and cultural context inseparable from its colonial past.

Bibliography

Andaya, B. W. and L. Y. Andaya (1982) *A History of Malaysia*, Macmillan, London.

Ariffin, J. (1992) *Women and Development in Malaysia*, Pelankduk Publications, Selangor Darul Ehsan, Malaysia.

Banerji, R., N. Mehotra and W. L. Parish (1993) *Gender Wage Gap in Malaysia and Taiwan*, Report No. 93-1, Population Research Center Discussion Paper Series, NORC and University of Chicago, Chicago, IL.

Dancz, V. H. (1987) *Women and Party Politics in Peninsular Malaysia*, Oxford University Press, Oxford.

DaVanzo, J. and J. Haaga (1991) *Women in Development: Issues for the Latin American and Caribbean Region*, Report No. 2, Latin America and the Caribbean Technical Department Regional Studies Program, RAND, Santa Monica, CA.

DaVanzo, J. and A. Chan (1994) 'Living arrangements of older Malaysians: who coreside with their adult children', *Demography* 15 (1).

Department of Statistics (1992) *Yearbook of Statistics 1991*, Government of Malaysia, Kuala Lumpur.

Fifth Malaysian Plan 1986–1990 (1986), National Printing Department, Kuala Lumpur.

Govindasamy, P. (1991) *Ethnic Fertility Differentials in Peninsular Malaysia: The Impact of Government Policies*, doctoral thesis, Department of Sociology, Michigan State University, Michigan.

Hirschman, C. (1975) *Ethnic and Social Stratification in Peninsular Malaysia*, Monograph Series, American Sociological Association, Washington, DC.

King, E. M. and A. Hill (eds) (1993) *Women's Education in Developing Countries: Barriers, Benefits, and Policies*, Johns Hopkins University Press/World Bank, Baltimore, MD.

Knodel, J. (1994) *Gender and Schooling in Thailand*, Working Papers No. 64, Population Council, New York.

Knodel, J. and G. W. Jones (1996) 'Post-Cairo population policy: does promoting girls' schooling miss the mark?', *Population and Development Review* 22 (4), December.

Liang, Y. (1987) 'Malaysia's new economic policy and the Chinese community', *Review of Indonesian and Malaysian Affairs* 21.

Lillard, L. A. and R. J. Willis (1994) 'Intergenerational educational mobility: effects of family and state in Malaysia', *Journal of Human Resources* 29 (4), Fall.

Loh, P. F. S. (1975) *Seeds of Separatism: Educational Policy in Malaysia 1874–1940*, Oxford University Press, Oxford.

Mason, K. O. (1985) *The Status of Women: A Review of its Relationships to Fertility and Mortality*, Rockefeller Foundation, New York.

National Clearinghouse on Women in Development (n.d.), 'National Clearinghouse on Women in Development (Malaysia)', Kuala Lumpur.

Pong, S. (1993) 'Preferential policies and secondary school attainment in Peninsular Malaysia', *Sociology of Education* 66, October.

— (1994) 'Sex preference and fertility in Peninsular Malaysia', *Studies in Family Planning* 25 (3), May/June.

— (1995) 'Access to education in Peninsular Malaysia: ethnicity, social class and gender', *Compare* 25 (3).

Post, D. (1994) 'Education stratification, school expansion, and public policy in Hong Kong', *Sociology of Education* 67 (2), April.

Saw, Swee-hock (1988) *The Population of Peninsular Malaysia*, Singapore University Press, Singapore.

Sixth Malaysian Plan 1991–1995 (1991), National Printing Department, Kuala Lumpur.

Takei, Y., J. C. Bock and B. Saunders (1973) *Educational Sponsorship by Ethnicity: A Preliminary Analysis of the West Malaysian Experience*, Southeast Asian Program Papers in International Studies, Southeast Asia Series, 28, Ohio University Center for International Studies, Athens, OH.

United Nations (1995) *Priority Themes: Development Promotion of Literacy, Education and Training, Including Technology Skills*, Report of the Secretary-General, Commission on the Status of Women, document released in electronic format, United Nations, New York.

Waston, J. K. P. (1980) 'Cultural pluralism, nation-building and educational policies in Peninsular Malaysia', *Journal of Multilingual and Multicultural Development* 1 (2).

Winzeler, R. L. (1985) *Ethnic Relations in Kelantan: A Study of Chinese and Thai as Ethnic Minorities in a Malay State*, East Asian Social Science Monographs, Oxford University Press, Oxford.

PART FOUR

South Asian Contrasts

CHAPTER 11

Gender, Education, Development: Sri Lanka

Swarna Jayaweera

'Modern' educational institutions were established in Sri Lanka under British colonial rule in the nineteenth century. Privileged groups enjoyed an elitist education, which led to remunerative employment in the colonial economy. With universal franchise in 1931, national policy-makers embarked on programmes to reduce socio-economic inequalities. In the 1940s a package of free education and health services and subsidized food was introduced and the demographic transition to low mortality and fertility rates followed. Thus the reforms contributed to the relatively high physical quality of life indicators (PQLI) in the contemporary period in a low-income country with low economic growth.

Policy framework

Free education at primary, secondary and tertiary levels was introduced in 1945. The private sector in education shrank to about 2 per cent of the school age population. An island-wide system of scholarships, free midday meals and subsidized transport to schools provided further incentives to less affluent parents. The mother tongue (Sinhala/Tamil) was enforced as the medium of instruction in primary schools in 1945, progressively in secondary schools in the 1950s, and in many of the faculties in the universities in the 1960s to extend equal educational opportunity to all social strata.

The network of schools grew from 4,537 in 1945 to 8,937 in 1963. Central schools offering free secondary education to aspiring rural students from 'feeder' primary schools in the neighbourhood became agents of upward mobility in the occupational hierarchy. Co-educational schools increased to 89.2 per cent in 1963 and to 96.5 per cent by the 1980s. Single-sex schools remained in major urban centres for children of elite and middle-class families. In 1942 the University of Ceylon was established by amalgamating the university and the medical college. Vocational education has been a low priority throughout the period. Public educational expenditure rose from 2.9 per cent of the GDP in 1950 to 4.6 per cent in 1964/65, with 16 per cent of the national budget allocated to education, rising to 20 per cent. With economic stagnation in the 1970s the percentage of GDP fell back to 3.5 per cent (Alailima 1995).

Progress slowed in the 1980s, particularly with the implementation of the IMF–World Bank-sponsored structural adjustment programmes. Reduction in social sector expenditure led to the allocation of around only 2 per cent of GDP in the mid-1980s and even less in the early 1990s, and to 6 per cent to 8 per cent of the national budget for education. The 'delivery system' developed in the earlier decades survived under great strain but the quality of infrastructure, services and content deteriorated. While primary schools of varying quality are available to around 80 per cent of children within 2 kilometres of their homes, the expansion of quality secondary education was stymied. Only 5.4 per cent of the approximately 10,000 schools in the country offer senior secondary education in the full spectrum of subject areas, including science. Educational opportunities are inequitably distributed, with fewer than 2 per cent of such schools in economically disadvantaged districts.

Policy changes such as the abrupt liberalization of the economy in 1977, decontrol of prices, devaluation of currency, reduction in subsidies and the conversion of food rations to unindexed food stamps led to spiralling costs of living. The incidence of poverty rose from an estimated 19 per cent in 1979 to 27 per cent in 1987 (Edirisinghe 1990). The state attempted to mitigate the consequences of these harsh measures by providing free textbooks up to Grade 10 (1980), support for school midday meals (1989) and two free uniforms per year (1993). Yet increases in the incidence of child prostitution and child labour and in the number of street children are manifestations of the impact of these policies on the children of vulnerable groups. The juxtaposition of policies that increased disproportionately the burdens of women and children (Commonwealth Secretariat 1989; CENWOR 1995) with special ameliorative measures reflects the dualism in the IMF–World Bank policy package, which increased poverty through macro-economic policies and subsequently added poverty alleviation projects as artificial appendages. Meanwhile the pressure on the state to introduce 'cost recovery' and 'user fees', and to give primacy to market forces in education, threatens, albeit unsuccessfully as yet, to erode the social gains of the past decades.

Sadly, the country has also been engulfed in social conflict with insurgent youth in the south in the late 1980s and ethnic conflict for over a decade in the north and east. Defence expenditure has escalated. Disruption and trauma among families in the conflict areas have affected educational opportunities.

In recent years the positive international climate has created a momentum for policies to promote equal educational opportunities. The ratification of the UN Convention on the Rights of the Child (1989), the endorsement of the Jomtien Declaration on Education for All (1990), and the World Declaration on the Survival and Development of Children (1990) resulted in the formulation in Sri Lanka of a Plan of Action for Children and a Children's Charter (1992). Sri Lanka's Women's Charter, formulated and accepted as national policy in 1993, was based on the UN Convention on the Elimination of All Forms of Discrimination Against Women (CEDAW), which was ratified in 1981. In the South Asian region many girls are severely disadvantaged, except in Sri Lanka and the Maldives. The South Asian Association for Regional Cooperation (SAARC) Year of the Girl Child (1990) and the SAARC Decade of the Girl Child (1991–2000) stimulated interest in the education and all-round development of girls. In Sri Lanka, 1997 was named the 'year of educational reform' and compulsory education for the 5–14 year age group, more equitable distribution of senior secondary education opportunities, curriculum reforms and university reforms were introduced.

Educational experiences of girls and women

While gender differences in access to education have been virtually eliminated in Sri Lanka, the educational experiences of girls and women are often affected by their location in the social structure.

Only 3.5 per cent of rural schools are well-equipped senior secondary schools, as compared with 23.2 per cent of the urban schools. Around 15 per cent of the country's schools are small and impoverished, but the percentage of such schools is as high as 30 per cent in less developed districts and rural areas.

The high aspirations of parents for the education of their sons and daughters and the aspirations of girls themselves have ensured near gender equality in enrolment. At the last census in 1981, 83.6 per cent of girls and 83.7 per cent of boys in the 5–14 age group and 42.7 per cent of girls and 41.2 per cent of boys in the 15–19 age group were enrolled in schools (see Table 11.1) Since then participation rates in the 15–19 age group and 20–24 age group have been virtually stagnant due to the rising costs of living.

In 1991 average years of schooling were 10 years (male) and 9.7 years (female) among the most affluent and 5.4 years (male) and 5 years (female) among the poorest (World Bank 1994). Around 8 per cent of children never enter the system. The incidence of 'dropping out' is high at secondary level. 'Drop-out' rates are slightly higher for boys, largely because they have easier access to employment. The major reason for non-schooling is poverty – the cost and opportunity costs of education. Poor families do not have the capacity to support their children through secondary and tertiary education despite the wide range of incentives that have been

Table 11.1 Urban and rural educational participation rates, Sri Lanka, 1981

	Total			Urban			Rural		
	Total	Male	Female	Total	Male	Female	Total	Male	Female
5–9	84.4	84.5	84.2	86.6	86.4	86.9	83.8	84.1	83.6
10–14	82.4	82.9	81.8	85.2	86.4	84.4	81.6	82.1	81.1
5–14	83.7	83.7	83.6	85.9	86.4	85.6	82.7	83.1	82.4
15–19	41.9	41.2	42.7	46.7	44.9	48.0	40.6	40.02	41.3
20–24	8.9	8.7	9.0	9.7	9.4	10.2	8.7	9.1	8.7
5–24	55.8	56.0	55.6	56.6	55.3	57.3	55.7	56.3	55.1

Source: Based on Census Report 1981.

Table 11.2 Age-specific enrolment rates in Sri Lankan schools by gender, 1991

Age group	Male (%)	Female (%)	Total (%)
5–9	90.1	87.3	88.7
10–14	86.6	87.5	87.1
5–14	88.3	87.4	87.9
15–19	37.5	42.6	39.9
20–22	3.1	4.6	3.8
5–22	62.1	63.4	62.8

Note: Excludes North and part of Eastern Province. Data based on population projections.
Source: School Census 1991, Ministry of Education, Statistics Division.

Table 11.3 Enrolment in Sri Lankan schols by level and gender, 1985 and 1993

School years	1985			1993		
	Total enrolment	Female enrolment	Female (%)	Total enrolment	Female enrolment	Female (%)
1–5	1,898,434	914,209	48.2	1,979,968	954,766	48.2
6–8	850,421	421,354	49.5	1,094,051	540,868	49.4
9–11	758,440	397,719	52.4	906,494	470,494	51.9
6–11	1,608,856	819,073	50.9	2,000,452	1,011,362	50.5
12–13						
Science	49,144	22,682	46.2	46,551	21,176	45.5
Arts	49,924	35,186	70.5	89,031	61,183	68.7
Commerce	33,722	18,836	55.9	55,563	28,278	50.9
Total	132,790	76,704	57.8	191,144	110,647	57.9
1–13	3,640,080	1,809,986	49.7	4,172,897	2,077,282	49.8

Source: Annual School Census, Ministry of Education.

provided. Non-attendance is concentrated chiefly in pockets of disadvantage in low-income urban neighbourhoods and remote or deprived villages and plantations. The labour inputs of girls are required for household chores and childcare in families where the mothers are employed, and for income support, chiefly in domestic service in affluent homes, in agriculture, or, in the case of older girls, in low-skill, low-pay jobs in industry (Jayaweera 1993a).

Performance levels in education appear also to illustrate the nexus between socio-economic background, school facilities and achievement. Studies have indicated that gender differences hardly exist in abilities. A test of competencies at entry level to schools at five years found that the total index was higher for girls and that boys scored higher in only one of the nine tests of different competencies (Abhayadeva 1991).

University education is the apex of the education system and the goal of around 85 per cent of secondary school students of both sexes. (Rupesinghe 1991). The number of universities has increased from one in 1942 to twelve in 1996, with the social composition of the university becoming more egalitarian following the abolition of fees and changes in the medium of instruction. The percentage of women students has increased from 10.1 per cent in 1942 to about 45 per cent since 1970.

The universities are highly selective. Students qualify at a very competitive GCE Advanced Level examination and are then selected on cut-off marks based on a quota system of 40 per cent merit, 55 per cent district and 5 per cent disadvantaged district quotas. Only around 20 per cent of qualified candidates gain admission, breeding considerable frustration among aspirants and confining university education to around 3 per cent of the 20–24 age group. Admission statistics indicate that while a higher percentage of girls than boys qualify for admission, a lower percentage of girls than boys of those qualified are admitted on the basis of the complex admission criteria.

Micro-processes of learning and socialization

The Sri Lankan education system has been examination-centred for over a century, and co-curricular activities have been virtually crowded out of institutional programmes in an increasingly competitive ethos dominated by imperatives of academic success. A common curriculum has been organized for Grades 1 to 11 with uniform curricula, textbooks, and guidelines for teachers prepared by the national curriculum development authority, thus stifling teacher initiative and student creativity. Streaming into arts, science and commerce courses occurs in Grades 12 and 13, with little flexibility in options directly linked to university courses.

This dominance of rote learning in a context in which girls have relatively less access than boys to out-of-school 'recreational' programmes has meant that girls have less opportunity for all-round personality development through activities that involve creativity, initiative and group participation. One study found that 40 per cent of school-age girls did not participate in extra-curricular activities in schools, while 71 per cent of the 15–17 age group had spent their evenings in private tuition classes in examination subjects (Jayaweera 1993a). Those who did so were engaged in sports, music, dancing, drama and handiwork (Jayaweera, Sanmugam, Jayatileke and Mendis 1992).

Certain education processes reinforce gender role stereotypes that perpetuate inequality. A common curriculum in life skills in the first two years of secondary school is followed by home science for girls and woodwork and metalwork for boys. The percentage of girls enrolling in science courses in Grades 12 to 13 is lower than that of those selecting arts courses. Moreover, girls tend to be enrolled in biological science courses required for medical-related employment while boys are concentrated in physical science courses that are avenues to technology-related employment.

Unlike other South Asian countries there is no strong 'son preference' in Sri Lanka. Nevertheless, girls experience a dual agenda in socialization. Both at home and at school girls are expected to be passive, modest and obedient. In one study (Jayaweera 1993c) adolescent girls perceived that they were restricted in physical mobility and social behaviour and that parents did not approve of girls choosing their own marriage partner. The majority of these girls had internalized stereotypical behaviour, the unequal gender division of labour within the household and the concept of gender-appropriate jobs. They had a low level of self-confidence and felt inferior to boys. They were not convinced that they should exercise their autonomy in selecting marriage partners. However, they rejected patriarchal control of the household, believed in joint decision-making by spouses and in achieving economic independence, and were confident in confronting problems as individuals rather than as girls.

These contradictions stem from the dual agenda of high educational and vocational aspirations and socialization in passivity and 'femininity'. They reflect the absence of overt gender discrimination juxtaposed with the impact of gender role assumptions based on presumed gender differences. The study indicates that all girls do not necessarily conform to stereotypes and that the instrumental value of education has an overarching influence. It also underscores the fact that education at all levels has not empowered the majority of girls and women to challenge social norms and practices that negate human dignity and women's rights.

Distribution of skills

Studies over four decades have noted that the aspirations of secondary schoolgirls have not changed, with primacy given to teaching, medical-

Table 11.4 Distribution of Sri Lankan students by faculty, 1985/86 and 1991/92

Faculties	1985/86			1991/92		
	Total	Female	F (%)	Total	Female	F (%)
Medicine	2,345	1,009	43.02	3,869	1,662	42.9
Dentistry	289	161	55.7	407	212	52.1
Veterinary science	170	73	42.9	261	115	44.1
Agriculture	775	279	36.0	1,517	676	44.6
Engineering	1,762	264	14.9	3,082	377	12.2
Architecture	108	49	45.4	211	100	47.4
Science	3,125	1,306	41.8	5,604	2,330	41.6
Management studies	3,367	1,426	42.3	5,555	2,450	44.1
Law	461	219	47.5	924	526	56.9
Social science/humanities	6,511	3,377	51.9	9,207	5,144	55.9
Total	18,913	8,160	43.1	30,637	13,592	44.4
Total: prof. science-based courses	5,449	1,835	33.7	9,347	3,142	33.6
Total: science courses	3,125	1,306	41.8	5,604	2,330	41.6
Total: arts-based courses	10,339	5,019	48.5	15,686	8,120	51.8

Source: Statistical Handbook 1985, 1990, University Grants Commission, Planning Division.

related employment and secretarial services (Green 1952; Jayaweera 1976; Rupasinghe 1991). While there are no legal barriers to entry to any programme, the gender distribution of university students among faculties indicates a relatively high percentage of women students in arts, law, medical-related, and in recent years, agriculture and management courses, and low and static representation in engineering courses over two decades. (see Table 11.4). At the tertiary level, the main alternatives to university education are programmes associated with servicing and nurturing roles such as teacher education, paramedical services, library services, social work, accountancy, management and computer services.

Despite the increasing dominance of technology in the economy vocational education remains poorly developed in Sri Lanka, with wide gender imbalances in vocational training programmes. Seventy per cent of women students in technical colleges have opted to follow commerce-related courses and a small proportion enrol in technical courses. There are also a very small number of innovative vocational programmes provided by NGOs to train women for non-traditional jobs (Jayaweera 1991b, 1995b). The consequence of these gender imbalances is that women are equipped with a narrow range of skills, further disadvantaging them in seeking employment in a country that is endeavouring to industrialize rapidly.

Gender dimensions of education and development

A major objective of the International Decade for Women (1976–85) was 'to integrate women in development'. This phrase becomes a shibboleth in economically developing countries such as Sri Lanka, in which women have always been integrated in development on unequal terms. Dichotomous perceptions of the 'reproductive' and 'productive' roles of women have had their repercussions in the differential impact of social and economic development programmes on women and men.

Far-sighted 'social' policies that focused on the extension of educational opportunity to all social strata have produced a relatively literate female population (see Table 11.5) able to access health and family planning services extensively. Outcomes of the rising educational levels of women have been a steep decline in death rates to 6 per 1,000, and particularly in infant mortality rates to 15 per 1,000 and maternal mortality rates to 0.6 per 100,000, and a steady decline in the annual average population growth rate from 2.3 per cent in the 1950s to 1.2 per cent in the 1990s. Life expectancy has risen to 70 years for men and 74 years for women – all indicators that are favourable in the context of slow economic growth. Their participation in education and employment has delayed marriage to an average of 25 years for women, and rising educational levels have increased contraceptive use, contributing to reducing family size (Abeykoon 1996; Caldwell 1996).

The PQLI was estimated to be 79.7 per cent for men and 78.1 per cent for women by the 1970s. Women have benefited from the intrinsic value of education in widening their horizons. In the political sphere they have exercised their right to vote *en masse*, but few have sought to contest national or local elections. The percentage of women in the national assembly – now parliament – was only 5 per cent in 1931 and 5 per cent at the last general elections in 1994, although Sri Lanka had the world's first woman prime minister in 1960 and currently both the executive president and prime minister are women. There appears to be no correlation between education and political participation, and middle-class professional women are generally cynical about politics (De Silva et al. 1994).

Neither macro- nor micro-studies have found a positive linear relationship between education and employment among women. Women have always made a crucial contribution to household and national economies. Until the 1960s access to education facilitated their entry to the higher levels of the occupational hierarchy, but the relationship between educational attainment and employment has become increasingly complex for women in recent decades. The female labour force has increased rapidly since the 1960s, largely due to the rising educational levels of women and economic pressures on families. Since then falling commodity prices and the consequent low absorptive capacity of the economy have created

Table 11.5 Literacy by sector and gender, Sri Lanka, 1946–91

	Census 1946	Census 1953	Census 1963	Census 1971	CF&SE Survey 1981/82	Census 1981	LF&SE Survey 1985/86	HI&E Survey 1991
All island								
Total	62.8	69.0	76.8	78.5	85.4	86.5	84.2	86.9
Male	76.5	80.7	85.6	85.6	89.9	90.5	88.6	90.0
Female	46.2	55.5	67.1	70.9	81.1	82.8	80.0	83.8
Urban								
Total	76.2	82.6	87.7	86.2	89.7	93.3	89.1	92.3
Male	84.5	88.5	91.8	90.3	92.9	95.3	92.4	94.0
Female	65.7	74.1	82.7	81.5	89.8	91.0	86.1	90.6
Rural[1]								
Total	60.1	66.4	70.1	76.2	86.0	84.5	84.6	87.1
Male	74.7	79.0	83.9	84.1	90.1	89.0	88.5	89.9
Female	43.0	52.4	63.6	67.9	82.1	79.9	80.7	84.3
Estate								
Total					64.8		59.4	66.1
Male					78.0		74.5	79.0
Female					52.6		45.9	52.8

Note: 1. Estate sector included in rural in Census.

CF & SE Survey: Consumer Finances and Socio-economic Survey, Central Bank of Ceylon.

LF & SE Survey: Labour Finance and Socio-economic Survey.

HI & E: Household Income and Expenditure.

Source: Department of Census and Statistics, Central Bank of Ceylon.

massive unemployment. Structural adjustment programmes fuelled the growing demand for low-cost female labour in the 1980s and 1990s. The female labour participation rate increased from 25.8 per cent in 1980 to 39.4 per cent in 1990 (Labour Force Surveys 1980/81, 1990) and the female labour force in the 20–34 age group almost doubled in the 1980s, but at all educational levels – that is, regardless of educational attainment. High unemployment has been a significant feature in Sri Lanka since the late 1960s, but female unemployment rates have been at least double male unemployment rates consistently – 8.8 per cent (male) and 19.7 per cent (female) in 1995 (see Table 11.6). Another trend has been the poor absorption of youth or entrants into the labour market. In the labour force in 1995 31 per cent of men and 48 per cent of women in the 15–19 age group, 26 per cent and 41 per cent respectively in the 20–24 age group and 12 per cent and 26 per cent respectively in the 25–29 age group were unemployed (Labour Force Survey 1995). Unemployment rates are higher for both men and women secondary school leavers and university

Table 11.6 Unemployment rates, Sri Lanka, 1963–95

Year	Total	Male	Female
1963[1]	7.3	8.9	7.6
1971[2]	18.7	14.3	31.1
1980/81[3]	15.8	12.4	23.0
1985/86[4]	14.1	10.8	20.8
1990 1st quarter[5]	14.0	9.1	23.4
1990 quarters 2–4[6]		11.8	23.4
1995 2nd quarter[7]	11.9	8.8	18.4

Notes: 1. Census of Ceylon 1963; 2. Census of Ceylon 1971; 3. Labour Force and Socio-Economic Survey 1980/81; 4. Labour Force and Socio-Economic Survey 1985/86; 5. Labour Force Survey 1990 1st quarter – all island; 6. Labour Force Survey 1990 2nd–4th quarters – excluding Northern and Eastern Provinces; 7. Labour Force Survey 1995, 2nd quarter, excluding Northern and Eastern Provinces.
Source: Department of Census and Statistics, Colombo.

graduates than for the non-schooled or primary school leavers, but female unemployment rates have been and are much higher than male rates in the former group (see Table 11.7). The highest female economic activity rates are those of plantation women workers, who have the lowest literacy rates and educational attainment.

A new phenomenon has been the vocational trained unemployed, and around one-fifth of the unemployed have received some form of vocational training, mainly at craft level (Alailima 1992). These young women seek training in one centre after another while making unsuccessful efforts to find jobs, but are then compelled to be unemployed or to seek employment as overseas domestic labour (Jayaweera 1991b). Besides their vulnerability to unemployment, it appears that the employment opportunities available to large numbers of women in the 1980s have been in marginal, low-paid economic activities. The percentage of women in paid employment declined from 80 per cent of the female labour force in 1981 to around 55–60 per cent in the 1980s, and the percentage of unpaid female labour increased from 6 per cent to around 20–25 per cent during this period.

Women are also disadvantaged by the horizontal gender segmentation of the labour market. They are concentrated chiefly in peasant and plantation agriculture, in 'feminine' domestic and assembly-line industries, in the education and health services and in domestic service. They are under-represented at managerial level despite the relatively high proportion of women in higher education institutions and in management courses. Education has not, therefore, increased access to remunerative employment for the majority of women. Sectoral analyses point to a deterioration in

Table 11.7 Unemployment rates by educational level and gender, Sri Lanka, 1985/86 and 1994

Level	1985/86			1994*		
	Total	Male	Female	Total	Male	Female
No schooling	6.1	7.7	4.8	2.5	3.7	1.6
School years 1–5	7.7	7.0	9.4	8.9	8.3	10.2
School years 6–8	11.2	9.5	16.5	12.7	9.6	21.2
School years 9–10	20.8	15.4	34.9			
GCE O Level	22.3	14.4	35.6	18.4	12.2	29.6
GCE A Level	32.0	18.7	44.9	25.2	14.7	34.1
Degree	6.3	3.3	10.2			
Postgrad. degree	3.9	4.2	3.2			
All levels	14.1	10.8	20.8	13.6	9.9	20.8

Note: * Excluding Northern and Eastern Provinces.
Source: Department of Census and Statistics, Colombo, Labour Force Surveys 1985/86, 1994 (1st quarter).

the situation of women in the economy since 1978 as a consequence of the much-publicized demand for cheap female labour.

The restructuring that took place in the industrial sector has had a significant impact on women. With the sudden opening of the economy in 1978 and removal of subsidies for production, several local industries collapsed. 'Feminine' industries were strongly affected by competition. Forty thousand women engaged in handloom production lost their livelihoods in 1979–80 (Atukorale 1986). Failure to revive local industries since then has deprived rural secondary school-educated women of employment opportunities outside agriculture.

Priority has been given to export-oriented industrialization. The international division of labour based on the 'comparative advantage' of low-cost female labour has led to the relocation of labour-intensive industries in developing countries such as Sri Lanka. Eighty per cent of the labour force in factories within and outside export-processing zones are women. The majority are young women secondary school-leavers between 18 and 25 years with 10 or 12 years of education. They are engaged in fragmented, semi-skilled jobs with minimal transfer of technology and lack of facilities to upgrade skills, denying them any opportunities of upward occupational mobility (see Table 11.8). While they have access to income, their working conditions are insecure and exploitative (Goonetileke et al. 1988; Rosa 1989; Weerasinghe 1989; CENWOR 1994). The majority of home-based workers in sub-contracting industries are also women, both secondary

Table 11.8 Employment in the Greater Colombo Economic Commission industries, Sri Lanka, 1992

Occupational level	Male	Female	Total	Female (%)
Administration	617	216	833	25.9
Technical staff				
Executive	594	131	725	18.1
Non-executive	433	87	520	16.7
Supervisory				
Technical	718	511	1,229	41.6
Non-technical	621	1,349	1,970	68.6
Clerical and allied	1,511	2,076	3,587	57.9
Skilled	4,659	6,675	11,334	58.9
Semi-skilled	3,369	33,209	36,578	90.8
Unskilled	3,366	9,096	12,462	72.9
Trainees	2,069	17,068	19,137	89.2
Others	1,583	337	1,920	17.6
Total	19,540	70,755	90,295	78.4

Source: GCEC Colombo.

school-leavers and 'drop-outs', who are at the bottom of a process of inequitable distribution of profits (Jayaweera and Dias 1989).

In the services sector, the number of women in professional and semi-professional employment increased to 49.5 per cent by 1985/86 as a consequence of their participation in secondary and higher education. With the reduction of public sector employment brought about by the structural adjustment programme the number declined to 43.9 per cent in 1994. As in many other countries, public service in education, health and administration has been a favoured niche for women for decades.

The majority of women in the informal sector continue to be in casual employment in domestic service and petty trade. A new trend since the late 1970s has been the exodus overseas of women migrant workers from low-income families struggling for survival in the informal sector, to meet the demand for domestic labour in the affluent countries in West and Southeast Asia, and even in Western Europe. These women, whose remittances make a significant contribution to national revenue, are vulnerable to economic and sexual exploitation (Dias and Weerakoon 1995; Hettige 1992).

Self-employment is seen by policy-makers as a way of reducing unemployment. 'Income-generation projects' have been implemented under a variety of donor-supported WID projects. Unemployed, secondary-educated, rural and urban women have formed the majority of participants. They have access to credit and many have mobilized for innovative group activities such as women's banks, but the majority have had little significant increase in income or upward mobility as they lack the crucial inputs of technology, skills training and access to markets. They also tend to be isolated from mainstream development.

The relationship between gender, education and development has several facets in the context of Sri Lanka's experience. Women have made a substantial contribution to national development, in new settlement areas, in the plantations, in industrialization, in the public sector and in their contribution in earnings to reduce the negative balance of payments. Their labour inputs have been crucial to family survival, maintenance and mobility. But it is a moot point as to whether they themselves have benefited proportionately in terms of their own advancement. An inter-generational study in six representative locations affected by specific development programmes (CENWOR 1987; Jayaweera 1995) found that there has been a reversal in occupational and socio-economic mobility for secondary-educated women in recent years as a consequence of the demand for low-cost female labour in macro-economic policies. Except for those in the upper and middle classes they no longer had access to teaching or other equivalent jobs but were unemployed, self-employed (in low-skill, low-income activities), semi-skilled workers, unpaid family labour or wage labourers. The inequitable distribution of senior secondary and higher education facilities has led to bifurcation in 'career paths' – upward vertical mobility for those from families with resources and horizontal mobility at the lower levels of the employment structure for the majority. There is clearly an interface of social class factors and the social construction of gender. Women from different socio-economic classes with the same educational attainment have access to jobs at different occupational levels. Men and women with the same educational attainment reach different levels in the occupational structure.

Finally, it is important to examine the issue of whether education changes the lives of women and gender roles and relations within the family. It is apparent that education has improved the status of women within the family, reduced family size and expanded their economic roles. There is, however, no simple relationship between education and the empowerment of women. All the evidence points to the fact that economic independence through employment or otherwise enables women to share in decision-making and to exercise their autonomy as individuals with rights and aspirations (CENWOR 1987).

Education is an enabling factor in the development of capabilities, but it is not necessarily a facilitator unless women have control of resources. The unequal gender division of labour within the household continues, although professional dual earner families are seen to share tasks more equitably. Education, even higher education, does not appear to have motivated large numbers of women to challenge gender role assumptions and obscurantist social practices pertaining to marriage. Control of female sexuality is a visible manifestation of gender inequality. Domestic violence and sexual abuse occur irrespective of the educational levels of family members. Clearly access to education is insufficient unless education is used consciously to socialize girls and boys, women and men to reject negative gendered norms and to accept and practise gender equality, social justice and the observance of human rights, all of which are in essence indicators of human development.

Bibliography

Abeykoon, A. T. P. L. (1996) *Population Trends in Sri Lanka: The Post-War Experience*, Working Paper No. 10, CENWOR, Colombo.

Abhayadeva, C. (1991) 'Gender and competences of children at entry to primary school', *Gender and Education*, CENWOR, Colombo.

Alailima, P. J. (1992) 'Education–employment linkages', *Journal of the Social Sciences*, 15.

— (1995) *Post-Independence Evolution of Social Policy and Expenditure in Sri Lanka*, Working Paper No. 9, CENWOR, Colombo.

Atukorale, P. (1986) 'The impact of 1977 policy reforms on domestic industry', *Upanathi*, 1 (1).

Caldwell, B. (1996) 'Female education, autonomy and fertility in Sri Lanka', in R. Jeffery and A. Basu (eds), *Girls' Schooling, Women's Autonomy and Fertility Change in South Asia*, Sage, London.

CENWOR (1987) *Women's Work and Family Strategies*, CENWOR, Colombo.

— (1993) *Shadows and Vistas: On Being a Girl Child in Sri Lanka*, CENWOR, Colombo.

— (1994) *Export Processing Zones in Sri Lanka: Economic Impact*, ILO, Geneva.

— (1995) *Structural Adjustment and Women: the Sri Lanka Experience*, CENWOR, Colombo.

Commonwealth Secretariat (1989) *Engendering Adjustment for the 1990s*, Commonwealth Secretariat, London.

— (1990/1991) *Household Income and Expenditure Survey*, Sri Lanka.

De Mel, G. (1994) 'Perceptions of women teachers in selected teachers' colleges regarding gender issues', unpublished MA thesis, University of Colombo.

Department of Census and Census of Population Statistics (1981, 1980/81, 1990, 1995) *Labour Force Survey*, Sri Lanka.

De Silva, W. et al. (1994) *Women, Political Empowerment and Decision Making*, CENWOR, Study Series No. 8, Colombo.

Dias, M. and N. Weerakoon (1995) 'Migrant women domestic workers from Sri Lanka: Trends and Issues', in CENWOR, *Facets of Change*, CENWOR, Colombo.

Ederisinghe, N. (1990) *Poverty in Sri Lanka: its Extent, Distribution and Characteristics of the Poor*. Employment and Poverty Alleviation Project, World Bank, Washington, DC.

Goonetileke, H. et al. (1988) 'Industrialization and women workers in Sri Lanka', in N. Heyzer (ed.), *Daughters in Industry*, Asian and Pacific Development Centre, Kuala Lumpur, Malaysia.

Green, T. L. (1952) 'Education and social needs', *University of Ceylon Review*, 10.

Hettige, S. (1992) 'From dependent housewives to breadwinner. Some aspects of migration of female workers to the Middle East', *Women, Poverty and Family Survival*, CENWOR, Colombo.

Jayasena, A. (1991) 'Sexism in the post primary school curriculum', *Gender and Education*, CENWOR, Colombo.

Jayaweera, S. (1976) 'Vocational preferences of secondary school girls in Sri Lanka', *Modern Ceylon Studies*, 7 (1, 2).

— (1984a) 'Universalization of elementary education', *Journal of the National Education Society of Sri Lanka*, 24.

— (1984b) 'Access to university education: the social composition of university entrants', *University of Colombo Review*, 1 (4).

— (1991a) 'The education of girls in Sri Lanka: opportunities and constraints', *Half our Future. The Girl Child in Sri Lanka*, Sri Lanka Federation of University Women, Colombo.

— (1991b) *Women, Skill Development and Employment*, Institute of Policy Studies Research Studies, Women in Development, Series 2.

— (1993a) 'Education of the girl child', in CENWOR, *Shadows and Vistas*.

— (1993b) 'Functional literacy and the education of the girl child', in CENWOR, *Shadows and Vistas*.

— (1993c) 'The socialization of the girl child', in CENWOR, *Shadows and Vistas*.

— (1995a) 'Women, education and occupational mobility', in *Facing Odds: Women in the Labour Market*, CENWOR, Colombo.

— (1995b) 'Women and education', *Facets of Change*, CENWOR, Colombo.

— (1996) 'Sri Lanka', in G. L Mark (ed.), *Women, Education and Development in Asia*, Garland, New York.

— (1997) 'Women, education and empowerment in Asia', *Gender and Education* 9 (4), 411–24.

Jayaweera, S. and T. Sanmugam (1987) *Women Engineers in Sri Lanka*, Sri Lanka Federation of University Women, Colombo.

Jayaweera, S. and M. Dias (1989) *Subcontracting in Industry: Impact on Malsiri Women*, Commonwealth Secretariat, London.

Jayaweera, S., S. Rupesinghe and S. Perera (1991) 'Gender differences in performance at secondary school examinations in Sri Lanka', *Gender and Education*, CENWOR, Colombo.

Jayaweera, S., T. Sanmugam, W. Jayatileke and S. K. Mendis (1992) *Women Graduates in Agriculture*, Study Series No. 3, CENWOR, Colombo.

Kumar, S. (1987) 'The Mahaweli scheme and rural women in Sri Lanka', in N. Heyzer (ed.), *Women, Farmers and Rural Change in Asia*, Asia and Pacific Development Centre, Kuala Lumpur, Malaysia.

Kurian, R. (1982) *Women Workers in Sri Lanka Plantation Sector*, ILO, Geneva.

— (1989) 'Women's work, male domination and controls of income among plantation workers in Sri Lanka', in H. Afsher and B. Agarwal (eds), *Women, Poverty and Ideology in Asia*, Macmillan, London.

Rajapakse, D. (1989) 'Agricultural transformation and changing labour relations: implications for peasant women in Sri Lanka', *Hidden Face of Development*, CENWOR, Colombo.

— (1995) *The Great Sandy River: Class and Gender Transformation among Pioneer Settlers in Sri Lanka's Frontier*, Het Spinhuis Publishers, The Netherlands.

Rosa, K. (1989) 'Export oriented industries and women workers in Sri Lanka', in

H. Afsher and B. Agarwal (eds), *Women, Poverty and Ideology in Asia*, Macmillan, London.

Rupesinghe, S. (1991) 'Gender differences in the career aspirations of students in GCE (OL) grades in Sri Lanka', *Gender and Education*, CENWOR, Colombo.

Rupesinghe, S. and L. S. Perera (1987) 'An assessment of the academic abilities of students studying at junior secondary level in Sri Lanka', *Sri Lanka Journal of Social Sciences* 9.

Sri Lanka Federation of University Women (1980) *Unemployment Among Women Arts Graduates*, Colombo.

Strauss, M. (1951) 'Family characteristics and occupational choice of university entrants', *University of Ceylon Review* 9 (2).

University Grants Commission (1984–94) *Statistical Handbook*, Planning and Research Division.

Uswatte, A. G. (1974) 'University admissions in Ceylon: their economic and social background and employment expectations', *Modern Asian Studies* 8 (3).

Weerasinghe, R. (1989) 'Women workers in the Katunayake investment promotion zone in Sri Lanka', *Women and Development in Asia*, Macmillan India Ltd.

Wijesuriya, G. (1994) *Participation and Performance in Primary Education*, National Institute of Education, Maharagama.

World Bank (1994) *Poverty Assessment Study*, World Bank, Washington, DC.

CHAPTER 12

From WID to GAD: Experiences of Education in Nepal

Mo Sibbons

Nepal is one of the poorest countries in the world (real GDP per capita US$1,137, compared to $26,379 for the USA) with one of the lowest levels of human development, ranked 154th of 175 countries in the *Human Development Report* 1997. While agriculture dominates the economy, much of Nepal is so mountainous or thickly forested that less than one-fifth is actually under cultivation. The pressure of the rapidly expanding population on the available arable land is intense, causing considerable migration. Nepal is a land-locked country totally dependent on its routes into India for all exports and imports, including all important fuel oils (Karan and Ishii 1996). It is a country characterized by great diversity: geographical diversity from the low-level, flat north Indian plain of the Tarai to the highest mountains in the world in the Himalayan chain; cultural and religious diversity from Buddhist to Hindu with many variations and other religions making up the rich tapestry of difference; and numerous ethnic groups, associated with location and religious-cultural systems. It is this rich and varied mix that influences perceptions towards education and, consequently, educational outcomes. The result is generally (but not universally) to produce an education system which favours males more than females – in access, participation and achievements.

This chapter looks at one particular project being implemented in Nepal: the Secondary Education Project. The approach adopted in this project ensures that all project activities include social appraisal at all stages; this identifies the areas where positive actions need to be taken, enables development of responsive activities and provides formative monitoring during implementation. The purpose is to provide an inclusive secondary system, which allows access to all children and, more importantly, equal opportunities for positive outcomes. This chapter is an interim consideration of the practice and results. The project is continuing. No formal evaluation has yet taken place, but qualitative and formative monitoring of the equity-related aspects of component activities has been carried out. The particular component of the project described in detail is a

Table 12.1 Regional distribution of girl students, Nepal, 1995 (per cent)

Development region	Mountain	Hill	Terai	Total
Eastern	39.2	38.1	37.6	37.9
Central	27.8	40.0	30.1	35.8
Western	47.4	42.0	35.2	40.8
Mid-Western	11.2	25.5	35.3	29.0
Far-Western	15.6	13.8	27.6	19.7
Total	27.7	38.1	34.2	35.9

Source: Ministry of Education 1995.

series of participatory, decentralized, activity-prioritization workshops, designed to identify local perceptions of gender inequity and ways to address them through specific local activities – at community, school, district office and regional administration levels.

The background to this approach is the strong incentive to concentrate on gender equity because the current situation is so poor. Girls are educationally so disadvantaged compared to boys that there are very few educated women available to be trained as teachers. As in Papua New Guinea, Ethiopia and Niger (see Chapters 3, 6 and 7), this is a powerful factor perpetuating girls' educational disadvantages. Girls are 2.6 times more likely to be kept out of school, 20 per cent more likely to repeat a year, and 89 per cent more at risk of dropping out of school. Some of this is related to the fact that they are more than twice as likely to be involved in household chores. Specifically in terms of secondary education (years 6 to 10), the gross enrolment rate for 1995 is 22 for girls against a total GER of 32. This is an improvement from 1985, when the figures were 12 and 24 respectively (CERID 1997). The national statistics mask the vast differences among the regions, and within regions among the different climatic zones.

Projects for girls are popular with donors supporting education in Nepal. Recognizing the unfair outcomes of a system where few girls get beyond the first few years of schooling, and the fact that some parts of the country have poorer results (inadequately measured by the School Leaving Certificate) than others, programmes and inputs have been targeted at the most disadvantaged areas. By concentrating on female students and teachers these projects have failed to challenge the existing system in any meaningful way – they have attempted to make the existing system better while leaving the institutions and mechanisms of educational delivery intact and unreformed. The male-dominated power base that controls the education system is not affected by 'projects for girls'. Any gains are limited and short-term.

This chapter looks at attempts that have been made to move from 'projects for girls' to a gender-responsive project aimed at quality improvements to the secondary system. The approach parallels the general moves there have been in development work from a women in development (WID) approach to a gender and development (GAD) approach. Marginalization of development for one half of the population in small 'add-on' projects is to be avoided in favour of placing women centrally with men in development approaches that address relationships preventing all from benefiting equally. This change in approach is necessary but not sufficient to ensure women's ability to meet their full potential. Challenges to the status quo are required if sustainable advances are to be seen. That is where the problem lies, as well as the solution. The initiation or even suggestion of changes or activities that are perceived to undermine existing power relations are not going to be accepted by those who hold power unless convincing arguments can be made for the long-term benefits for all.

The first part of this chapter provides a brief description of the main gender differences that exist in the social structures in Nepal and the way these impact on girls' and women's lives. While this demonstrates the importance of introducing gender-responsive policies, the extent of social and cultural diversity is such that generalized, unitary approaches are unlikely to meet the needs of all groups. The second section explores the relationship between donor-supported education projects and current development paradigms. A description of the Nepal Secondary Education Project (SEP) follows, with an outline of two particular sub-components that challenge traditional approaches to female education. Finally, a general conclusion is drawn.

Nepal: socio-cultural constructs

There are four geo-ecological zones in Nepal: the Great Himalaya, including Mount Everest; the Middle Mountains, a plateau between 3,000 and 5,000 metres bisected by four main rivers; the Outer Himalaya, between 1,000 and 2,000 metres; and the Tarai in the south, related to the Ganges valley. The last two contain important fertile valleys, some of which became habitable only from the 1950s after DDT spraying to eradicate malaria-carrying mosquitoes. Since then migration to the Tarai has increased rapidly in response to the pressure of a rapidly growing population on increasingly impoverished land (Karan and Ishii 1996). The geographical diversity of Nepal also reflects cultural differences. These are in part a reflection of religious affiliations, but they also owe their existence to ethnicity and historical influences. A full exploration or explanation will not be attempted here. What will be described, very briefly, are the main cultural influences on gender and education.

First, the most marked difference is that between the Buddhist mountain communities and the 'conservative' Hindu communities of the Terai. The former includes matriarchal societies who in the past have practised polyandry; in the Terai, patriarchal and polygynous households are predominant. This is not solely a consequence of religion, but a complex of economic, social, cultural and religious influences. As far as access to schooling is concerned, the geographical as well as the cultural aspects of communities together create an interesting pattern of attendance at school. Boys and girls in the scattered, remote communities in the mountains have very poor physical access to schools. Seasonal migration patterns with domestic animals to the high summer pastures affect boys' ability to attend school. In the mountainous areas school enrolment is low. However, drop-out rates also tend to be low. It seems that only parents who value school send their children and that, once in school, they complete the primary grades, with a number of girls progressing to secondary schooling.

In the relatively densely populated, flat plain of the rural areas in the Terai, physical access is less of a problem. Purdah (segregation and veiling of females post-puberty) is practised in many of the villages. The pattern of school attendance is almost the reverse of that seen in the mountains. Relatively high enrolment at primary level of both boys and girls is followed by rapid and marked drop-out of girls, and very low transition rates to secondary school. The need to hide older girls from exposure to boys and men restricts their access to secondary schools, as they are co-educational and the vast majority of teachers are men. The data in Table 12.1 indicate the differences in enrolment.

Current development paradigms as a context for education projects

Meeting the needs of the majority is the main priority of the principal stakeholders, the donor organizations and the government of Nepal. Donor-supported education programmes which work with larger populations exhibiting significant disparities have the potential to provide healthy statistics that 'prove' the effectiveness of projects and programmes. Percentage changes in enrolment rates and/or the ratio of boy:girl enrolment are notable examples. Meeting the needs of minority groups is rarely cost-effective because the numbers are always too small compared to the inputs required. In Nepal concentrating on the urban Terai, the highest population density, produces the most dramatic statistical evidence of changes in access to school. This evidence suggests that project-induced changes are not long-lasting and do not produce a robust change in attitudes towards education, particularly that of girls. They also fail to address the very different constraints that exist for children in the sparsely populated and remote mountain areas. The very different gender issues of the Terai and the mountains are also not captured in data selected to maximize results. The consequences of this, it is argued here, are that the children of the remote areas cannot benefit from such projects and programmes, which do not address gender disparities or challenge inequity. Empowerment and autonomy are not achieved. Consequently reductions in fertility, often high on the agenda for donors, are unaddressed.

Examples of projects failing to achieve robust changes are considered below. Official government statistics suggest that the most lasting changes have occurred in the Kathmandu valley, in response to socio-economic change rather than development projects. In Kathmandu, the ready availability of private schools and higher disposable income enable parents to send their children to school. Although the evidence about the quality of the education provided in the private institutions is equivocal, there is a perception among the local communities that the quality of education provided is superior to that of the government schools. The higher ratio of girls in Central Region, which includes the Kathmandu valley, is replicated in the larger conurbations of the Terai. It is tempting to conclude that socio-economic change of itself will create the necessary preconditions for improvements in access to schooling for both boys and girls, again with a greater impact on the numbers of girls able to attend school. However, this is too simplistic. The example of Sri Lanka (Chapter 11) demonstrates that government investment in health and education is as necessary as economic growth for encouraging a positive attitudes towards education and gender equity (Jeffery and Basu 1996).

Neither should we conclude that no attempts should be made to stimulate a more rapid economic transition and greater gender equity. Examples of positive outcomes should be used to facilitate processes of change that are favourable to the most disadvantaged. The purpose of research and evaluation is to provide evidence of positive and negative responses to interventions – to facilitate policy development.

Analysis of the impact of capitalist transformations on the marginalization of women demonstrates multiple manifestations. Turshen and Holcomb (1993: 54) have argued that capitalism inevitably marginalizes and subordinates women: the separation of reproduction and production into different locations, away from the integrated sets of activities within the domestic arena that dominated pre-capitalist and subsistence economies, encourages and provides the stage for domestication of women and their subordination in the male- (wage-earning) dominated household. This view is not substantiated by the evidence of Elson and Pearson (1981), who give examples of women benefiting from economic change. Sen argues that the vast majority of women continue to take a subordinate role to that of men. However much they may benefit from improvements to their 'bargaining power' from the acquisition of personal income, they inevitably bargain from a situation of inequality (Sen 1990).

It could be argued that equal access to effective schooling provides an additional benefit for girls, from which as adults they can further enhance their bargaining power. This should not be viewed solely from the functionalist perspective as skills with which to enter the labour market. Depending on the nature and content of education it can act as a means of emancipation, adding to women's autonomy and hence independence from male oppression.[1] This broader perspective, taking the argument beyond the economic, has its critics. The view that education can act as an instrument of democratization and social equity is 'countered by "conflict" theorists who underscore the role of education as an agent of social reproduction and control' (Jayaweera 1997). The context of heterogeneity, so significant in Nepal, suggests that education has the potential to 'reduce, reproduce or widen gender inequalities' (ibid.), depending on its form and content.

The benefits that accrue to society from the education of girls seem to be well established. Improvements such as a decline in the infant mortality rate, increases in contraceptive prevalence rates, and lower fertility are often cited as reasons for the emphasis on improving enrolment and retention rates of girls in school. This is very much the efficiency argument that was used throughout the 1980s, and is still used, for mainstreaming concerns for the inclusion of women in development programmes. The move from the marginalizing 'women in development' (WID) approach (small, discrete, poorly funded, income-earning projects for women) to the 'gender and development' (GAD) approach is well described in Moser (1993). The recognition by the international development community that half the potential workforce were, inefficiently, being left out of the development equation prompted the emphasis on inclusion of women throughout the development agenda. New analytical tools were developed for the purposes of ensuring that 'the truth' about the existing specific and local situation was understood sufficiently to incorporate this analysis in the development of the gender sensitive projects. These tools have their critics, as does the approach (Kabeer 1994).

A quotation from a World Bank Report (1997) provides an example of the instrumentalist way in which education for girls is seen in the 1990s. This concerns Africa, but the message is a clear indication of the attitude of a leading multilateral organization, replicated in many other bilateral and multilateral programmes:

> Message 1: Basic education is fundamental to Tanzania's efforts to speed up economic growth and distribute the benefits of growth widely throughout the society. Basic education is a catalyst that increases the impact of other investments in health, nutrition, family planning, and water.
>
> Message 2: Women in Tanzania are the primary agents of human capital investment. The litmus test of an effective social investment is whether it improves the ability of women to carry out this task.

One of the recommendations that result from those conclusions is:

> A new commitment to getting a large share of the next generation of girls through secondary school.

In the same way the exclusion of girls from schools was seen to be contributing to a failure of certain states to develop – as measured by GDP, IMR, TFR and LE. Projects for girls were introduced, funded by the international community. In Nepal, initiatives promoting girls' education are similar to those in other developing countries. Targeting of girls in the most disadvantaged districts with incentives such as scholarships, encouraging more female teachers, and hostels for girls to board in order to allow those from the remotest areas to attend school are combined with free textbooks and free midday meals. Disappointingly (perhaps predictably) these measures have not reduced inequalities and the districts targeted continue to show the poorest representation of girl students and women teachers.

A recent report on gender and secondary education in Nepal (CERID 1997) reports that, when questioned, senior education staff were of the view that despite the numerous programmes being implemented the benefit from them has been insignificant. Programmes conceived and implemented at the central level face problems such as uncertainty of disbursement of funds for approved programmes, delay of the distribution of scholarships for girls, and rules in place being replaced by an arbitrary selection process. Poor coordination, supervision, monitoring and dissemination of information about schemes result in no positive change for the most disadvantaged communities.

The establishment of a special section in the Ministry of Education – the Women's Education Unit – is a telling example of such laudable attempts at improving female educational opportunities failing to produce results. Far from this unit creating a dynamic force for change, it has resulted in the marginalization of gender concerns. The fact that a women's unit exists means that it deals with all issues to do with women and that general projects can therefore ignore gender issues. There is little or no evidence of the Women's Education Unit being used by projects to help with the development of gendered programmes of activities by using its expertise when designing and planning development projects.

The Nepal Secondary Education Project

The Secondary Education Project (SEP) is a project of the Ministry of Education in Nepal, supported by a loan from the Asian Development Bank and a grant from the UK government Department for International Development (DfID). The components of the project supported by DfID are concerned with quality aspects of education and are managed by

Cambridge Education Consultants. They include support for institution-building in the ministry, for those sections particularly involved in implementation of other project components, including planning of secondary education, in-service teacher training, textbook writing and production, testing and assessment, monitoring and evaluation.

The overall aim of the project is to improve access to a better-quality secondary education system, and especially to reduce the disparity between girls and boys. Access issues include any constraint that prevents girls or boys going to school, not only the physical availability of schools. A key feature of the project has been gender analysis of all activities and their context, and the inclusion of gender-specific activities where relevant. This agenda is accepted by some of those working in the project as addressing an issue of human rights – that all children should be entitled to the same access to and benefits from an education system. Two examples provide illustrations of the difficulties faced in trying to develop policies and activities at the centre and a possible way forward towards inclusive education.

In-service teacher training A programme of subject-specific teacher training has been designed and is being implemented through the Secondary Education Development Units throughout Nepal. Schooling in Nepal is co-educational (other than in a few private, single-sex schools). The lack of female teachers in schools has a direct correlation with the achievement levels of girls. Schools where there are no female teachers have lower enrolments of girls and poorer performances. There are several possible explanations for this, one of which is that male teachers favour the boys in their classes and exclude girls from participation. This is (presumably) not intentional. Some male head teachers are aware of problems of not having female teachers on their staff, especially when they are teaching girls going through puberty who need a staff member to confide in. However, the majority of teachers are unaware of this problem and do not know that their teaching style disadvantages the small number of girls in their classes.

Girls do particularly badly in science subjects and mathematics. There is a general consensus among education sector staff that this is a function of biology. This assumption that girls cannot do these subjects is readily transmitted to the girls themselves, who believe they cannot, therefore should not, succeed. While girls are out-performing boys in all subjects in many industrialized countries, undermining this myth, cultural attitudes in countries like Nepal will not be transformed easily. Expectations of teachers, parents and students of failure results in just such an outcome. The in-service programme therefore included a unit on gender issues in teaching. This was accepted by the project managers and by the consultants advising on INSET. Subsequently the content of that unit became rather contentious.

It was the view of the social development advisers, supported by most of the subject specialist advisers, that a generic unit that aimed at training first the trainers and then the teachers in social analysis skills should be included. This would enable them to determine for themselves what differences there are in boys' and girls' lives and the roles they are expected to play, which influence their entry to school and their ability to benefit from the learning process. Although the time allotted to this training session was inadequate, results of training the trainers in the use of the unit were encouraging. Participants saw the relevance of what they had been asked to do and suggested ways in which school practices could easily be modified to address gender constraints. New activities that could be undertaken by the teachers in school or in the community were also forthcoming. As an outcome of their workshop activity they provided interesting and sometimes unexpected ideas on how they could tackle the issues they had themselves identified.

However, this apparent early success was not borne out by subsequent events. The unit was not included in the set of printed training notes.[2] When questioned on why it had been excluded, the answer was that it was not relevant to the subject teachers' training programme. What was required was an exercise that provided teachers with examples of how they could enhance girls' learning of science, or of mathematics, or of English (the three subjects included in the first in-service training programme). Attempts to explain the rationale for a unit that provided teachers with a method of exploring their own practice, in a way that enabled them to develop inclusive teaching approaches specific to their own context, fell on stony ground.

It was profoundly disappointing that such a lack of gender awareness should exist within the international advisers' group, although less surprising that government education sector officials should have problems in understanding the concept and approach, given their lack of exposure to such ideas. Attempts to 'train' the project and ministry staff through on-the-job support and counter-parting have had a minimal effect, although after two years of constant but gentle (mostly) reminders of issues, support in the appraisal of interventions and help in amendments to activities do seem to be bringing about some permanent if slow change in understanding.

The project is continuing. Monitoring the use of the gender training unit helps to remind the trainers of its value, and to support their further development in gender analysis. Readers with experience of gender training may be familiar with the outcome. Some trainees are very enthusiastic and have become great advocates; the majority go through the motions and have some understanding; others are hostile to this challenging change required of them, their attitudes and their understanding.

Regional workshops for locally specific strategy development   The second example of gender awareness-raising activities in the SEP is a series of strategy development workshops, one in each region of Nepal. The diversity that is Nepal, described above, provided the incentive for the following approach to strategy development for quality improvements to education. As part of the SEP project a research study was commissioned to look into gender issues in the secondary education system in Nepal. It was felt that a traditional dissemination of the findings of this study to a group consisting of project staff, Ministry of Education and other government officials and academics was unlikely to produce anything beyond an agreement that there were things that could be done.

An alternative approach was developed using the findings of the research to structure participatory action planning workshops in the regions. Participants were invited from parent representatives of school management committees, teachers, head teachers, teacher trainers, supervisors and district and regional ministry educational officers. It was hoped to maximize female participation, although this is difficult in the context of so few female teachers and officers. Representatives from mountain, hill and Terai were included.

In broad outline, the objective of the workshops was to produce locally specific practical steps that could be taken at different levels of the education system to address the various constraints on educational achievement identified by the participants. The research results were used to reinforce what the members of the workshop groups were identifying as problems, and where appropriate to give them additional information or corroboration of their views from other examples.

Although the purpose was to raise awareness of gender issues, this was not used as the title of the workshops, nor did the workshop start with this as a theme. The first group exercise was to ask participants what they knew about current education policies that were available to help encourage school enrolment. The whole group was sub-divided into small, homogeneous, working groups, i.e. parents in one group, teachers in another, head teachers in another, and so on. The reasons for doing so were twofold: first, so that, for example, parents were not intimidated by having to work with high-level government officials; second, so that differences in knowledge about policies and understanding of and perceptions about them by the various groups could be highlighted. An interactive plenary session explored the policies: which groups knew of them, what they understood by them, and how well they thought they worked in practice.

As an outcome of this first session, the topics for the next small group discussions were identified. Each group was asked to look at a different set of questions related to different aspects of the schooling system: school/community linkages and opportunities; current patterns of school attendance and the reasons for these patterns; issues associated with the recruitment and training of teachers; and the effectiveness of the school system. At the feedback session from these discussion the other groups were asked to comment on the conclusion that had been drawn and to provide different views or examples if appropriate. For the trainers the important outcome was for participants to recognize the differences that exist in their experiences and contexts, and for them to provide a rich set of information to add to the evaluation.

A third workshop activity concentrated on children's socialization through the school system and the way in which texts used in schools influence children's perceptions and reinforce social and cultural norms; not all of these are necessarily supportive of an equitable society. The final sessions were devoted to looking at possible strategies that could be developed by different groups and at different levels to address the problems and constraints that they had identified. The outcomes of the first sessions were synthesized, and the main areas that they had identified in their group work as priority areas where actions needed to be taken were reiterated in the form of 'purpose statements', for groups to develop into strategies. For example, where groups had identified difficult access to physical facilities as a disincentive to school attendance they were asked to develop a strategy that would enable all children to have ready access to school. These tasks were again sub-divided between groups, each group having a different purpose to achieve. Sharing of the results was interactive. An action committee was formed from the workshop to develop the strategies into action plans. These were then taken to a national symposium, where representatives from the regional workshops presented their findings. The participants at the national meeting were from each of the regions and from the relevant institutions of the ministries involved in education sector development.

Process

At the time of running these workshops, the practical difficulties of getting significant numbers of people together from diverse locations in a protracted monsoon season seemed to outweigh the results achieved! Many of the participants travelled on foot for considerable distances before being able to pick up any form of transport.[3] Isolated village schools do not have road access. Getting messages to them in the first place to request their participation is difficult, as telephone connections are uncertain or non-existent. Achieving substantial numbers of participants, who were representative of a considerable diversity of locations and interests, was represented as the first significant success for the process, largely due to the efforts of supportive ministry staff.

The next significant success was the enthusiastic participation of all those attending, given the use of an untried methodology with groups of people unused to workshop environments. For most of the parents and some of the teachers, being asked to express their own opinions in a public environment for the first time was a risky endeavour. How it would work in practice was an unknown. In the event we were extremely satisfied, and impressed by the sophistication of the debates and ideas that were being put forward. After the first regional workshop, each subsequent event was refined and improved. The process as a whole gave a range of stakeholders the opportunity to express their own views and to get them heard by others in positions of higher authority, and for their ideas to feed into policy debates at national level.

Outcomes

One of the most important outcomes was the clear articulation of local constraints on secondary schooling. The following is an illustration of the type of sophisticated and open debate that resulted. Gender disparities in enrolment had been identified as of significance in some schools. A head teacher from a school in the Eastern Region was able to give an excellent anthropological explanation of the socio-cultural constraints that prevent daughters rather than sons from going to school. Parents value education for boys more highly than education for girls; there is an expectation that girls will continue to play their main role as wives and mothers; parents are unwilling to invest in a child who will become someone else's property. He was particularly concerned that the betrothal of young girls was a significant contributor to perpetuating this view. Despite his insightful exposition, when asked he willingly admitted that he had arranged an early marriage for his daughter, thus becoming one of the perpetuators of a situation he had acknowledged as being in need of change. This was a forceful example of how passionately a person may claim disagreement with the status quo, but be a contributor to its continuation. Social and cultural norms are powerful forces that require significant efforts to change.

The final session, in which the groups provided practical ideas on policy options and some strategies that could be adopted within the communities, schools or elsewhere in the education system, did provide some interesting and innovative ideas; these have been passed on to those at the centre, in the project and in the ministry, for incorporation in the development of secondary education.

Conclusions from the regional workshops

The fact that the headteacher described above, along with a number of peers and other education sector personnel, was given the opportunity to express his opinion may provide the incentive for change; obviously structural and institutional supports for change are a concomitant need.

Raising awareness of gender issues in a non-confrontational way in a constructive context where opportunities are provided to develop locally specific policies and sector responses would seem to be an obvious way forward. However, this requires a considerable change of attitude of senior officials at the centre. Although decentralization is on the statute books, the threat of devolving power to 'minor' officials at the periphery, or even more so to teachers in schools, is such that it remains a paper promise. The excellent responses of the district-level officers, teachers and head teachers, their perceptiveness and their willingness and openness to address schooling problems provide an ample platform from which to launch innovative and responsive policies.

Conclusion

The Nepal Secondary Education Project provides an example of an attempt to place gender at the heart of all activities in a Ministry of Education-owned programme. The reason for doing this is to enable the diversity of gender relations in Nepal to be reflected in school-level delivery of policies responsive to local needs. The significant educational disadvantage of most girls (and some boys in mountain areas) should be addressed if the government is to be able to claim equity of educational opportunities. Some societal benefits of such equitable access may be the motive behind donor-supported projects of such kinds: addressing the 'population problem'. However, the societal benefits are not restricted to the narrow confines of this goal: democracy and empowerment are surely to be added to them. All children in Nepal should be equally entitled to an education.

Notes

1. Note that this does not deny the existence of class (economic) oppression. As others have argued, a Marxist analysis that places female oppression exclusively in the domain of class relations obscures the universal subordination of women by men throughout time and place (see Kabeer 1994 for a critique of Marxist feminist analysis of gender relations). The argument here addresses women's subordinate role *vis-à-vis* men, irrespective of their social, economic or cultural location.

2. To call what was produced a manual would be giving it undeserved status.

3. Remote communities in the Great Himalaya may be three days' walk from the nearest road-head.

Bibliography

CERID (Research Centre for Educational Innovation and Development), with CEC (Cambridge Education Consultants) (1997) *Gender and Secondary Education: A Study Report*, Tribhuvan University, Kathmandu.

Elson, D. and R. Pearson (1981) 'The subordination of women and the internationalisation of factory production', in K. Young, C. Wolkowitz and C. McCullagh (eds), *Of Marriage and the Market: Women's Subordination in International Perspective*, CSE Books, London.

Jayaweera, S. (1997) 'Higher education and the economic and social empowerment of women: the Asian experience', *Compare* 27 (3): 245–61.

Jeffery, R. and A. Basu (1996) *Girls' Schooling, Women's Autonomy and Fertility Change in South Asia*, Sage, New Delhi.

Kabeer, N. (1994) *Reversed Realities: Gender Hierarchies in Development Thought*, Verso, London.

Karan, P. and H. Ishii (1996) *Nepal: A Himalayan Kingdom in Transition*, United Nations University Press, Tokyo.

Moser, C. (1993) *Gender Planning and Development Theory Practice and Training*, Routledge, London.

Sen, A. (1990) 'Gender and co-operative conflicts', in I. Tinker (ed.), *Persistent Inequalities*, Oxford University Press, Oxford.

Turshen, M. and B. Holcomb (eds) (1993) *Women's Lives and Public Policy*, Praeger, Westport, CT.

UNDP (1997) *Human Development Report 1997*, Oxford University Press, New York.

World Bank (1997) *Tanzania Social Sector Review*, World Bank, Washington, DC.

CHAPTER 13

Closing the Gender Gap? The Informal Sector in Pakistan

Christine Heward

The gender gap in Pakistan

The notion of the 'gender gap', the poorer access to educational provision of girls compared with boys, dominated debates about gender, education and development in the 1980s. In many developing countries fewer girls than boys enrolled in primary schools. They dropped out more frequently, creating a widening gender gap in secondary and tertiary education. The educational achievements of girls also compared adversely with that of boys (Kelly and Elliott 1982). By the 1990s it was clear that in many regions girls were actively closing this gap (King and Hill 1993). Indeed, in the Caribbean (as in some countries in the North) girls' enrolment and performance are superior to that of boys at all levels. By the late 1990s the annual data from the UNDP and UNICEF suggest that the gender gap is now confined to certain parts of Sub-Saharan Africa and South Asia. With gender gaps closing in many African countries, southern India and Sri Lanka, the problem is increasingly seen as a feature of poor South Asian societies that practise seclusion. Pakistan is one of the countries with a wide and apparently intransigent gender gap in access to educational provision at all levels. The glacial speed of progress is demonstrated in the changes from 1960, when 39 per cent of boys and 11 per cent of girls enrolled in primary schools, to 1980, when 38 per cent of men and 15 per cent of women were literate (UNICEF 1997). In 1995 the male literacy rate was 50 per cent and the female 24 per cent. Gross primary enrolment was 57 per cent for boys and 30 per cent for girls, with 48 per cent reaching Grade 5. Secondary enrolment was 28 per cent for boys and 13 per cent for girls.

As Chapter 11 shows, the sharpest contrast with another state in South Asia is with Sri Lanka, where welfare spending goes back 70 years to the colonial era, when universal suffrage was introduced. In 1995 primary school enrolment in Sri Lanka was 105 per cent of boys and 106 per cent of girls (i.e. children younger and older than the 'normal' primary school age range were enrolled in primary schools) with a completion rate of 92 per cent. Seventy-eight per cent of girls and 71 per cent of boys attend secondary schools. The literacy rate is 93 per cent for men and 87 per cent for women (UNICEF 1997).

Sri Lanka has a higher GDP per head than Pakistan – $640 compared with $430. Far more significant in closing the gender gap has been the devotion of a much larger proportion of its budget to a wide range of human development policies, which have improved the health and education of its children, women and men over several generations.

Pakistan's miserable record on narrowing the so-called 'gender gap in education' is one of the most visible features of one of the poorest records of investment in human development in South Asia. Explanations are not hard to find. Corruption, defence spending and huge inequalities stand out among the causes. Despite 50 years of independence, Pakistan's democracy is fragile, its power centres controlled by tiny feudal, military and industrial elites. For many of them the populace represent only an opportunity for self-aggrandisement, sometimes on a truly breathtaking scale (Grey and Syal 1998). Since the country's foundation as a Muslim state in 1947, Pakistani politics have been dominated by the presumed threat posed by big brother India. For more than half of its history Pakistan has had military governments. Popular elections were first held in 1970 and the northern areas were finally enfranchised in 1992. While state intervention in the economy in the 1960s and 1970s was reversed in the 1980s and 1990s, investment in the social sector has remained low. The first priority of General Zia ul Haq's military regime from 1977 to 1988 was to strengthen the defence sector. Despite the introduction of a fragile democracy in 1988, total state expenditure on education rose from a dismal 1.3 of GNP in 1972–73 to a miserable 2.3 per cent in 1989–90. The annual UNDP *Human Development Report*s reveal that Pakistan has consistently had one of the lowest levels of expenditure on human development and the highest on military spending of countries classified as having low human development. In 1985 defence spending in Pakistan was four times that on health and education. This was cut to 125 per cent in the mid-1990s. In 1994 defence spending accounted for 6.7 per cent of GNP, 2.7 per cent on education and 1.8 per cent on health. Chronic under-funding in health and education is exacerbated by one of the highest birth rates in the world.

School enrolment rates rose during the early 1970s and declined during the 1980s, at first gradually, then more rapidly in the late 1980s. Enrolment also increased among girls in the 1970s and declined in the 1980s (Erce-lawn, Mahmood and Nadvi 1994). A recent survey by the Federal Bureau of Statistics shows a further decline of 2 percentage points in the net enrolment rate of 5–9-year-olds between 1991 and 1996 (Gazdar 1997). While female literacy has more than doubled in the last two decades and the percentage of female to male enrolment has risen from 37 per cent to 61 per cent in primary schools and 26 per cent to 44 per cent in secondary schools, the gender disparity in years of schooling remains 0.7 years for girls and 2.9 for boys, demonstrating that girls drop out long before they have a sufficient education to gain the all-important secure grasp of literacy. Adult literacy among women is 47 per cent of that of men. Although there has been some narrowing of Pakistan's gender gap, it remains one of the largest among developing countries. One of the main reasons for this is the low priority accorded to primary education compared with secondary and higher education in government spending. In 1988 primary enrolment was 65 per cent below the average for low-income countries; secondary enrolment was 18 per cent lower while that in tertiary education was well above average. The share of total education expenditure given to primary education has barely changed. Indeed, it declined from 34 per cent in 1980–81 to 26.9 per cent in 1998–99 while the expenditure on secondary and tertiary education increased. Poor provision and wide inequalities particularly disadvantage the rural poor and women. The lowest school enrolment and literacy rates are among girls and women in remote rural areas (Ercelawn, Mahmood and Nadvi 1994). How far the rise in primary school enrolment of girls from 15 per cent in 1980 to 24 per cent in 1995 is due to the government's efforts or to those of parents and their daughters 'carrying it on their backs' is an open question. Universal primary education remains a distant dream in the face of resources that are hopelessly inadequate for a population doubling every 24 years.

In mid-1998 the political and economic situation is set to deteriorate further. The politically popular nuclear arms race with India will once more ensure that defence spending and debt repayment are major priorities, with human development neglected. While privileged young men, educated in English-medium schools, appear in the Northern media saying that no sacrifice is too great in the contest with India, the girls and women in the villages struggle to survive without basic services of clean water, primary healthcare and education.

Pakistan is a society of huge inequalities, duly reflected in educational provision. Regional disparities are glaring. Female literacy rates are highest in urban Sindh at 41 per cent and lowest in rural Baluchistan at 3 per cent, where the disparity between literacy rates for men and women is also the greatest (ul Haq 1997). The private English-medium schools dominate the system while the government schools are demoralized with an inappropriate curriculum, poorly trained teachers, rote learning from poor-quality materials and a high drop-out rate. A recent field visit made by the author to a government school in a village in the remote dry part of Southwest Punjab provides an example. The village consisted of 150 households whose main means of livelihood is the production of grindstones. Our driver located the village by following the electrical power lines, which had been installed immediately before the last election but remained 'purely decorative'. A new water-pump and latrines have recently been installed under the government's Social Action Plan. On the day of this unannounced visit 14 boys between grades 1 and 4 were present.[1] They were sitting on the porch of the large schoolroom, learning their lessons from the ubiquitous Punjabi primers. The two male teachers came on a motorbike from the town of D J Khan about three-quarters of an hour away. They said that the school had been started in 1961 and only ten boys had reached Grade 5, none of whom had gone on to matric. A young man accompanying us round the village told us, in faltering Urdu, that the school was often closed for long periods because there was no teacher and that most boys left after a year or two to find work. A group of women gathered and were asked by the development worker why so few children went to school. They said they would send all their children, including the girls, to school if it was good and the teachers attended regularly. The group also emphasized that any school would have to be free as they were much too poor to afford any fees.

Recent research shows that one of the pressing issues is the way teachers are appointed through a process of political patronage. Some cannot teach properly. Many teachers see remote rural areas as 'hardship postings' and do not attend. Parents have no redress against such abuses. Rural schools may be closed for long periods because they have no staff. The buildings may be inconveniently placed in poor condition without boundary walls, drinking water or latrines. Teachers, head teachers and educational officials are unapproachable and unaccountable to parents (Akber 1997). In a survey of government primary schools in 1997 in rural areas of Sindh and Punjab, Gazdar found that 40 per cent of schools were closed because of teacher absenteeism. The proportion of girls' schools closed was two-thirds (Gazdar 1997).

Gender relations in Pakistan

The reasons for the large, intransigent gender gap in Pakistan lie in the politics of gender, education and development. The dominant explanation is low demand among families for girls' education. Parents' reluctance to send their daughters to school is attributed to the low cultural value of girls compared with their brothers and the high opportunity cost for families in replacing girls, who carry a heavy burden of domestic responsibilities (Jaffer and Jaffer 1997). The labour market for educated adult women, where any educational investment might pay off, is poorly developed in most areas of Pakistan. For every 100 men who are eco-nomically active, there are only 16 women, the lowest percentage in South Asia (ul Haq 1997). Where there is paid work in the major cities, purdah, the social segregation of women, is more strictly observed than in many parts of the countryside and women are confined to insecure outwork at the lowest rates of pay in their own homes (Shaheed 1989). Any investment in a daughter's education benefits the family into which she marries, not her parents who supported her. Sathar and Lloyd (1994) found that poor families are much less likely to send their children to school. Parental education, especially that of mothers, is an important factor determining whether children attend. Within families boys are more likely than girls to be sent to school. The length and difficulty of the journey to school is also much more salient for girls than boys (Gould 1993).

Pakistan has the most rapidly developing economy in South Asia. In the last two decades GDP per head has trebled (ul Haq 1997: 39). The benefits of this astonishing performance have been very unequally distributed among the country's population. Urban elites and men have seen their standards of living rise, while the lives of women, especially those of rural women in remote areas, have changed little. A WB study, *Women in Pakistan*, published in 1989, documented the way in which their lives are dominated by childbirth and child-rearing without the basic amenities of safe water, sanitation and healthcare. In other low-income countries infant and maternal health are improving faster than in Pakistan. The fertility rate has remained at 6 per woman for 30 years. If this rate is sustained Pakistan will, by 2050, be the third most populous country in the world after China and India. Under-five mortality is 137 per 1,000. Only 35 per cent of births were attended by trained personnel in 1992 and the maternal mortality rate (MMR) is variously estimated at 350 to 600 per 100,000. Whereas infant mortality fell by an average 43 per cent between 1965 and 1985 in the low-income countries, the figure was only 25 per cent in Pakistan. In marked contrast with most other countries boy babies are more likely to survive than girls, whose under-five mortality rate is 12 per cent higher. Pakistan also has the lowest percentage of women in its population of all the South Asian countries, only 93 per cent (ul Haq 1997).[2]

For those who do survive, providing basic services for their families dominates their lives. Fetching water remains one of the most onerous responsibilities for women. Half of the population of Pakistan do not have a safe water supply. Fifty-five per cent do not have access to primary healthcare and two-thirds have no sanitation. Ibraz and Fatima (1993) characterize the plight of the women in Pakistan as 'Uneducated and Unhealthy', confined by their extremely low cultural value to their 'natural roles' in an 'endless cycle of disregard' and excluded from decision-making and the control of resources at all levels.

Since the 1970s girls' schooling has been the single most important correlate of fertility in Pakistan. Fertility rates among educated women, who are largely confined to urban areas, are falling. The extremely slow expansion of girls' education, especially in rural areas, where the mass of the population live, is arguably the principal cause of Pakistan's stubbornly high birth rates (Sathar 1996). Pakistan has a rapid rate of urbanization (ul Haq 1997; *The Economist* 11 April 1998).

High fertility is related to women's lack of autonomy in their personal lives and in the household. The importance of purdah varies among the various sub-cultural groups, with the Pathans of North West Frontier Province (NWFP) being the strongest adherents. One of the greatest difficulties women face in 'finding a voice' in Pakistan is their high level of illiteracy, which confines them to their spoken mother tongue. They cannot communicate with women from other communities, whereas the majority of men have access to the national language, Urdu. Ironically Pakistan was the first Muslim state to elect a woman prime minister. Benazir Bhutto came from a feudal family and enjoyed an education at Oxford and Harvard. Her rhetoric about helping the poor left a legacy of corruption on a stupendous scale (*The Nation* 11 January 1998). Despite a century of attempts to gain greater rights by the women's movement in Pakistan, in 1994 only 1.6 per cent of MPs were women, the lowest in South Asia (Mumtaz and Shaheed 1987; ul Haq 1997). The Women's Department of the government is marginalized and ineffective (Kazi and Raza 1992).

The Social Action Plan

In 1992 the government of Pakistan formulated a Social Action Plan to accelerate spending on neglected social services, targeting primary education, primary healthcare, family planning, rural water supplies and sanitation. Budget allocations in 1988–93 were doubled for 1993–98, with the government undertaking to cover 80 per cent of the budget while a multi-donor package was negotiated for the remaining 20 per cent. Despite this increase in social spending from 1.7 per cent of GDP in 1992 to 2.2 per cent in 1993, the Social Action Plan is facing increasing problems of budget cuts, ineffective implementation at local level and allegations of corruption (ul Haq 1997: 109).

In early January 1998 the newly elected government proposed a new educational initiative, including legislation to make primary schooling compulsory. It proposed to double the education budget, with half of the funds coming from the Social Action Plan and the rest from a new loan of 4.5 million rupees from the World Bank (WB). The government's actions were confused and uncoordinated, with a group of 300 assorted experts receiving proposals from all interested parties with the aim of distilling a policy at a three-day convention later that month. The debate was dominated by concerns about the inculcation of Islamic values, the reform of higher education and the need to introduce English from the first year to help government schools compete with the prestigious private

English-medium schools (*The News* 17 January 1998). Key issues about how to universalize basic education, increase literacy by reducing drop-out rates, improving quality and effectiveness, upgrading teacher training and addressing issues of girls' education have been ignored. In the mid-1990s basic education, especially that of girls, has formed a central plank of priorities of such important donors as the World Bank and the UK's newly created Department for International Development. The major donor to education in Pakistan, the World Bank, works through governments. One may speculate just how much of the WB loan will benefit the poorest communities. In Pakistan it seems that the Bank's new director has so far not managed to fulfil his objective of turning round its previous appalling record on monitoring the outcomes of loans. A former high-ranking official of the WB in Islamabad is quoted as saying: 'We made a mantra out of the phrase "good governance" as though we intended to try to stamp the corruption out. But the truth is that we turned a blind eye, telling ourselves this is the way things are done in Pakistan and it's not our business to stop it' (*The Nation* 11 January 1998).

NGOs and informal schools

An even more telling comparison can be made between Pakistan's seemingly intransigent gender gap and the progress that has been made in Bangladesh (the former East Pakistan) since independence in 1971. Bangladesh is one of the poorest and most densely populated countries in the world, with a mean GDP per head of $220, less than half that of Pakistan. In 1960 only 31 per cent of girls enrolled in primary school compared with 80 per cent of boys. In 1995 84 per cent of boys and 73 per cent of girls enrolled, with a completion rate variously estimated at between 47 per cent and 55 per cent. In 1980 41 per cent of men and 17 per cent of women were literate, and this rose to 49 per cent and 26 per cent in 1995. The economic activity rate among women in Bangladesh has risen steadily to twice the average in South Asia. By far the most impressive gains have been made in fertility rates, which had fallen from 6.7 in the 1960s to 4.1 by 1995 (UNICEF 1997; ul Haq 1997).

In 1983 the Bangladesh Rural Advancement Committee began to establish so-called informal schools in villages. Government schools were seen as remote and out of touch with the needs of local communities. BRAC schools were nearby, the calendar and hours determined by parents. The schools meet six days a week, 50 weeks a year. The day is short (to allow for domestic chores). Classes are limited to 30 pupils, who are taught in blocks of three years. The curriculum is specially designed and all materials are free. Teachers are hired by and responsible jointly to BRAC, the community and parents. They are given two weeks' initial training and one in-service training day every month. BRAC schools measure their success by their ability to serve as a bridge to the formal government school system. They are seen as a successful model, now being popularized by the World Bank, and are being adapted in many countries, including Pakistan.

A number of NGOs have entered partnerships with local communities to start informal schools. These tend to be one-room, one-teacher community schools with shorter, more flexible hours and flexible age of admission. In recruiting a teacher, residence in the community is considered more important than academic qualifications. The schools emphasize basic literacy and numeracy rather than state certification. Many such schools try to reach those who would never have an opportunity to go to school (Akber 1997).

The National Rural Support Programme (NRSP) was started in 1991. Its aim is poverty alleviation through a 'bottom-up' approach in which community organizations are formed and activists identified with whom development needs are discussed and priorities negotiated. Feasibility studies follow. Resources are then made available for the village organization to carry out their programme. 'Community school needs are assessed through Social Sector Surveys, conducted by the NRSP staff with the help of the community members' (NRSP 1997: 70). Where a school is needed and prioritized by the community organization, a Village Education Committee (VEC) is formed of five or six members, who must include women. The NRSP provides an initial grant for school supplies of basic furniture, registers, mats, blackboard, register and small library and a single grant to supplement the teacher's honorarium in the first year. The VEC draws up a list of children, finds suitable rent-free accommodation and identifies a teacher (a woman if possible). It is responsible for the financing and administration of the school. It decides on the school fee, keeps the accounts, sets the school times and monitors attendance. The NRSP provides a two-week course of teacher training (NRSP 1997: 70–1).

New understandings of girls and their schooling in Pakistan

Experience in the informal sector has changed understandings of the issues surrounding girls' education in Pakistan. Contrary to the long-accepted view that parents are unwilling to educate their daughters, it is now widely understood that most parents do want to educate their daughters. It is poor provision of suitable schools that prevents them from sending their daughters to school. Parents want their daughters educated in schools near to their homes so that they do not have long journeys over main roads or through areas controlled by different clans. They prefer women teachers, although those in rural areas are often willing for their daughters to be taught by a man, especially if he is from the community and is therefore seen as trustworthy. Parents want a quality education for their sons and daughters and do not support schools perceived as ineffective, where teachers do not attend and pupils do not learn. Community involvement in the establishment and running of girls' schools is an effective way of raising girls' enrolment even in the most remote and conservative areas. Sending children to school is a considerable burden on already over-stretched domestic budgets. Educational costs are a potent issue and one of the most important causes of children dropping out of school. Costs include books, uniform, travel and opportunity costs, including domestic chores in the case of girls and possible earnings in the case of boys. Parents may be willing to pay for a quality education for their children. However, in Kohistan compensation for the cost of sending girls by giving a monthly bottle of cooking oil to those who attended regularly increased attendance by 273 per cent. While the evidence is sparse, it seems that parents in many areas expect to educate their sons for a longer period than their daughters. While most do not expect their daughters to enter the paid labour market, some express the hope that they will be able to educate them up to matric (Akber 1997; Action Aid Pakistan 1997; Jaffer and Jaffer 1997).

The issues

The NRSP is attempting to meet the needs of some of the most disadvantaged communities in the poorest areas of Pakistan. Some of the community schools are supported by a partnership with a UK-based NGO, Learning for Life, which receives National Lottery and DfID funding.

During a field visit to a village near Mirpurkhas in Sindh the author met the members of the Village Education Committee, who were all women. They had started a school two years ago under a tree. They built the pleasant one-room school building themselves. The men had helped with the roof. A fee of 10 rupees a week had been fixed. Some families had difficulty paying the fee and were given remission, especially if they had several children at school. The teacher was a woman from the community who had been educated to matric level in Mirpurkhas. There were 32 children in attendance at the school. All the older pupils were girls. The younger ones were boys and girls. She was teaching them in groups and individually, using the blackboard and primers, which the families had to buy. There was considerable evidence of progress towards literacy among the children. She taught the children in the mornings and then had a literacy group for the women in the afternoon, for which she received no payment whatsoever other than the gratitude and appreciation of the women. One told us how she kept a little shop and could now add the stock up properly in figures rather than making rough estimates with longer or shorter lines. In the evening the teacher was studying for a higher qualification. This caused problems for her with her domestic responsibilities, she said. Her discussion of the schoolwork was thoughtful and very positive. The first item on her 'wish list' was simple story-books to encourage the children to read.

At a village nearby, an informal school had been started a month before the monitoring visit. Twelve girls, some with their younger siblings, for whom they are responsible, sat in two rows on benches in front of a blackboard. They chanted the alphabet in Urdu and English as the young male teacher pointed to the letters with his stick. The oldest boy present acted as monitor, taking the stick and repeating the same process several times. Two very poor Hindu villages provided further evidence of the difficulties communities face in educating their children, especially daughters. In one a schoolroom was in the course of construction. Meanwhile the school was being conducted under a tree. Although the school was only three months old there had already been a change of teacher. The young man we met had been there only a few weeks. The VEC would prefer a woman, who would be more likely to stay. At the time of the visit five girls and 13 boys were present, doing numeracy work by copying the sums from the tattered poor-quality primers onto wooden boards. They came out in ones and twos to have their work corrected by the teacher. One girl had a little sibling with her. Another arrived late because she had had to collect grass for the animals as her mother was not well enough to do it. At another very poor Hindu village the women entertained us with tea and biscuits and loaded us with gifts, including examples of the earthenware water-pots that are such an important part of their lives. They told us that they wanted their daughters to have a better life than they had had. They had appointed a woman teacher from the community, and they were all anxious to show off the children's learning. A short programme of songs and recitations was presented. At the two-week course of training the teacher had made some large coloured flash-cards in Urdu and English. Some of the subjects – ducks, the Queen – were of dubious relevance to children in the semi-desert of rural Sindh. No other more appropriate objects had been added.

Quality, effectiveness and their relation to the very high drop-out rate are arguably the most important issues for popular schooling in Pakistan. Rote learning from limited poor-quality resources dominates schooling in all but the elite English-medium schools. Encouragement of active learning methods and the production of appropriate materials are crucial to breaking the present vicious circle of children attending for a brief irregular period to acquire such a tenuous grasp on literacy that they soon lapse back into illiteracy. Access remains the crucial issue for educators and policy-makers, but issues of teacher training, curriculum and materials are of equal importance. If children in rural areas are to learn effectively from enthusiastic teachers, regular methods of supporting them through visiting advisers, newsletters and regular in-service workshops are needed. Rather than furniture, schools need a wider range of interesting and attractive resources that teachers know how to use and supplement (Action Aid Pakistan 1997). The donor community has initiated a number of innovations including learning coordinators, hostels for women teachers and kits of instructional materials in attempts to break away from rote learning. A recent review of research on these issues showed the difficulties such innovations encounter in Pakistan. The status, pay and education of primary schoolteachers is very low. They are seen as people who got their jobs by political preferment. They are no good for anything else and no good at teaching. Teacher training is entirely theoretical and consists of learning notes copied from the blackboard. There is an administrative culture of carrying out orders from the top, which stifles innovation at local level. The most effective teachers are those with the highest levels of personal education, which has apparently given them enthusiasm and commitment (Warwick and Reimers 1995).

During the field visits we attended a meeting of local village organizations with the recently appointed government District Officer (DO). Their children's schooling generated the most pressing issues. There are a number of government schools, which are closed or moribund because there are no teachers. Representatives from several villages raised the issue of women teachers who are appointed to teach in local schools but do not take up their appointments because the journey is too difficult and they have no suitable chaperone to accompany them. The DO listened to them politely and told them he did not have to do even that. In any case the government had no money. We were all given more presents, including a partridge for the DO. After a truly sumptuous supper at which no village women were present, we drove off into the darkness in our four-wheel drives.

The lack of women teachers is now a 'critical barrier' to the expansion of girls' education in Pakistan (Jaffer and Jaffer 1997). In the remote rural areas the low enrolment, high drop-out rate and scarcity of secondary facilities for girls perpetuates the cycle of low female literacy. Field visits to villages in the mountainous desert above D J Khan in Southwestern Punjab provide telling evidence of the importance of these issues. The area had a length of tarmac road built with funds made available by the recently 'deposed' President Leghari, who was born nearby. A school building that had once housed a boys' secondary school stood beside the road. Both were deteriorating rapidly. The NRSP field officer was camped out in one of the dilapidated school buildings.

The villages were groups of stone 'beehive' huts with brushwood roofs. The villagers kept cattle, sheep and goats, which provided their entire diet of meat and milk products. The first school was not accessible by road and could be reached only by an indistinct path up a cliff. Some 20 boys and girls were sitting on mats in front of a male teacher who was rehearsing the numbers 1 to 100 in Urdu, pointing to the blackboard with his stick. A woman ran up and dumped a baby in one girl's lap. With water having to be carried 2 kilometres, the need to divest herself of an additional burden may have been irresistible. The children began to 'say their lessons' from their primers, while others went out to the teacher to go through the primer. Rote learning predominated. One young man stood out as a model of good practice. He was encouraging understanding by building Urdu words on the blackboard using liberal quantities of praise to encourage the children to respond. The only woman teacher in the area had never been to school, and had learned all she knew from her father and brothers. Her main difficulties, she said, were that she had no watch to tell her when to start and finish school and had to find the energy to complete all the domestic chores demanded by her mother-in-law as well as run the school. At one village a meeting of the men was started by firing guns into the air. Only six of the 32 men present were literate. They wanted schooling up to 'matric' for their children. At another village we were met with tea and biscuits by a delegation of women. The spokeswoman told us in the faltering Urdu she had learned from her father that the fee of 20 rupees a month was too much for them to pay.

Sustainability is one of the most insistent issues for the informal sector. The NRSP has given to each community a single payment as a start-up grant with an element towards the teacher's honorarium. If communities cannot continue to support the teachers through fees then the schools may close. Government support is equally uncertain. The government pledged 200 million rupees to the informal sector last year from the SAP, but then cut this to 86 million, resulting in school closures. Some informal schools may become part of the private sector run by individuals for profit (Akber 1997). Sustainability is rooted in the political constraints, political will and vested interests that so bedevil development in Pakistan.

For Village Education Committees to raise the finance, find the energy to administer their own schools and monitor their effectiveness through ensuring attendance and efficient teaching and learning is indeed a tall order. NGOs have invested in energizing them and building their capacities. Some are vibrant, while others are paper tigers (Gazdar 1997).

The crucial difference among the cultures of different areas for establishing literacy among rural men and women should not be overlooked. Sindhi is a written language with a high rate of urban literacy and a literature that includes daily newspapers. Literacy rates and secondary education rates among women make the recruitment of women teachers feasible but not easy. In Baluchistan the mother tongue is not written. Literacy demands Urdu. The politics of language and culture also complicate schooling in Pakistan. Urdu is the national language and the language of instruction in secondary education, with English dominating higher education. In NWFP and the northern areas Pashtu, a written language, is used among Pathan communities. School curricula are consequently overloaded with language studies. Many children begin school at five attempting to learn the alphabets of two completely new languages, at the same time devaluing their mother tongue as a vehicle for learning. It is little wonder that drop-out rates are so high and literacy rates rise so slowly.

Reconceptualizing the gender gap

The notion of the 'gender gap' is too narrow to conceptualize the relationship of gender, education and development, even in a country where the main issue appears to be inequalities of access. The analysis shows that wider educational issues of sustainability, quality and effectiveness must be considered in a political, economic and cultural context. It reinforces the main conclusion of the women's education and fertility debate that to be effective girls' education must be part of a wider platform of reform (Jejeebhoy 1995; Jeffery and Basu 1996). Many rural communities are too poor, with women's lives overburdened with the tasks of survival, for informal schools to be a long-term sustainable solution. Sadly, any possibility of the widespread introduction of clean water, sanitation, primary healthcare and basic education by the government has been forestalled by the disaster of the nuclear arms race between India and Pakistan. Defence has been re-established as the top spending priority with renewed enthusiam following India's nuclear tests. The 20:20 compact suggested at 1995 UN Conference on Poverty in Copenhagen would commit the aid agencies and the government of Pakistan to spending 20 per cent of aid on human development. While the North supplies arms the 20:20 compact remains a dream, consigning the girls and women of Pakistan to ignorance. The growing flight from the land to the cities gives women their main chance of a better life, including education.

Notes

1. In January 1998 I undertook monitoring visits to schools and projects in Sindh and SW Punjab on behalf of a UK-based NGO in partnership with NRSP, a Pakistani NGO based in Islamabad.

2. In India the proportion of women in the population has fallen to 94 per cent, the lowest ever recorded. The Indian government has become so concerned about this continuing rise in the number of 'missing' women that it has introduced a reward of 500 rupees for low-income families who have a daughter (*Independent*, 3 October 1997).

Bibliography

ActionAid Pakistan (1997) 'Report of ActionAid Pakistan's workshop on the "Access" project and research design', mimeo, ActionAid Pakistan, Islamabad.

Ainsworth, M., K. Beegle and K. Nyamete (1996) 'The impact of women's schooling on fertility and contraceptive use: a study of 14 Sub-Saharan African countries', *World Bank Economic Review* 10 (1): 84–122.

Akber, M. (1997) 'Do communities own non-formal schools?', *NGO News* 3, Fall, Asia Foundation, Islamabad.

The Economist (1998) 'Dangerous questions', 11 April, p. 62.

Ercelawn, A., M. Mahmood and K. Nadvi (1994) 'Social costs of economic restructuring in Pakistan' in UN Economic and Social Commission for Asia and Pacific Development Papers 15, *Social Costs of Economic Restructuring in Asia and the Pacific*, UN, Bangkok.

Gazdar, H. (1998) 'Policy prescription or political mobilisation?', *The News on Sunday*, 18 January, Islamabad.

Gould, W. T. S. (1993) *People and Education in the Third World*, Longman, London.

Grey, S. and R. Syal (1998) 'The hunt for Benazir's booty', *Sunday Times*, News Review, 12 April, pp. 1–2.

Haq, M. ul (1997) *Human Development in South Asia*, Oxford University Press, Karachi.

Ibraz, T. and A. Fatima (1993) 'Uneducated and unhealthy: the plight of the women in Pakistan', *Pakistan Development Review* 32 (4) Part II: 905–15.

Jaffer, R. and R. Jaffer (1997) 'Understanding the gender gap in Pakistan', *Education Action* 8, ActionAid, London.

Jeffery, R. and A. Basu (1996) *Girls' Schooling, Women's Autonomy and Fertility Change in South Asia*, Sage, New Delhi.

Jejeebhoy, S. (1995) *Women's Education, Autonomy and Reproductive Behaviour: Experience from Developing Countries*, Oxford University Press, Oxford.

Kazi, S. and B. Raza (1992) 'Women, planning and the government policies of Pakistan', *Pakistan Development Review* 31 (4) Part II: 609–20.

Kelly, G. and C. Elliott (1982) *Women's Education in the Third World: Comparative Perspectives*, State University of New York, New York.

King, E. and M. Hill (1993) *Women's Education in Developing Countries*, World Bank, Washington, DC.

Mahmood, N. and G. Zahid (1992) 'Measuring the education gap in primary and secondary schooling in Pakistan', *Pakistan Development Review* 31 (4) Part II: 729–40.

Mumtaz, K. and F. Shaheed (1987) *Women of Pakistan: Two Steps Forward and One Step Back?*, Vanguard, Lahore.

The Nation (1998) 'Bhutto clan leaves a trail of corruption in Pakistan', 11 January.

The News (1998) 'Education policy urges compulsory primary education', 17 January.

NSRP (1997) *Annual Report for 1996.*

Sathar, Z. (1996) 'Women's schooling and autonomy as factors in fertility change in Pakistan: some empirical evidence', in R. Jeffery and A. Basu (eds), *Girls' Schooling, Women's Autonomy and Fertility Change in South Asia*, Sage, New Delhi.

Sathar, Z. and C. Lloyd (1994) 'Who gets primary schooling in Pakistan: inequalities among and within families', *Pakistan Development Review* 33 (2): 103–34.

Shaheed, F. (1989) 'Purdah and poverty in Pakistan', in H. Afshar and B. Agarwal (eds), *Women, Poverty and Ideology in Asia*, Macmillan, London.

UNICEF (1997) *The State of the World's Children 1997*, Oxford University Press, Oxford.

Warwick, D. P. and F. Reimers (1995) *Hope or Despair? Learning in Pakistan's Primary Schools*, Praeger, Westport, CT.

World Bank (1989) *Women in Pakistan: An Economic and Social Strategy*, World Bank, Washington, DC.

— (1995) *Priorities and Strategies for Education: A World Bank Review*, World Bank, Washington, DC.

Index